Disorderly Women in Eigh

WOMEN AND MEN IN HISTORY

This series, published for students, scholars and interested general readers, will tackle themes in gender history from the early medieval period through to the present day. Gender issues are now an integral part of all history courses and yet many traditional texts do not reflect this change. Much exciting work is now being done to redress the gender imbalances of the past, and we hope that these books will make their own substantial contribution to that process. This is an open-ended series, which means that many new titles can be included. We hope that these will both synthesise and shape future developments in gender studies.

The General Editors of the series are *Patricia Skinner* (University of Southampton) for the medieval period; *Pamela Sharpe* (University of Bristol) for the early modern period; and *Penny Summerfield* (University of Lancaster) for the modern period. *Margaret Walsh* (University of Nottingham) was the Founding Editor of the series.

Published books:

Masculinity in Medieval Europe
D.M. Hadley (ed.)

Gender and Society in Renaissance Italy
Judith C. Brown and Robert C. Davis (eds)

Gender, Church and State in Early Modern Germany: Essays by Merry E. Wiesner
Merry E. Wiesner

Manhood in Early Modern England: Honour, Sex and Marriage
Elizabeth W. Foyster

Disorderly Women in Eighteenth-Century London: Prostitution and Control in the Metropolis 1730–1830
Tony Henderson

Gender, Power and the Unitarians in England, 1760–1860
Ruth Watts

Women and Work in Russia, 1880–1930: A Study in Continuity through Change
Jane McDermid and Anna Hillyar

The Family Story: Blood, Contract and Intimacy, 1830–1960
Leonore Davidoff, Megan Doolittle, Janet Fink and Katherine Holden

Disorderly Women in Eighteenth-Century London

Prostitution and Control in the Metropolis 1730–1830

TONY HENDERSON

Longman
London and New York

Pearson Education Limited
Edinburgh Gate,
Harlow, Essex CM20 2JE, United Kingdom
and Associated Companies throughout the world.

*Published in the United States of America
by Pearson Education Inc., New York.*

First published 1999

ISBN 0-582-26421-9 PPR
ISBN 0-582-26395-6 CSD

Visit our world wide web site at http://www.awl-he.com

British Library Cataloguing in Publication Data

A catalogue entry for this title is available from the British Library

Library of Congress Cataloging-in-Publication Data

Henderson, Tony, 1959–
Disorderly women in eighteenth-century London : prostitution and
control in the metropolis, 1730–1830 / Tony Henderson.
p.   cm. — (Women and men in history)
Includes bibliographical references and index.
ISBN 0–582–26395–6. — ISBN 0–582–26421–9 (pbk.)
1. Prostitution—England—London—History—18th century.
I. Title. II. Series.
HQ186.L66H46   1999
306.74'09421—dc21   98–31244   CIP

Set by 35 in 10/12pt Baskerville
Produced by Addison Wesley Longman Singapore (Pte) Ltd.,
Printed in Singapore

Contents

List of Figures

List of Tables

Acknowledgements

The completion of the Ph.D. thesis upon which this book is based owed much to the financial backing of the Economic and Social Research Council and to the generous award of a Scouloudi Research Fellowship by the Institute of Historical Research at the University of London. Yet more invaluable were the support, encouragement and informed criticism of the following: my doctoral supervisor, Professor Penelope Corfield, whose critical and incisive readings of the text were invariably helpful; the Metropolitan History Seminar and the British History, 1689–1848 Seminar at the Institute of Historical Research; the staff of the Westminster City Archives, the Corporation of London Record Office, the Guildhall Library and Muniments Room, the Institute of Historical Research, and the British Library; numerous friends and colleagues, including Tony Claydon, Edmund Green, Timothy Hitchcock, Fatima Luis, David Omissi, Dominic Omissi, Sarah Palmer, Roy Porter, Maria-Sophia Quine, Jim Sharpe, John Styles, Timothy Wales and Liz Wander. My wife, Sarah Booth, has given me love, encouragement and criticism throughout, for all of which I am deeply thankful. Finally I would like to express my gratitude to Hilary Shaw and Bill Jenkins of Pearson Education and to Pamela Sharpe – such patience and perseverance deserve a greater reward than this small book.

Conventions

BL	British Library
C.J.	*Commons Journals*
CLRO	Corporation of London Record Office
GJR/M	Guildhall Justice Room Minute Books of Proceedings
GL	Guildhall Library
GMR	Guildhall Muniments Room
OBSP	*Old Bailey Sessions Papers*
Police Committee	Reports from the Select Committees on the State of the Police of the Metropolis
P.P.	*Parliamentary Papers*
WCA	Westminster City Archives

To my parents
Robert and Doreen

The arrest of a prostitute in Covent Garden c.1740
Reproduced by kind permission of the City of Westminster Archives Centre

CHAPTER ONE

Introduction

What! must not a Woman of the Town walk in the Town Streets?
These men think they do things so meritorious in taking up light
Women; why a light Woman hath a right of Liberty as well as another
to walk about the Streets. The Life of a Man, and the Liberty of the
Subject, is a tender thing.[1]

By 1700 London had long spilled over the ancient boundaries of
a medieval city. Alongside the growing industrial districts to the
east and south of the City had arisen a more elegant, wealthy area
extending west towards Westminster – the home of government.
The seventeenth century saw Soho and Leicester Fields enclosed by
houses and much of St. Giles in the Fields and Covent Garden built
over. By the close of the century, the first of the great squares and
thoroughfares had been laid out, beginning with Bloomsbury Square
in 1680, to be followed within twenty years by Grosvenor Street,
Red Lion Square and Golden Square. The eighteenth century saw
the continued development of such magnificent schemes west of
the old City, while much unobtrusive building took place to its
north and east, around Clerkenwell and along the course of the
Thames. New roads were laid to open up the surrounding countryside for building, north and south of the river. Between 1700 and
1820, London's population grew from approximately 674,000 to
1,274,000 and its area increased to around twelve square miles.[2]

1. Lord Chief Justice the Rt. Hon. Sir John Holt summing up at the trial of three
soldiers for the murder of a constable, attacked by them to prevent his arresting a
prostitute; quoted in T. Bray, *The Tryals of Jeremy Tooley, William Arch and John Clauson,
three Private Soldiers, for the Murder of Mr. John Dent, Constable, in the Parish of St. Paul's
Covent Garden, March 18 1708–9* (1732), p.19.
2. For short, useful descriptions of the growth of London in this period, see
R. Porter, *English Society in the Eighteenth Century* (1982), pp.60–1; P.J. Corfield, *The
Impact of English Towns 1700–1800* (1982), pp.66–81, G.E. Eades, *Historic London*

1

London was a major European capital. Standing head and shoulders above other English towns, it possessed an almost irresistible attraction, drawing in vast quantities of food, produce and, most importantly, people – many of them girls and young women with the hope, rather than the certainty, of finding employment. The city was perceived by many contemporaries not just as the political, the social or the economic, but equally as the degenerate heart of the nation.

This is a study of female prostitution in London in the eighteenth and early nineteenth centuries. It has three central concerns. It begins by attempting to recover and gain some understanding of the diverse experiences of the capital's prostitutes; to identify the dominant social characteristics and the motives of those who entered prostitution; to describe the organisation and finances of the trade, the relative importance of the street and the brothel; and to locate the whole within the wider social and economic context of the city.

This leads into a discussion of the distinctly urban nature of prostitution, principally through an examination of the part played by the capital's policing agencies in shaping the trade. A survey of the history of the laws touching on prostitution is followed by a detailed examination of the execution of those laws during the eighteenth and early nineteenth centuries. For the magistracy and for the parish watch, prostitution was a prime component of the chronic problem of public order. The attempts of the authorities to impose varying degrees of control on the capital's prostitutes, and the latters' ability to exploit loopholes in the law and in the policing system in order to continue working, vividly illuminate many of the dilemmas and opportunities facing individuals and groups in a rapidly urbanising society.

Thirdly, this study charts the changing attitudes towards the trade and towards the women engaged in it. These are most clearly, though not uniquely, expressed in the writings and activities of social commentators such as Bernard de Mandeville and Jonas Hanway. The period saw fundamental changes in society's conceptions of prostitution, the penitent magdalen, of respectable if impoverished origin, gradually taking her place alongside the vicious harlot as one of the archetypal images of the prostitute. The final chapter in particular is concerned with describing and analysing this transformation.

The structural division of the book into three main areas is of course artificial and it will swiftly become plain that a large degree

---

(1966), pp.201–6. See also G.E. Mingay, *Georgian London* (1975), and M.D. George, *London Life in the Eighteenth Century* (1925).

of overlapping between them is both necessary and beneficial. Nevertheless, I hope that, in retaining the divisions, while making their boundaries permeable, the study will successfully reflect both the distinctiveness and the unity of the numerous ideological and material realities of prostitution in the London of the period between 1730 and 1830.

A line has been drawn around the subject by the adoption of a fairly precise definition of what constitutes prostitution. Male same-sex prostitution has not been examined. This is principally because buggery was a capital offence and it is with the act itself rather than its commercial or non-commercial nature that the legal sources were concerned in any specific case. Hence, for example, a watch book entry of 1777 for the arrest of two unnamed men for 'sodomytical practices' or one of 1778 noting the charging of an anonymous man by one John Jones with 'taken hold of him By his Privet Parts & want him to be a Grebel [sic] to him' tell us nothing about prostitution.[3] The fact that in the latter case, as in others, the prosecutor failed to appear to press the charge before the magistrate is equally unhelpful (though not of course to the perpetrator, who was discharged). Nor is this a study of the eighteenth-century demi-monde, with its actresses, mistresses of the rich and powerful, and celebrated courtesans. Rather it is a study of the majority – the streetwalkers and inmates of bordellos who, if contemporary observers are to be believed, thronged the streets and alleys of the Georgian city.

The work has a more general purpose than those studies which concentrate on the campaigns of social reformers and their opponents. While the writings and activities of men such as Jonas Hanway and John Fielding, the members of the Societies for the Reformation of Manners, the founders of the London Female Penitentiary and others are discussed, the bulk of this study is given over to recovering and examining the experiences of the prostitutes themselves – who they were, how they lived, and how they stood in relation to their peers and to those set in authority over them.

Chapter 2 describes the changing face of the capital over the period, before going on to build up a picture of the social characteristics of the women who moved into prostitution in the eighteenth and early nineteenth centuries. The often haphazard creation and fitful survival of sources dealing with the earlier part of the period means that much of this picture relates most directly to the

---

3. WCA D2108 Charge book of the parish of St. James, Piccadilly, entry 10 Jan. 1778.

years after 1800. The geographical and social origins of London's prostitutes are examined, together with their likely ages at entry and exit from the trade, and these provide the basis for a comparison with the findings of demographic and social historians with regard to the city's population at large. The chapter goes on to describe the organisation and economics of prostitution. The relative importance of brothels, common lodging houses and streetwalkers is investigated, together with the relationships that developed between bawdy house keepers, bullies and prostitutes, throwing important light upon the degrees of independence and exploitation experienced by the women who entered the trade.

The chapter also attempts to place prostitutes within the context of the wider 'community'. Can anything be discovered of plebeian attitudes towards prostitutes? The often hostile treatment meted out to pilloried bawds by crowds is well documented, as is the infrequent occurrence of riots directed against bawdy houses such as that which engulfed Peter Wood's Strand brothel in 1749. But is this the whole picture? Are the capital's prostitutes best understood as part of a wider 'criminal underworld' (itself a concept that does not wholly withstand critical scrutiny) or as declassed victims of lower-middle-class poverty – both views common among eighteenth- and early nineteenth-century commentators. Or was prostitution no more than one option among many open to the female poor in an urban economy of makeshift, attracting little, if any, censure from within the ranks of London's lower orders?

The third chapter maps the social geography of commercialised sex in Georgian London. Watch committee charge books and the presentments by City wards of disorderly and bawdy houses are used to locate the capital's red light districts. In the light of that work, the reasons for both the endurance and the shifting locations of such districts can then be examined. Chapter Four considers the history of the laws governing prostitution in England from the earliest known royal decrees of the tenth century, leading to a more detailed rehearsal of the common and statute law operating in the eighteenth and early nineteenth centuries.

The fifth and sixth chapters deal with the policing of prostitutes and of their houses of resort. Chapter Five discusses the implementation of the laws governing streetwalkers. After describing the operations of those agencies most responsible for policing prostitution in London, the chapter concerns itself primarily with prostitutes' relationships with the various parts of the legal system and their ability to exploit the conflicts occurring within it. Chapter Six similarly examines the policing of disorderly and bawdy houses and other 'houses for the reception of prostitutes'.

Chapter Seven discusses the changes in attitudes – toward both the trade and the women involved – that are apparent in the writings of various commentators and the responses of those in authority. The break-up of a generalised conception of 'lewdness' is suggested. With the increasing reluctance to acknowledge the existence of female sexual appetite and the recognition of economic factors in the decision of women to turn to prostitution (that is, that they became prostitutes through poverty rather than lust) came a denial of prostitutes' ability to act as free agents. In conclusion, the implications of these changes, for prostitutes and for other women, are considered.

The nature of the sources used in this book, and the peculiar difficulties and challenges they present, are discussed in the text where it is most relevant. What follows here is no more than a brief introduction to the types of material employed.

There is no central core of evidence upon which to base a study such as this. A considerable body of material has, however, been drawn from the records of the parish and ward watches of Westminster and the City of London. Of equal importance have been the notes of the cases heard before the City aldermen sitting at the Guildhall Justice Room, the annual presentments of the ward inquest juries to the Common Council of the City, and the accounts of those held for trial in the Southwark compter in the early nineteenth century. The descriptions of trials at the Old Bailey of prostitutes accused of theft and assault have been used extensively, as have the minutes and reports of the House of Commons Select Committees on the Police of the Metropolis sitting between 1812 and 1828. Further sources that have been employed include the reports of a number of other parliamentary Select Committees (on vagrancy, prisons, burglary and the like); the minutes of the committees on prostitution set up by the City in the early nineteenth century in response to a series of petitions against the trade; reference books and case histories produced for the guidance of justices of the peace and parish officers; various newspapers and magazines; the great mass of pamphlets and small books published on the question throughout the period; and a small number of more personal papers including, of course, James Boswell's London journal covering the years 1762 and 1763, and the Francis Place collection.

Of the manuscript sources, by far the most important are those generated by the various agencies responsible for policing the capital in this period. For the purposes of governance, Westminster was divided into parishes, the City into wards. The survival of records relating to the Westminster parish watch, or police, forces is sporadic: no records remain from two or three parishes while others, such as those of St. Margaret and St. James, have survived in relative bulk. No parish, however, has retained even individual examples, much less extended runs, of every type of watch record. Those records that do exist, and that are relevant to a study of prostitution, can be divided into three sorts – charge books; 'beadles' and patroles'' [sic] report books; and watch committee minutes.

Apart from a single book for the parish of St. Margaret relating to the years 1793–94, charge books survive only for St. James, covering most of the period 1773–79.[4] Prefaced by an injunction to the watchmen to be sober and vigilant and to enter all charges within its pages alone, the charge book resided in the parish watch house. The name of the person brought to the house and charged with an offence was entered by the constable of the night, along with that of the person making the charge (usually a watchman). Also recorded were the date, time and place of the offence, the formal charge and frequently a short description of the circumstances surrounding the alleged crime's commission. Later entries generally include a cryptic indication of the subsequent fate of the accused, including the date of their appearance before a named justice of the peace and the nature of the verdict handed down (usually this took place early the following morning although it is clear that a large number of women did not even proceed that far into the judicial machine, being ejected from the watch house before dawn with a simple caution against repeating their offence). These books record events at the lowest possible level of the legal system and as such offer the historian a unique, though by no means uncomplicated, insight into the activities of streetwalking prostitutes and their relationship with the law.

Twice each night the beadle was expected to walk the streets of the parish, in the company of the constable of the night if he was present, checking on the conduct and attention to duty of the watchmen and patrols. The principal events of the night were then

4. St. James's charge books also survive from 1800–03 and 1818–29. With the exception of statistical sampling of charges from the years 1821–25, these have not, for the most part, been used here. This is partly because a brief examination of them suggested that the great amount of time that would have to be expended in fully researching them would not be rewarded with any substantial addition to the knowledge acquired from the earlier runs of charge books, and partly because their use would have tilted the evidential balance of the book too much in favour of the already well-sourced post-1800 period.

recorded in the beadles' report book. Captains of the patrol appear to have served much the same function as beadles and their report books are for the most part indistinguishable. Some report books survive from three Westminster parishes. St. James possesses the most comprehensive collection, its earliest book covering the period from 1739 to 1742, while St. Margaret and the Liberty of the Rolls have smaller runs of books from later in the century. The longer entries make frequent reference to the presence and activities of prostitutes on the streets of the parishes, although the majority consist either of a comment on the wakefulness or lack thereof of various named watchmen or a laconic 'all well'.

Watch committee minute books survive for six of the ten Westminster parishes. They record attempts to organise and reorganise the watch, efforts to deal with newly perceived problems in the parish, the hearing of complaints against the constables, beadles and watchmen, the passing of accounts and the like. The placing of watchmen's stands and beats is usually discussed, as is the occasional mounting of extra patrols, often to deal with a perceived increase in the number of prostitutes soliciting for trade. The earliest minute books date from 1736 although the majority originate from the second half of the century.

Nothing akin to the watch house charge books survives for the part of the capital under the jurisdiction of the City of London. The records of the twenty-six wardmotes, however, perform a similar function to that of the watch committee minutes. Of greater importance for an understanding of the prostitution within the City are the annual presentments of the ward inquest juries and the accounts of trials held at the Guildhall Justice Room.

Each year, on Plough Monday, the inquest jury of each of the city wards processed to the Court of Aldermen, there to present a document giving, among other things, the names and addresses of any persons they believed ran disorderly and bawdy houses for the reception of prostitutes in the ward, together with a request that such individuals be prosecuted at the expense of the City. Of 3,380 lists of presentments made between 1700 and 1829, fully 3,336 survive, allowing for an exceptionally detailed picture to be built up of the incidence and location of those houses seen by the authorities as being especially troublesome, as well as of the processes by which they were policed.[5]

5. As with all other sources (especially those of judicial origin) mentioned here, the degree to which these documents accurately reflect the actual incidence or nature of that which they record is discussed more fully elsewhere in this study.

The Guildhall Justice Room minute books survive in an occasionally broken sequence from 1758 to 1796. These record the judicial business conducted by the aldermen of the City who from at least the 1730s sat in daily rotation (as members of the commission of the peace), complementing the longer-established activities of the Lord Mayor at the Mansion House.[6] Those before them included a large number of prostitutes, brought from the Wood Street and Poultry compters, or prisons, to be accused of soliciting in the streets of the City.

Illustrating a degree of bureaucratic inquisitiveness seemingly unparalleled elsewhere in the capital, the records of those women held at south London's Southwark compter before being committed to the sessions in the years from 1814 to 1829 are especially useful when employed with a proper sense of caution. As a matter of course, the commitments book for each sessions recorded the name, age, physical appearance, place of birth and residence of the prisoner. This was supplemented with information as to the nature and location of the offence, the date of commitment (and by whom committed), the date of trial, verdict of the jury, where appropriate the sentence, and the date of subsequent discharge. A final entry recorded the court's 'observations as to character' of each of the accused.

The entries in these books stating the nature of the offences with which the women were charged are terse and formulaic. As such, they provide scant evidence of the more quotidian events leading up to the point at which the law was deemed to have been broken. While the St. James charge books are more useful in this respect – a description of the event itself frequently being preferred to the strict terminology of a formal charge – and many of the other records discussed above also contain fruitful narrative scraps, it is necessary to turn to one of the most important of the published sources used in this study to garner a great deal more such information.

The *Old Bailey Sessions Papers* (*OBSP*) reported the trials conducted at the eight sessions held each year at the Justice Hall adjoining Newgate prison. They were originally printed and sold as a commercial venture, being hawked in the streets for a few pence within days of the conclusion of the sessions.[7] They gained the

---

6. J.H. Langbein, 'Shaping the eighteenth-century criminal trial: a view from the Ryder sources', *University of Chicago Law Review*, 50 (1983), p.77.
   7. Ibid., p.4.

status of official court records in 1775.[8] The court tried serious
offences (that is, felonies) committed in the City of London and
the county of Middlesex. The majority of prostitutes who appear in
the pages of the *OBSP* stood accused of stealing privately from the
person, although some found assault included in the charges laid
against them. The publisher of the *OBSP* aimed at completeness
and from at least the mid-eighteenth century the report of each
of what were felt to be the most interesting trials would be in the
form of a supposedly verbatim transcript of the exchanges heard
in the court. Clearly such 'transcripts' have to be used with care.
The court's proceedings were deliberately designed to intimidate.
Witnesses, prosecutors and accused were understandably anxious
to construct their accounts in such a way as to make them more
acceptable to the bench and the jury. The *OBSP* were aimed at a lay
readership which sought to be entertained as well as informed.
Paradoxically, this carries with it an advantage for a study of prostitution as any case containing matters of a sexual or possibly
scandalous nature was sure to be reported at length. The certain
omissions and probable alterations made by the *OBSP*'s publisher,
however, serve to increase the reader's distance from descriptions
of events already reshaped by the formalised procedure and language
through which they were told.

It would nevertheless be a mistake to see in the difficulties of
interpretation that thus arise a reason for repudiating the usefulness of the *Old Bailey Sessions Papers* as a source. Setting narrative
complexities aside for the moment, beginning in 1791 the *Papers*
record the ages of those found guilty. These can be combined with
data derived from other sources to build up a picture of the age
profile of London's streetwalkers. The exact location at which prostitute and client met is almost always given and rarely contested
and can be used to map the changing geography of the trade in
the capital. That both parties were able to agree on this, while
each usually attempted to lay the initiative in making contact on
the other, is indicative of the need to adopt a sceptical yet not
wholly disbelieving approach when employing these accounts. In
J.H. Langbein's words, the *OBSP* 'touch on countless facets of the
social and economic life of the metropolis and give us sustained
contact with the lives and language of the ordinary people of the
time'.[9] Thus the trial narratives are rich in incidental detail, giving

8. T.R. Forbes, 'A study of Old Bailey sentences between 1729 and 1800', *Guildhall Studies in London History*, 5 (1981), pp.26–35.
9. Langbein, 'Shaping the eighteenth-century criminal trial', p.271.

much-needed information as to the activities and, with added caution, the motivations and attitudes of prostitutes, clients, police and, of course, the court itself.[10]

Another essential source has been the collection of reports and, more especially, the printed minutes of evidence produced by the various Select Committees on the Police of the Metropolis that sat between 1812 and 1829. Each committee tended to concern itself with a particular aspect of the capital's policing. The committee of 1812 largely restricted itself to considering the basic organisation of London's night watch; that of 1816 heard evidence as to the relative efficiency of the various forces; the first report of the 1817 committee dealt principally with the question of public houses and the licensing laws, the second with rewards and the increasingly fashionable topic of child offenders; those of 1818 and 1822 looked most closely at the supposed decline in public morals and the related growth of prostitution, while the report of 1828 returned to the questions of juvenile crime and the bounty system. All the committees, however, took such matters as no more than starting points for their investigations and almost all dealt at some length with the question of prostitution. Such were the manifest ramifications of the sex trade that many other committees also discussed the issue in their reports, including the committee on burglaries of 1770, that on the watch two years later, the eight committee reports on various facets of the judicial and prison system that were produced between 1811 and 1828, and those of 1814 and 1821 on vagrancy. These have also all been used in this study.

Many of the caveats noted with regard to the *OBSP* apply with equal force to these documents. Present-day readers have to pick their way with care through the tangle of hidden, and not-so-hidden, agendas of those whose testimony is recorded. The Police Committee of 1816, for example, persisted in the belief that female child prostitution was widespread in the metropolis, despite the repeated denials of members of the judiciary and policing authorities who gave evidence before it. Evidence from alternative sources suggests that in this instance the witnesses' views were closer to the reality of the situation than those of the committee. The same can also be said of a number of other matters on which the committee was disappointed by the statements made to it.

10. For a detailed and intelligent analysis of the advantages and shortcomings of the *OBSP* for the historian, see Langbein's 'Shaping the eighteenth-century criminal trial', and his 'Criminal trial before the lawyers', *University of Chicago Law Review*, 45 (1978).

Such disagreements are not necessarily a disadvantage to the historian, as they obliged both sides to support their claims with argument and example. The committee rooms did not always reverberate to the sound of axes being noisily ground, however. More frequently, the committee members were happy to admit their ignorance, encouraging the witnesses to supply them with the most basic information regarding a particular matter as well as to digress at length on one or other of its facets – to the profit of the committee and of the present-day reader. Such information has been used in this study to confirm, to qualify and in some cases to fill the gaps in the evidence collected from other sources.

The great number of pamphlets published in this period on the subject of prostitution has also proved invaluable. Such little books, often provoking others into print in denial or support of the author's argument, have formed the basis of the discussion in Chapter Seven of changing attitudes towards the trade.[11]

Many studies of prostitution have been built on such sources. More often than not, they have turned out to be histories of prostitution, of reformation, of the police – but rarely of prostitutes. This book is not the first to attempt some kind of history of the latter. No doubt, like others, it has failed. But that failure does not negate the need for a history of prostitution that escapes from the domination of those who placed themselves in authority over prostitutes – the agents of the law and the moralisers. In constructing such a history, we may break free from the languages of sexuality and criminality that together form the restrictive vocabulary of vice. To do so points to the deployment of concepts drawn neither from the histories of sex nor of deviance, but from economic and labour history.

By concentrating on such concepts, we can attempt much more detailed – though probably far more mundane – reconstructions of the experience of prostitution. Magdalenes and reformatories, for instance, along with workhouses and charities, will come to be seen as only a part (and perhaps a very minor part at that) of prostitutes' lives – subverted as much as submitted to, formed and reformed as much by their inmates as by their managers. Via what might be termed a prostitute-centred history, the relationship between

11. Of course, the number of replies generated by a particular pamphlet is far from being a reliable indicator of its relative influence. No publication produced a greater response (in terms of published rejoinders) than the Reverend Martin Madan's *Thelyphthora* of 1780 in which it was argued that the introduction of polygamy would lead to the disappearance of prostitution.

prostitutes and their reformers – indeed, between prostitutes and their historians – may be plausibly, and more sympathetically, portrayed as one in which the latter were simultaneously an irritation and an opportunity for the prostitutes rather than – as has often been the case – the other way around.

CHAPTER TWO

The Experience of Prostitution

Over the course of the eighteenth century, commentators and social reformers became increasingly keen to impress their readers with the depth of their understanding of prostitution. In particular, they put forward a number of theories as to the types of women and young girls who would be most likely to enter the trade and which combinations of circumstances made their doing so probable. Some blamed what they saw as increasing frivolity and indiscipline in the manner in which female children were raised. Corrupted by novels and the general luxury and opulence of the nation, such children soon exhibited tendencies towards impudence and idleness.[1] 'And then it is', wrote one author, 'that a Wench of Fourteen, fancys herself as fit for Man, and ripe for Joy, as a woman of Five and Twenty.'[2] A subsequent failure of parental vigilance would quickly result either in the 'ruining' of the girl by a 'rampant Rake', leading ineluctably to a career on the streets, or to her more immediate seduction into a brothel by an aged procuress. By the later eighteenth century, however, it was the innocence, rather than the appetites, of the young victims of bawds and lechers that was emphasised, with some writers arguing that it was not from the ranks of dissolute masses that prostitution drew its recruits but from the respectable families of the impoverished lower middle classes.

---

1. See, for example, Anon., *The Evils of Adultery and Prostitution; with an Enquiry into the Causes of their Present Alarming Increase, and some Means Recommended for Checking their Progress* (1792).
2. Father Poussin, *Pretty Doings in a Protestant Nation. Being a View of the Present State of Fornication, Whorecraft, and Adultery, in Great Britain, and the Territories and Dependencies thereunto belonging* (1734), p.6.

The social origins of prostitutes

Sources which allow us to construct our own image of the women who entered prostitution in the eighteenth and early nineteenth centuries are fairly thin. Nevertheless, those that do exist unsurprisingly suggest a more complex picture than that suggested above. Throughout this period, most prostitutes appear to have been born into the poorest sections of the community and to have acquired few skills while growing up that would allow them to escape poverty. Thomas Pellatt, secretary to the London Female Penitentiary, told Parliament in 1817 that the prostitutes who applied to his institution for aid were 'chiefly persons who have lived in service, maid-servants, orphans, persons who have been left with one parent, and that parent under the necessity of going out to work'.[3] John Fielding, the London magistrate, found that most of the twenty-five prostitutes he had arrested and questioned on the night of 1 May 1758 were born into pauperism. It is also perhaps significant that the parents of twenty-two of the young women were either dead or had deserted their children.[4]

Although Fielding did not record the occupations, if any, in which his interrogatees had engaged before their entry into prostitution, there was general agreement amongst most commentators that certain trades were responsible for the introduction of a disproportionately large number of women to a career on the streets. The clothing industries were held to be particularly culpable in this respect. Criticisms of the clothing trades' role took two apparently contradictory forms. One blamed a combination of bad working conditions, low pay and the essentially trivial nature of the industries' products. In 1783, the writer Charles Horne warned parents against allowing their daughters to become milliners, mantua-makers (dress-makers), haberdashers and other 'dealers in vanity' as such trades were not merely held in generally low esteem but were 'actually seminaries of prostitution'.[5] The other, and by the close of the eighteenth century more common, form of complaint attacked the diminishing opportunities offered to women by these occupations as they came increasingly to be dominated by men. All but a few trades had become 'shamefully engrossed' by men, complained

3. *P.P.* (1817), Vol.VII, Police Committee, 2nd report, p.505.
4. B.L. Add.Mss.27825, Place Papers, ff.240–45.
5. C. Horne, *Serious Thoughts on the Miseries of Seduction and Prostitution, with a full Account of the Evils that produce them; plainly showing Prostitution to be contrary to the Laws of Nature* (1783), p.51.

The Times in 1786: 'We have men mantua-makers, men milliners, men stay-makers, men shoe-makers for women's shoes, men hair-cutters for ladies' hair; and, to the shocking indecency of the sex, even men corn-cutters! . . . Such are some of the many causes to which we owe that awful excess of female prostitution'.[6]

How far the supposed connection between the clothing and fashion trades and prostitution was a causal one, and how far merely coincidental, cannot be determined with any certainty. But that such fears were not wholly misplaced is suggested by an examination of the occupations claimed by some of those arrested as prostitutes in Southwark between 1814 and 1829. Of the fourteen women for whom a trade is recorded, nine are connected to the clothing industry, including shoe-binders, a mantua-maker, a satin stitch worker, a glove maker, a straw-bonnet maker, a stay trimmer, a hat binder and a needle woman. The remaining five women include a sack maker, a charwoman, a costermonger (a seller of fruit and vegetables from a barrow), a fruit seller and a former domestic servant.[7]

It is a little surprising that only one woman, Sarah Jones, who is described as having been formerly servant to a Mr Humphreys of Tooley Street, appears to have spent any time in service, as this was another occupation which the authorities considered a common route into prostitution. Pellatt's statement to the 1817 Police Committee that most of the women applying to the London Female Penitentiary had been domestic servants echoed that made in a proposal to a committee of the Common Council of the City that had been set up in 1814 in response to a petition against streetwalking signed by many of the City's householders.[8] The proposal, by Captain Torkington of the Royal Marines, desired the creation of an asylum for those unemployed female servants, discharged without money or character references (essential if another post was to be obtained) by unthinking employers, who formed 'the greater part' of the capital's prostitutes.[9] John Lavender, a patrol

---

6. *The Times*, 8 Dec. 1786.
7. CLRO 225E SC1\8 (Southwark compter). Commitments for trial at the sessions, Jul. 1814 to Oct. 1842.
8. CLRO Petition Roll No.12, Petition of the Inhabitant Householders of the Principal Streets in the City of London against Female Prostitutes, read in Common Council 16 Dec. 1813.
9. CLRO Misc. Mss 283.4. Committee papers 1814–25 (Committee appointed 16 Dec. 1813 to consider petition of inhabitant householders), Letter from Capt. R. Torkington of the Royal Marines relative to providing an Asylum for Female Servants out of place, read in Committee 21 Jan. 1814.

officer of Queen's Square police office, also criticised the 'caprice' of employers who discharged female servants without reason and refused to supply references, thus driving their former employees into prostitution.[10] Defoe, too, writing in 1725, believed many of London's prostitutes to be out-of-work maidservants, although he blamed the women's own greed and lack of foresight. More especially, he complained of their 'amphibious' lifestyle, moving from 'Bawdy-House to Service and from Service to Bawdy-House again', thus rendering themselves unfit for either position.[11]

Economies of makeshift

Defoe's comments, among which is also a complaint at the demands such women made on parish funds, highlight an aspect of the trade about which the available sources are more than usually silent: that is, the degree to which many women may have moved in and out of prostitution, or combined it with another occupation or periodic calls on private charity and parish relief, in order to cover periods when 'respectable' employment was unavailable or to supplement the inadequate earnings such employment brought. Martin Madan's *An Account of the Triumphant Death of F.S. a Converted Prostitute*, although its protagonist was almost certainly fictional, suggests that periodic resort to prostitution was common enough for it to form a convincing part of a stereotypical narrative of a prostitute's life.[12] F.S., having received the genteel and liberal education befitting the daughter of an army officer, is reduced to poverty, seduced, impregnated and deserted. After a brief time spent on the stage and as a strolling player, she works at her needle to support herself. Failing to meet her modest needs in this way she turns to prostitution, the shame she feels at her way of life leading to habitual drunkenness. Driven from her lodgings she spends three months in the Magdalen Hospital for Penitent Prostitutes. From there, appalled at the prospect of returning to prostitution, she joins the harvest gathering in Kent. Come the end of harvest, she gains a place in a tradesman's house in Canterbury. Falling ill, she is

10. *P.P.* (1816), Vol.V, Police Committee, p.229.

11. Andrew Morton (pseud. for Daniel Defoe), *Every-Body's Business is No-Body's Business; or Private Abuses, Public Grievances: Exemplified in the Pride, Insolence, and Exorbitant Wages of our Women Servants, Footmen, etc.* (1725), p.7.

12. M. Madan, *An Account of the Triumphant Death of F.S. a Converted Prostitute, who Died Apr. 1763, aged Twenty-Six Years* (1763).

dismissed and reduced to beggary and reliance on the charity of the cathedral clergy. By now consumptive and fearing approaching death, she returns to London, obtains cheap lodgings through a former fellow prostitute and sends for her mother. The mother in turn desires the presence of the author, Madan himself, and the narrative closes with Madan leading F.S. in the singing of hymns as, wholly repentant, she dies.

Gothically embroidered as it is, F.S.'s story in some part echoes those more prosaically related by many prostitutes charged with theft at the Old Bailey. Anne Lumley, accused in January 1753 of the theft of John Pixley's watch, told the court that she had explained to Pixley that she was not 'a common person in that way' when he had solicited her but that she was reduced to poverty (her husband having been killed in battle abroad) and 'a little money would be of service' to her. It was only Pixley's subsequent refusal to pay that had led her to keep the watch he had given her as guarantee of later payment.[13] Elizabeth Hammond, charged with a similar crime in 1754, informed the Old Bailey court that she got her living by winding silk but that she had accepted a silver watch from John Jolly in order to lie with him.[14]

An income generated from various sources in this way could also include money, food or clothing, won from the parish authorities and private philanthropic concerns. Thomas Frinnagan, master of St. Giles's Catholic Free School, regularly distributed oatmeal and old clothes to the poor of the St. Giles district in the winter months. As he told the 1814 Select Committee on Vagrancy, he frequently noticed the very women whom he had relieved in the morning, painted and gaudily dressed the same evening 'offering themselves to the notice of the unthinking, as prostitutes'.[15] Although there is no suggestion that Frinnagan subsequently refused charity to these women, there is no doubt that the parish authorities at least were reluctant to supplement prostitutes' income in this way. The parish officers of Bishopsgate, for example, refused relief to Mary Johnson in 1751, telling her that she 'might go a whoring or a thieving' to get her bread.[16] That such a reaction by the authorities was fairly common is suggested by the remarks made by the clerk of the peace for Surrey to the 1828 Select Committee on the Police. He

13. *OBSP*, 11–15 Jan. 1753, p.63.   14. *OBSP*, 23–28 Oct. 1754, p.308.
15. *P.P.* (1814–15), Vol.III, Minutes of the Evidence taken before the Committee to enquire into the State of Mendicity and Vagrancy in the Metropolis and its Neighbourhood, 23, p.137.
16. *OBSP*, 16–21 Oct. 1751, p.287.

stated that many parishes refused more than temporary relief to any applicant not blind, lame, impotent or otherwise unable to work and that women were in consequence 'driven upon the town'.[17]

Not all parishes could afford such severity, however. The parish of St. Giles, covering some of the most wretched streets in the capital, attempted to enquire into the background of every applicant for relief in order to ascertain their character and term of residence in the parish but was faced with the landlords of slum lodging houses who were willing to swear to any tenant's possession of a good character and several months residence.[18] Certainly, the parish distributed relief to women its officers knew to be prostitutes; women like Hannah Ragin who shared a room with several others in a notorious house of ill fame and yet received regular relief from the parish funds in addition to occasional extra payments of up to eighteen pence a time.[19]

The geographical origins of prostitutes

St. Giles's was known as a strongly Irish district and the parish's concern with the length of time an applicant for relief had been resident in the parish draws attention to the fact that throughout this period the proportion of immigrants in London's female population was extremely high, with most estimates placing it at around two-thirds to three-quarters of the whole.[20] From this fact alone it may be supposed that many of London's prostitutes were born and raised outside the capital. Although the majority of Fielding's small group were Londoners by birth,[21] and the Reverend Henry Budd, chaplain of Bridewell in the early nineteenth century, found the prostitutes in the prison to be equally divided between those born within the capital and those born without,[22] César de Saussure, writing around the same time as Fielding, concluded that most of London's streetwalkers were from the country, come to London to

17. *P.P.* (1828), Vol.VI, Police Committee, p.152.
18. *P.P.* (1817), Vol.VII, Police Committee, 1st report, p.155.
19. Ibid., pp.153–4.
20. P.J. Corfield, *The Impact of English Towns, 1700–1800* (1982), p.103; M.D. George, *London Life in the Eighteenth Century* (1925; all citations refer to the 1985 edition), p.118.
21. B.L. Add.Mss.27825, Place Papers, ff.240–45.
22. *P.P.* (1814–15), Vol.III, Select Committee to enquire into Mendicity and Vagrancy, p.64.

TABLE 2.1 *Birthplaces of prostitutes (Southwark) 1814–29*

Region of origin	Number of prostitutes	%
Ireland	10	12.82
W. Counties	9	11.53
Home Counties	6	7.69
North-east	4	5.12
North-west	4	5.12
N. Midlands	3	3.84
South	3	3.84
Scotland	3	3.84
Wales	2	2.56
Abroad	2	2.56
S. Midlands	1	1.28
E. Counties	0	0.00
(Total migrants	47	60.25)
London	31	39.74
Total	78	100.00

Source: CLRO 225E SC1\8 (Southwark compter). Commitments for trial at the sessions, July 1814 to October 1842. Regions as in P. Earle, 'The female labour market in London in the late seventeenth and early eighteenth centuries', *Economic History Review*, 2nd ser., XLII, 3 (1989), pp.328–53

W. Counties = Gloucs, Wilts, Somerset, Dorset, Devon, Cornwall, Worcs, Hereford
Home Counties = Middlesex, Herts, Surrey, Kent, Essex
North-east = Yorks, Northumberland, Durham
North-west = Lancs, Cheshire, Shropshire, Cumberland, Westmorland
N. Midlands = Warwicks, Notts, Derbys, Staffs, Leics
South = Sussex, Hants
S. Midlands = Bucks, Beds, Oxon, Berks, Northants
E. Counties = Cambs, Lincs, Rutland, Hunts, Suffolk, Norfolk

NB. London = urban, built-up area only
    Abroad = 1 from Portugal and 1 from America

seek their fortunes.[23] Such women were, wrote William Hutton, 'a sacrifice to the metropolis, offered by the thirty-nine counties'.[24]

Of those prostitutes arrested in Southwark between 1814 and 1829, seventy-eight had their place of birth recorded. These have been grouped together in Table 2.1. Although London-born women formed much the largest single group, immigrant prostitutes made up over sixty per cent of the entire group. That a relatively high

23. C.de Saussure, *A Foreign View of England in the Reigns of George I and George II* (translated and edited by Mme. van Muyden, 1902), p.203.
24. W. Hutton, *A Journey to London; Comprising a Description of the most Interesting Objects of Curiosity to a Visitor of the Metropolis* (2nd edn., 1818), p.47.

number came from Ireland should not be taken as representative of the capital at large as Southwark was, like St. Giles to the north of the river, an area with a substantial Irish community. More interesting, perhaps, is the fact that those parts of the British Isles most geographically distant from London combined to produce a high proportion of the Borough's streetwalkers, to some extent confirming Bernard Mandeville's assumption in his proposal for legalised prostitution that recruits to the state-run brothels would be predominantly drawn from the northern and western parts of the kingdom.[25]

Of the two women born outside these islands one was American by birth while the other, Lodiana Rose, was described as a 'Negro . . . a native of Portugal'. Black prostitutes were not unknown in London in this period, Lord Pembroke telling Boswell in 1775 of a brothel that at one time had been entirely staffed by black women.[26] While Pembroke's brothel was an expensive establishment intended for the use of upper-class men, black prostitutes could also be found working in the poorer neighbourhoods along the river.[27] It seems most likely that Lodiana Rose, described in the records as 'a common street-walker' and sharing a room in Dover Street, one of the most notorious parts of Southwark, with her compatriot Augustin Dilima (a former soldier and sailor turned shoe-maker) was one of these.

The ages of prostitutes

Rose was twenty-two years of age when she was arrested and sentenced to a month's imprisonment in the summer of 1819. She was thus older than many of the women arrested for prostitution in Southwark in this period (see Figure 2.1). The youngest women held in the Borough compter were the sixteen-year-old Martha Burges and Mary Ball, the former living with her mother in Kent Street. The existence of still younger prostitutes soliciting on the streets of London was a matter of great concern to observers and to the authorities throughout the eighteenth and early nineteenth centuries. Charles Horne complained that girls of twelve and thirteen

25. B. Mandeville, *A Modest Defence of Public Stews: Or, An Essay Upon Whoring. As it is Now Practis'd in These Kingdoms* (1724), p.64.

26. L. Stone, *The Family, Sex and Marriage in England, 1500–1800* (1977), p.601.

27. See, for example, the print depicting a riverside bawdy house, 'The Wapping Bagnio', in Stone, *The Family, Sex and Marriage* (1977), print 41 between pp.576 and 577.

FIG. 2.1 *Age structure of prostitutes arrested in Southwark, 1814–29*

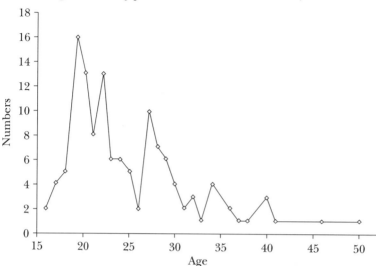

Source: CLRO 225E SC1/8 (Southwark Compter) Commitments for Trial at the Sessions, Oct. 1814–Oct. 1842

years old who were thought of as far too young for marriage were nevertheless considered perfectly fit for prostitution.[28] Others lamented the presence along the Strand of 'infant prostitutes' as young as nine or ten years of age 'offering their persons . . . to every passenger'.[29] One wrote of such children inviting men to the bagnios, or Turkish baths, of Catherine Street and Bridges Street.[30] The Select Committee on the Police of 1816 was itself anxious to discover the whereabouts of child bawdy houses. The magistrates and police officers it questioned, however, generally denied any knowledge of such houses, despite the committee's insistence that brothels 'devoted to children alone' were notoriously known to exist.[31] This suggests that although there almost certainly were some very young streetwalkers in this period, their numbers were much exaggerated by commentators.[32]

28. Horne, *Serious Thoughts on the Miseries of Seduction and Prostitution* (1783), pp.6, 32.
29. *The Times*, May 10 1786 and 14 Oct. 1788; see also 17 Jun. 1788 and 29 Dec. 1789.
30. Ibid., 14 Oct. 1788.
31. *P.P.* (1816), Vol.V, Police Committee, pp.127, 147, 252.
32. It has been plausibly argued that the even stronger conviction held in the late nineteenth century that child prostitution abounded in London had equally little basis in fact. See J.R. Walkowitz, *Prostitution and Victorian Society* (1980), p.17.

That this was so is further indicated by the policies of the various reform houses set up to induce women to leave the trade – policies laid down very often by reformers keen to win general sympathy for London's prostitutes and thus tending in their public statements to emphasise the extreme youthfulness and innocence of the objects of their philanthropy. In his *Proposals for Establishing a Public Place of Reception for Penitent Prostitutes*, Robert Dingley also spoke of 'another set of Objects', that is, girls of 'the lower Class of people' aged from twelve to fifteen years who were at risk of ruination. His decision that they should be kept entirely isolated from the prostitutes in the proposed asylum carries the strong implication that he expected few of that age to have already embarked upon a career in prostitution.[33] A proposal of 1770 advocating the establishment of a similar institution stipulated that only women aged between fifteen and twenty-one were to gain admittance.[34] The average age of those applying for entry into the Magdalen Hospital for Penitent Prostitutes and the London Female Penitentiary was between seventeen and eighteen years.[35] While younger than those held, for example, in the Southwark compter, this is still considerably older than the supposed mass of child prostitutes for whom the Select Committee demonstrated such concern.

The information available from various records of arrest and punishment confirms a generally older age profile for the bulk of London's prostitutes than that the Select Committee on the Police, and others, were anxious to establish. The youngest group of which we have evidence was that taken up out of the bawdy houses in Hedge Lane in 1758 by John Fielding (see Figure 2.2). Eleven of the twenty-five women were aged between eighteen and nineteen, the group's median age being eighteen and its mean age 18.1. Fielding also asked the women how long they had been 'upon the Town'. Twelve of them had entered prostitution at the age of eighteen or above although the fact that some, such as the fifteen-year old who had been on the streets since she was twelve, had done so very much earlier in life brings the mean age for the group down to 16.4 (see Figure 2.3).

33. R. Dingley, *Proposals for Establishing a Public Place of Reception for Penitent Prostitutes* (1758), p.7.

34. R. Challoner, *Proposals for Opening a Subscription in Favour of an Asylum to Receive Poor Young Maids, Destitute of Places; for Preserving their Virtue and Innocence, 'till Proper Places can be Procured for Them* (c.1770).

35. *P.P.* (1817), Vol.VII, Police Committee, 2nd report, pp.332, 505.

FIG. 2.2 *Age structure of prostitutes questioned by John Fielding, 1758*

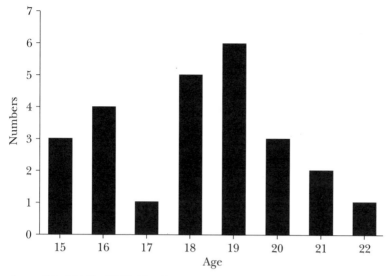

Source: B.L. Add.Mss.27825, Place Papers, ff.240–45

FIG. 2.3 *Ages at entry into prostitution of prostitutes questioned by John Fielding, 1758*

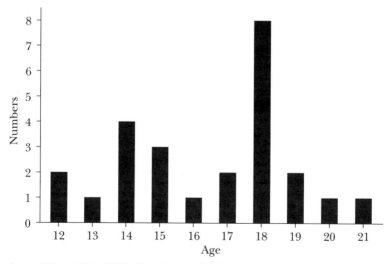

Source: B.L. Add.Mss.27825, Place Papers, ff.240–45

FIG. 2.4   *Age structure of prostitutes held in Bridewell and questioned by the Guardian Society, 1816*

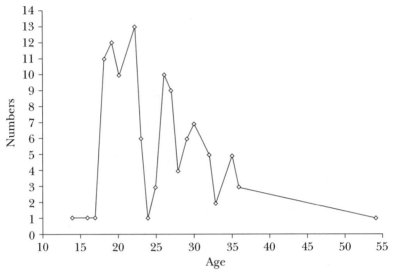

Source: P.P. (1817), Police Committee, 2nd Report, VII, p.459

A breakdown of the ages of the 111 prostitutes questioned by the Guardian Society while serving terms of imprisonment in the Bridewell in 1816 produces figures that more nearly agree with those mentioned above drawn from the Southwark compter, or gaol, records. Although the largest single cohort was slightly older, at twenty-two years of age, than that at Southwark, the mean age of those questioned exactly coincides with the latter's figure of 24.8, while the median age is only marginally greater at twenty-four (see Figure 2.4). We can compare this in turn with figures derived from listings of all women imprisoned in the Bridewell as 'disorderly' between 1815 and 1817. Although other evidence confirms that this was the term used within the prison (and outside it) to describe prostitutes, it is probable that some of the women so listed were not prostitutes and it is this which may account for the slightly higher set of averages thus produced, with a mode age of twenty years, a median of twenty-five and a mean of 26.3 (see Figure 2.5).

Finally, there are the ages of those women found guilty at the Old Bailey from 1791 (when such information is first included in the records) to 1799 and from 1820 to 1825. These women were not tried as prostitutes but rather for offences related to prostitution

FIG. 2.5 *Age structure of female disorderly offenders: Bridewell, 1815–17*

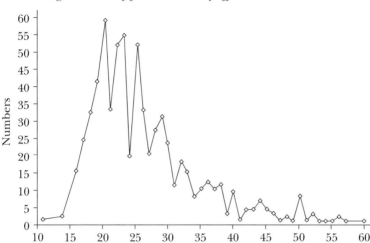

Source: *P.P.* (1818), First Report from the Select Committee on the Prisons within the City of London and Borough of Southwark (275), VIII, App. 27

– overwhelmingly theft from, and occasionally assault on, clients. There are grounds for believing that this was something of a specialist activity and that many of the women regarded themselves not as prostitutes but rather as thieves who used the methods of prostitution to gain access to their victim's person. Perhaps for this reason, as well as a possible tendency on the part of juries to acquit more youthful offenders (the ages of those acquitted not being recorded), analysis of the figures results in a relatively advanced age profile, with the mode ages of those convicted in the 1790s standing at twenty-seven and thirty years (against a mean of 28.2 and a median of twenty-seven) while those found guilty between 1820 and 1825 are, interestingly, somewhat younger with a mode age of twenty-two, a mean of 25.4 and a median age of twenty-three (see Figures 2.6, 2.7 and 2.8).

It is just possible, from the above information, to sketch a rough social characterisation of London's streetwalkers and brothel in-mates in the eighteenth and early nineteenth centuries, although it is clear that the nature of the trade, and of the sources, is such that many prostitutes would not conform to any such generalisation. Whilst acknowledging this, it can be said that most of the capital's prostitutes were born into relative poverty, if not outright pauperism.

FIG. 2.6   *Age structure of prostitutes convicted at the Old Bailey,*
1791–99

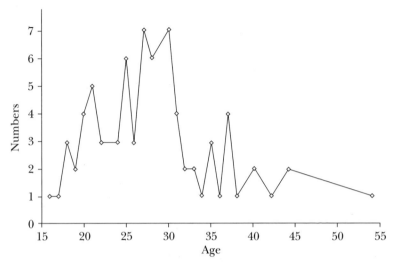

Source: OBSP

FIG. 2.7   *Age structure of prostitutes convicted at the Old Bailey,*
1820–29

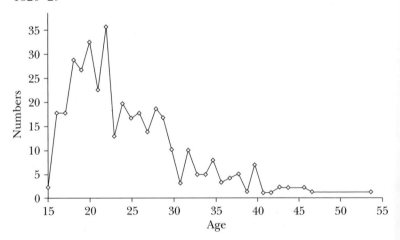

Source: OBSP

FIG. 2.8   *Age structure of prostitutes convicted at the Old Bailey, 1791–99 and 1820–29*

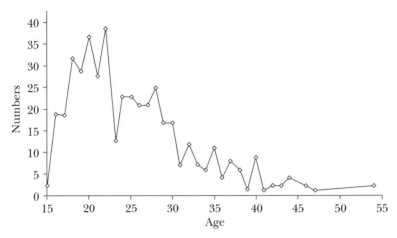

Source: OBSP

The likely death or desertion of one or both parents compounded an economic plight made worse by the ability to gain only unskilled, or at best semi-skilled, and insecure employment. Despite the authorities' concern with child prostitution, most entered the trade in their late teens or early twenties, leaving the streets within a few years. Even a cursory glance at the Old Bailey records shows the great majority to have been unmarried. Just over half of them were born outside London.

The structure of the trade

It is appropriate at this point to examine the structure of the trade in which the women were engaged. The brothel keeper or bawd occupied the lowest place in the reformers' moral universe. John Disney wrote that 'the Lewdness of Common Whores, and such as frequent them, could never make so great a progress in the World, but by the avarice and wickedness of these vile Promoters' and called for ever more severe laws against 'such wicked Factors of Impurity'.[36]

36. J. Disney, *A View of Ancient Laws against Immorality and Prophaness* (1729), pp.13, 24.

By the turn of the century, the alleged monopolisation of bawdy houses in the City and the East End by Jews was used as further evidence of the keepers' iniquities, the authorities of Aldgate railing against the 'Jews of bad character' who by employing aliases and false addresses prevented the suppression of the parish's brothels.[37]

As we have seen, bawds were accused not merely of facilitating a woman's prostitution but often of being the cause of her initial fall. Hogarth depicted one such in the opening scene of *The Harlot's Progress*, meeting young girls newly arrived from the country and seducing them into a life of vice. The authorities seem to have found it difficult, however, to locate real – as opposed to fictional – victims of the practice. When Aldgate parish was asked to produce examples of such seduction into the paths of impurity it could only provide one instance, and that of a young boy seduced into theft from his employer through his association with prostitutes.[38] Nevertheless, the belief that bawds ensnared their reluctant and unknowing victims into prostitution was powerful enough (and became if anything more widely held over the course of the century) for scares to break out in the press from time to time. In the summer and autumn of 1788, *The Times* published a series of letters and articles claiming that London was ringed by female boarding schools, regularly visited if not actually run by bawds, the chief purpose of which was to supply recruits to the brothels of the West End. Once immured within these establishments and embarked on a career of prostitution, the young women's descent into degradation and disease was believed to be as rapid as it was inevitable. The brothel keeper, and her clients, growing tired of her, '. . . she is turned into the streets to catch at the casual chance of the evening, where, in a short time, she takes to gin-drinking, and at an age when the virtuous part of her sex are just entering into life, she pines out a diseased existence in some garret, or cellar'.[39]

In practice, it appears that only a small minority of London's prostitutes ever worked within the kind of brothel these writers so reviled. Undoubtedly, houses with a resident keeper (usually a woman, though male brothel keepers were not unknown) enjoying full control over the activities of a staff of women who lived on the premises, whose clients were effectively chosen for them by the bawd and who received either a set wage or a certain portion of the profits, did exist. The more expensive establishments, such as those

---

37. *P.P.* (1817), Vol.VII, Police Committee, 1st report, p.55.
38. Ibid., pp.54–5.   39. *The Times*, 17 Jun. 1788.

concentrated 'in that part of London where the court air is to be breathed' (that is, in St. James) were probably of this kind.[40] The keepers of these houses – often referred to as Mother Abbesses just as the houses themselves were known as convents or nunneries – were frequently well-known figures: the 'Little Harpy of iniquity from Germyn-street' accompanied her 'meretricious attendants' to the theatre and the pleasure gardens; Mammy Windsor of King's Place was renowned as 'the perfect mistress of the art of conversation';[41] while Mother Johnson attended the Queen's birthday parade in 1788 in an elaborate carriage and surrounded by the young inmates of her house.[42] At the other end of the scale lay those houses whose keepers were themselves so wretchedly poor as to render their prosecution a worthless exercise.[43]

Some bawdy house keepers coupled two or more occupations of varying degrees of respectability. William Newman, solicitor to the City of London, agreed with the members of the 1822 Select Committee on the State of the Police that many brothel keepers professed other trades such as the running of oyster shops and chandlers' shops.[44] John Fielding described the proprietors of Westminster's brothels and irregular taverns as 'Bawds, Thieves, Receivers of Stolen Goods, and Marshalsea Court and Sheriff's Officers'.[45] A Mr Dancer of St. Giles combined the running of three or four houses of ill fame in New Street with his position as clerk to the Bedford Chapel in nearby Charlotte Street.[46]

While the women living in Dancer's houses more nearly approached the status of paying lodgers than resident staff, in those brothels where the women were seen essentially as employees, the keepers used a variety of measures to ensure obedience on the part of the young prostitutes. The claim that brothel keepers made a practice of supplying their prostitutes with clothes in which to solicit, allowing the keepers to swear an action against the women for theft of the clothes should they abscond in them, was a common one.[47]

40. F.A. Wenderborn, *A View of England towards the Close of the Eighteenth Century* (2 vols., 1791), vol.1, p.291.

41. *The Times*, 2 Nov. 1786 and 5 Feb. 1788.   42. Ibid., 19 Jan. 1788.

43. *P.P.* (1816), Vol.V, Police Committee, p.127.

44. *P.P.* (1822), Vol.IV, Police Committee, p.88.

45. *C.J.* (1770), Vol.XXXII, Report from the Committee to enquire into the Several Burglaries and Robberies that of late have been committed in and about the Cities of London and Westminster, p.881.

46. *P.P.* (1817), Vol.VII, Police Committee, 1st report, p.152.

47. *The Times* of 10 May 1786 wrote of each prostitute being 'attended by an old ragged harradan, who supply them with cloathes for the purpose of enticing passengers'.

When Ann Smith was charged with stealing a number of articles of clothing from Elizabeth Ward in 1754, she claimed that Ward ran a bawdy-house and had given her the clothes 'to appear in company with', pointing out another woman in the court who had been similarly provided for.[48] Maria Ann Cooke, charged with a similar offence, made the same claim, adding that her prosecutor, Hannah Swinchurch, had allowed her but a shilling a week, had threatened her with death should she fail to bring home a man each night, and had recently turned out of the house three recalcitrant girls 'as naked as they were born'.[49] While Swinchurch evidently relied on threats of violence, ejection and prosecution to ensure her charges returned with clients, others were said to keep a closer watch, either following the women, or employing others to do so, as they solicited in the streets and public houses of the city.[50]

Actual as well as threatened violence against the inmates of brothels by their proprietors was probably fairly common. The prosecution of Elizabeth Moore in 1788 by the notorious bawdy house keeper Mother Wood for unpaid board and lodgings (Moore had quit Wood's establishment for that run by Mother Johnstone) brought to light the regular beatings Wood had inflicted on the nineteen-year old Moore when the latter had failed to earn sufficient money.[51] Another case came to the notice of the parish authorities of St. George, Southwark, when two young women, inmates of a bawdy house, applied to the parish for protection from the couple who ran the house and who had used 'a great deal of cruelty' against them. The authorities lodged the women in the parish workhouse until a prosecution (ultimately unsuccessful) for managing a disorderly house could be brought against the couple.[52]

Many houses employed one or more men commonly known as bullies and, more rarely, pimps. While it would be naive to imagine that they were not at least sometimes used to impose the brothel keeper's will on the prostitutes in the house, the little evidence that can be gathered suggests that their principal functions were to protect the brothel against invasion by the forces of the law and to eject the more unruly customers (including those who objected

48. *OBSP*, 24 Apr.–1 May 1754, p.146.
49. *OBSP*, 27 Oct. 1790, p.895.
50. *The Times*, 10 May 1786, 16 Apr. 1787 and 27 Nov. 1787; *P.P.* (1817), Vol.VII, Police Committee, 1st report, p.136; *P.P.* (1817), Vol.VII, 2nd report, pp.460–1; J.B. Talbot, *The Miseries of Prostitution* (1844), pp.12–14.
51. *The Times*, 2 Jun. 1788.   52. *P.P.* (1817), Vol.VII, 2nd report, p.465.

to being robbed of their money or possessions).[53] Many of the prostitutes soliciting in the street and enjoying a greater degree of independence from bawdy house keepers than those women described above also appear to have maintained some connection with bullies (frequently soldiers) but again the available sources indicate that the latters' principal role lay in the protection of the streetwalkers from the watch and in aiding the extortion and robbery of 'culls' or customers.[54]

For the majority of London's prostitutes, neither kept within a brothel nor soliciting under the watchful eye of a bawd, once a customer had been attracted a choice then, in theory, had to be made between a variety of locations at which the sexual act could be accomplished. In practice, financial and other circumstances limited the options open to each individual. Many undoubtedly made use of the darker corners of the capital's streets, alleys and parks. Jonathan Joel, having been picked up by two streetwalkers in Bishopsgate Street and having visited several of the City's public houses with them, was invited by one, the widow Ann Bains, 'to do that thing . . . called carnal conversation' with her in a nearby alley. She used the opportunity this gave to steal his watch.[55] Sarah Chapman was offered one shilling to go down an alley with James Mears, 'which I took, and, knowing that he had a wife and family, would not be concerned with him, so I ran away with the shilling'.[56] Boswell's well-known couplings with streetwalkers under the trees in St. James' Park, in Whitehall's Privy Gardens and even, on one occasion, in the middle of Westminster Bridge, have helped foster the idea that such extramural congress was, in terms of the dangers of interruption or arrest, relatively risk-free – at least before the widespread introduction of the gas-fuelled street lamp.[57] Nevertheless, a degree of seclusion was required if discovery was to be avoided and a number of couples can be found in the records of the Guildhall

53. Anon., *Low Life, or one Half of the World Knows Not How the Other Half Lives* (3rd edn., 1764), pp.2, 15, 86.
54. *Low Life*, p.9; *OBSP*, 8–10 Jul. 1719, trial of Mary Beal; *OBSP*, 9–10 Jul. 1718, trial of Mary Harris; *OBSP*, Oct. 1751, p.285; *P.P.* (1812), Vol.II, Police Committee, Appendix 8, quoting the testimony of Sir John Fielding to the 1770 Select Committee to enquire into the Several Burglaries and Robberies that of late have been committed in and about the Cities of London and Westminster; *P.P.* (1821), Vol.IV, Report from the Select Committee on the Existing Laws relating to Vagrants, 121, p.30; *The Times*, 22 Jul. 1786.
55. *OBSP*, 6–10 Sep. 1753, p.250.
56. *OBSP*, 6–8 Dec. 1752, p.4.
57. F.A. Pottle (ed.), *Boswell's London Journal, 1762–1763* (Yale, 1950), pp.49, 227, 231, 237, 255, 262, 272–3, 280.

Justice Room charged with 'being found together in an indecent situation'. The consequences of such prosecutions were almost universally more severe for the woman than for the man – she generally being committed to Bridewell prison as a disorderly person or common streetwalker, he gaining a discharge on promising never to repeat the offence.[58]

Bagnios or Hummums were popular establishments offering Turkish baths, steam rooms and temporary private accommodation. Much contemporary opinion saw little or no difference between such places and brothels: *Low Life, or one Half of the World Knows Not How the Other Half Lives*, an anonymous publication chronicling London's street-life from Saturday night to Monday morning, told of 'twelve-penny Harlots' being called to bagnios 'on fresh Duty'.[59] The inquest jury of Tower ward in the City presented 'the Bagnio or hot-house' on Tower Hill four times between 1742 and 1745 for 'entertaining Women of ill fame'.[60] Such places, then, were liable to be used by streetwalkers and their clients, although bagnios were just as likely to be the resort of adulterous couples and others whose sexual intimacies required a discreet location. The proprietors of many bagnios preferred to disassociate themselves from any suggestion of sexual impropriety. That in Bagnio Court off Newgate Street supported a reputable character, according to Thomas Penant, as did at least one of the Hummums in Covent Garden (this latter may be the same one for which an advertisement survives specifying that no women would be allowed entrance to the house after midnight).[61]

Bagnios began to decline in numbers toward the end of the eighteenth century, in part because of the spread of cheap hotels. Hotels had begun to appear in the 1780s when they were generally regarded as respectable places suitable for family accommodation.[62] By the early nineteenth century, however, many of London's hotels possessed reputations little different from the bagnios they had helped to replace (a development probably hastened by the fact that at least some hotels were former bagnios, unchanged in all but

58. See, for example, CLRO 204B GJR/M 1, sittings 1 Jun. and 19 Jun. 1752; GJR/M 2, sitting 16 Oct. 1761; GJR/M 6, sitting 9 Feb. 1778; GJR/M 12, sitting 2 Mar. 1781; GJR/M 21, sitting 5 Aug. 1783; and GJR/M 30, sitting 14 Feb. 1785.
59. *Low Life*, p.32.
60. CLRO 242–246 A–E Ward presentments, 1668–present date: annual presentments of All Hallows Barking precinct, Tower ward, 1742–45.
61. T. Penant, *Some Account of London – the fifth edition, with Considerable Additions* (1813), p.325; WCA Gardner Print Collection, Box 29, print 6b.
62. P. Langford, *A Polite and Commercial People: England 1727–1783* (1789), p.101.

name) and the Select Committees on the Police received numerous criticisms of the 'brothels near Covent Garden which the keepers call taverns and hotels' (the Union Hotel in Dean Street was particularly notorious) which were, as Nathaniel Conant, the chief Magistrate at Bow Street, complained, 'kept for the reception of men and women, for purposes which one cannot be blind to'.[63]

Public houses, of which Patrick Colquhoun estimated there to be 5,620 with licences (and many more without) within the Bills of Mortality in 1794, were a very common arena in which prostitutes might meet prospective customers or to which, given that many houses offered private rooms for hire, they might adjourn together. The authorities were particularly concerned with those houses where prostitutes gathered (rather than simply resorted to with clients) because it was in such houses that the women were able to mix freely with male thieves. Such places were commonly referred to as 'Flash Houses'.[64] On one of the few occasions on which Boswell chose to have sex with a prostitute indoors, he took two young streetwalkers into a back room at the Shakespeare tavern.[65] That this was a relatively common practice is confirmed by the records of the Old Bailey, which contain numerous examples of streetwalkers and their customers retiring to such rooms to complete the financial and sexual transaction. William Hale considered one cause of the absence of prostitutes from the streets of Spitalfields to be the decline in the number of public houses serving the parish, from 80 in 1780 to 55 in 1817 (this despite a rise in the parish's population).[66] By far the most usual place for prostitutes to take their clients, however, was to their own room in one of the many lodging houses in which London abounded.

The distinction between public house, hotel and lodging house seems frequently to have been little more than nominal. Public houses, as we have seen, commonly offered rooms for temporary hire; hotels and disorderly houses which lacked a licence to serve liquor might either do so illegally or have drinks brought in from a nearby public house;[67] while lodging houses might let out their rooms by the night or even by the hour as required.[68]

63. *P.P.* (1816), Vol.V, Police Committee, pp.21, 25; *P.P.* (1817), Vol.VII, Police Committee, 2nd report, p.478.

64. P. Colquhoun, *Observations & Facts Relative to Licensed Ale-Houses in the City of London and its Environs* (1794), p.3.

65. Pottle (ed.), *Boswell's London Journal*, p.264.

66. *P.P.* (1817), Vol.VII, Police Committee, 1st report, p.111.

67. *P.P.* (1816), Vol.V, Police Committee, p.255.

68. *P.P.* (1817), Vol.VII, Police Committee, 1st report, p.166.

Common lodging houses became increasingly numerous over the course of the eighteenth century, in part – according to Dorothy George – because of the large number of semi-derelict houses, claims to the titles of which were often murky.[69] Many of these houses undoubtedly relied on the trade of prostitutes to stay in business. De Archenholz reckoned that without the streetwalkers, 'thousands' of such houses would remain empty;[70] while Patrick Colquhoun agreed with the 1816 Select Committee on the Police that London possessed many lodging houses catering almost exclusively for prostitutes 'and the youths who naturally mix with that class of people'. Colquhoun's solution to the problem was to propose the setting up of a register of all lodging houses not paying above a certain rent in order that an eye might be kept on their inhabitants.[71]

One possible obstacle to the success of Colquhoun's plan (there is no evidence that it was ever put into practice) lay in the fact that it was by no means certain that it was to the very cheapest houses that prostitutes resorted. Alexander Russell, a resident of Dean's Court in the Strand, complained that although he and his neighbours had succeeded in using the law to drive disorderly houses out of Dean's Court, they had soon returned as the keepers were able to pay a far higher rent than that considered affordable by the middling sort of tradespeople.[72] Certainly it was possible to finance a considerable lifestyle on the proceeds from such houses. The profits from the disorderly house kept by Mr and Mrs Levi at 2 Cavendish Court were reckoned to average between £6 and £8 a day.[73] Mrs Cummins, owner of lodging houses in St. Giles', was able to maintain a well-furnished and respectable private dwelling in Camden Town and was reputed to be possessed of a great amount of property. Such substance was made possible, in Cummins's case, through charging rents that could reach as high as 18d. to 2s. per hour for one of the over 100 beds her houses contained. This was high even by the standards of such places and probably derived from the reputation her establishments possessed for protecting the customers of prostitutes from the otherwise ubiquitous risk of robbery.[74] Nevertheless, the keepers of quite ordinary houses were able to demand hugely inflated rents from the prostitutes who lodged with them. Compare Dorothy George's estimate of the average

69. George, *London Life*, p.97.
70. W. De Archenholz, *A Picture of England: Containing a Description of the Laws, Customs and Manners of England* (1797), p.303.
71. *P.P.* (1816), Vol.V, Police Committee, p.48.   72. Ibid., p.252.
73. *P.P.* (1817), Vol.VII, Police Committee, 2nd report, p.450.
74. *P.P.* (1817), Vol.VII, Police Committee, 1st report, p.166.

rent of a London artisan of around 2s.6d. a week with the 14s. Ann Thompson and Elizabeth Webb each paid weekly for board and lodging in the house of Jonathan Britt – with an additional 2s. due for every occasion on which a man accompanied them to their rooms.[75] Susannah Miller and Elizabeth Marsh, whose custom it was to rob their clients, paid over to their landlady, Mary Roberts, 5s. in the pound and 3d. in the shilling of whatever they managed to steal.[76] Carolina Brown paid James Ogden 1s.6d. per night for her room in his house in Darkhouse Lane in the City, rising to 3s. each time she brought home a man.[77] Clearly, the Levis – who sometimes played host to as many as fifty or sixty couples on a single night, according to the constable stationed outside their door by the irate parish authorities – were not unique in their ability to make vast profits from the trade.[78]

Income

That the keepers of brothels and common lodging houses were known to usurp the greater part of many streetwalkers' earnings was one reason why commentators generally emphasised the paltry financial rewards that prostitution won for its practitioners. Nevertheless, stories also circulated of the enormous riches accumulated by women operating at the more expensive end of the trade. Boswell toyed with the idea of arranging with some 'splendid Madam at fifty guineas a night';[79] while in 1786 *The Times* fulminated against one unnamed 'high kept woman of the town' who had reputedly spent £129 on pearl ornaments in which to mourn the death of the Princess Amelia.[80]

Although such anecdotes – of great wealth as well as extreme poverty – abound, they tell us little about how much the majority of the capital's prostitutes might expect to earn, and no source can be used to estimate their probable daily or weekly income. Sufficient evidence does survive, however, to allow us to state with some confidence the likely amounts to be gained from individual acts of prostitution.

75. George, *London Life*, p.100; CLRO 204B GJR/M 46, sitting 15 Jan. 1791.
76. *OBSP*, 12–15 Jul. 1721, trial of Mary Roberts, Susannah Miller and Elizabeth Marsh.
77. GMR MS 51/1 Billingsgate wardmote court minute book 1809–22: meeting 2 Oct. 1810.
78. *P.P.* (1817), Vol.VII, Police Committee, 2nd report, p.450.
79. Pottle (ed.), *Boswell's London Journal*, p.83.   80. *The Times*, 23 Nov. 1786.

A variety of things influenced the price a woman could levy on a customer. Clearly, among the factors influencing the prices levied by prostitutes were such large-scale trends as the overall state of the economy – perhaps particularly as reflected in the sum of money each woman required in order to subsist, the amount of disposable income available to prospective customers, and the numbers of women working the streets at any one time. Any meaningful interpretation of the effect of these would, however, require a fuller and more systematic knowledge of prostitutes' earnings and numbers than the sources can provide.

In part, at least, the price charged by a prostitute might depend upon whether the woman was hiring out her experience or skills, her physical attractiveness, youthfulness or companionship, or some other quality. More important than any of these in determining the amount charged, however, was the precise nature of the sexual act itself, while this was in its turn partially dependant on where it was to take place. Boswell appeared content to pay between 6d. and 1s. for his outdoor unions, although he pointedly described the two women who separately agreed to the lower price as 'a low brimstone' and 'a little profligate wretch'.[81] The woman who was able to offer her customers the seclusion of a private room was able to charge a higher amount. Some twelve years before Boswell's nocturnal ramblings, John Omitt paid 18d. to lie with Mary Maxwell in a room above a dram shop, while John Welch gave 2s. to Anne Jones 'because we was likely to be concerned together'.[82] As often as not, the woman would be forced to accept goods of a similar or greater worth, occasionally to be held as guarantee of future cash payment or more usually so she might pledge them at a pawnbrokers and receive part of the money raised. Thus Mary Wilks, also known as Mary Boswel or Mary Griffiths, accepted a white linen gown, a silk gown and two yards of fustian from William Mullings, a barber and periwig-maker and regular customer of hers, raising 8s. on them at Harris the pawnbrokers in Bride's Lane.[83]

Sexual practices

Many women preferred to solicit for custom in pairs. While it was usual for only one woman subsequently to enter into an agreement

---

81. Pottle (ed.), *Boswell's London Journal*, pp.50, 272.
82. *OBSP*, 5–11 Dec. 1750, p.18 and 27 Feb.–4 Mar. 1751, p.110.
83. Ibid., 17–19 Oct. 1749, p.161.

with the man, many men were willing to proffer a slightly larger sum of money to lie with both. Samuel Woodcock gave Mary Phillips and Elizabeth Preston (otherwise Tichbourn) 2s.6d. each that he might lie between them at their lodgings in Honey Lane in the East End.[84] Those who offered less were likely to lose their coin and be refused, as was Robert Colter, whose offer of sixpence worth of halfpennies to Sarah Holt and Mary Merrit led to his forcible ejection from the house minus his money.[85]

That Englishmen find flagellation a peculiarly satisfying sexual experience was a belief already well established in the eighteenth century and so it is unsurprising to find a number of accounts in the Old Bailey trial records of prostitutes being asked to batter their clients to orgasm. Amy Warrington, alias Chance, of St. Giles in the Fields broke a broom over the back of Bernard Kemble during a session involving two other prostitutes and for which Kemble had paid a total of 10s. The court acquitted Warrington of the theft of two guineas from Kemble, remarking that 'he an old clumsy Fellow deserved to be whipped for picking up Whores'.[86] Although Warrington was knowledgeable enough to give names to the various sexual positions desired by Kemble (names, such as 'lying in state', of which the court appeared ignorant), it is also apparent that the broken broom was an ordinary household instrument rather than something kept by her for the purpose of flogging clients and it is worth noting that none of the other cases of this kind coming before the court show prostitutes as wholly familiar with the sexual possibilities of scourging. John Tennant supplied his own rods when he paid Mary Wood to whip him in front and behind.[87] Abigail Smith refused to go out and buy the penny bundle of rods William Gotier wished her to use on him, while Grace Riley was compelled to borrow a whisk from her lodging house keeper's kitchen in order to satisfy Samuel Collins' hunger for punishment.[88]

Disease

Aside from the role it played in fulfilling a directly erotic preference, flagellation had the advantage for both parties of being a

---

84. Ibid., 30 May–1 Jun. 1754, p.198.   85. Ibid., 16–21 Jan. 1754, p.57.
86. Ibid., 23–26 Apr. 1718, trial of Amy Warrington, alias Chance.
87. Ibid., 3–5 Sep. 1719, trial of Mary Wood.
88. Ibid., 4–8 Dec. 1718, trial of Abigail Smith; and 16–21 Jan. 1754, p.67.

non-penetrative sexual activity, making the transmission of venereal disease from one to another much less likely. John Williams, for example, refused sexual intercourse with Bridget Noland 'saying she had the Pox, but gave her a Shilling to fetch Rods to flogg him with'.[89] Other forms of non-penetrative sex were probably more common. Mary Richmond masturbated John Cross for 3d. outside a public house in Poplin's Alley near Fleet Market, although here the motive appears to have been Cross's want of cash rather than any fear of disease.[90] Boswell 'toyed' with one woman he picked up on the Strand, praising himself for showing restraint in not attempting intercourse – he afterwards 'trembled at the danger I had escaped'. Although the woman had on this occasion only charged Boswell 1s., his well-justified fear of venereal disease meant he was prepared to go to much greater effort and expense to find 'some safe girl'.[91] And while he was unlikely to have gone so far as Christopher Hall who in 1717, according to Mary Long, offered her and her friend a guinea each if they could procure for him 'a Maidenhead' plus a further guinea to the woman they found as well as a settlement of £7 a year,[92] Boswell was ready to console himself with the thought that the money he spent in the winter of 1762 wooing a Covent Garden actress named Louisa was no more than the amount it would have cost him 'to be cured of what I contracted from a whore'.[93]

In the event, Boswell, to his horror and for the third time in his life, fell ill with the disease ('Too, too plain was Signor Gonorrhoea') either having contracted it from Louisa or through a resurgence of a previous infection.[94] In making his calculations as to the relative costs of an intrigue with Louisa against a cure for venereal disease, Boswell had figured the price of the latter to be about ten guineas (elsewhere remarking that the surgeons' fees ran very high in London).[95] For this reason he considered employing the services of a cheap quack doctor, but rejected the idea on the grounds that the dangers of an imperfect cure were too great. In fact, his friend Douglas, whom Boswell considered skilled but pricey, charged him five guineas for treatment lasting a little over a month.[96] Douglas

89. Ibid., 9–10 Jul. 1718, trial of Bridget Noland.
90. Ibid., 5–10 Dec. 1753, p.7.   91. Pottle (ed.), *Boswell's London Journal*, p.50.
92. *OBSP*, 11–14 Jan. 1716/17, trial of Mary Long. In the event, the offer proved illusory and 'the Maidenhead, having staid [sic] some time, and not getting the Guinea, went away in a Huff'.
93. Pottle (ed.), *Boswell's London Journal*, p.97.   94. Ibid., p.155.
95. Ibid., p.84.   96. Ibid., p.175.

prescribed a course of medicine, sexual abstinence, fresh air and exercise, which though painful eventually cured Boswell of all but 'a gleet' which gave him no discomfort and could be easily removed.[97] Although Boswell does not describe in detail the treatment he received from Douglas, it is probable that it included the regular administration of mercury, either internally in the form of a pill, or externally via ointment or a vapour bath.[98] While undoubtedly effective (until the 1830s mercury was the most common treatment for all venereal infections, in part because it was not until this date that gonorrhoea and syphilis were diagnosed as separate diseases rather than successive stages of the one disorder) mercury treatment was generally accompanied by the most unpleasant, and occasionally fatal, side-effects.[99] Medical practitioners were aware of the dangers to their patients of continued doses of mercury, Boerhaave's popular medical aphorisms, translated into English in 1724, warning physicians that 'as soon as the breath begins to stink, the gums to ake, the teeth to grow loose and stick out', the use of mercury should be halted or, at the very least, moderated in dosage.[100]

For those sufferers unwilling to risk – or unable to afford – mercurial cures at the hands of physicians, a range of alternative medicines was available, including lignum guaici, sarsparilla, cinchona, opium, cicota, walnut, ammonia, sulphuric and nitric acids.[101] Various curatives were advertised in the press, such as the Lisbon Diet Drink, Dr Solander's Vegetable Juice or Leake's Patent Pills, claimed to be sold at numerous outlets all over England, with full directions for use, at the low price, in 1793, of 2s.9d. per box.[102]

The very poor, among whose number an obviously infected and therefore probably customless prostitute might rapidly find herself, could turn to the parish for assistance as one of the sick poor whom local authorities were obliged to relieve under the Elizabethan Act of 1601. Should the infection not abate of itself once the woman had been admitted into the parish workhouse, it appears to have been common practice to arrange for her transfer for treatment at one of the London hospitals. The nineteen-year old Margaret Cock

97. Ibid., p.204.

98. See T.J. Wyke, 'Hospital facilities for, and diagnosis and treatment of, venereal disease in England, 1800–1870', *British Journal of Venereal Disease*, 49, 1 (1973), pp.78–85.

99. Ibid.; David Barlow, *Sexually Transmitted Diseases: the Facts* (1981), pp.13–15.

100. Quoted in Wyke, 'Hospital Facilities', p.81.   101. Ibid., p.81.

102. Stone, *Family, Sex and Marriage*, p.600; A. Fessler, 'Advertisements on the treatment of venereal disease and the social history of venereal disease', *British Journal of Venereal Disease*, 25, 2 (1949), pp.84–7.

entered Clerkenwell workhouse with venereal disease in January 1751, within a week she was transferred to St. Thomas' Hospital to be cured of her infection, as was Sarah Fox, who applied for admission aged 25 in 1748; while Elizabeth Wyatt was sent from the same workhouse to Guy's Hospital and Elizabeth Cox and Margaret Cooten were removed to the Lock Hospital in 1759.[103] Alternatively, prostitutes might attempt to gain admission directly into one of the hospitals, without going through the parish authorities (the latter route was in any case barred to those lacking a settlement in one of the London parishes). This was far from easy; as late as 1870, the six London hospitals that were prepared to take in syphilitic patients provided in total only 150 women's and 100 men's beds.[104] The situation in the eighteenth century was even more restrictive, with the Westminster Hospital refusing to accept cases of venereal disease and the Middlesex Hospital imposing a prohibitive fee on venereal patients of two guineas per week – although, as we have seen, Guy's and St. Thomas' Hospitals, as well as the London Hospital, did provide for such patients.[105]

Just one hospital treated exclusively venereal disease: the London Lock Hospital, opened in January 1747. Gaining access even to the Lock Hospital was not, however, a foregone conclusion for an infected prostitute. Sufferers presenting themselves for admission had to present a letter of recommendation, signed by a governor of the hospital, each of whom was allowed just one patient in the hospital at a time; although staff were forbidden to take money from any patient and the hospital did not insist on the prior provision of 'burial security money' against the possible death of the patient, each inmate was obliged to deposit the considerable sum of £1 11s. 6d. on entry into the hospital. However, perhaps the greatest obstacle in the way of prostitutes, who might expect to fall victim to venereal disease more than once during their time on the streets, was the Lock Hospital's refusal to readmit any patient for treatment once they had been pronounced cured and discharged.[106] Nevertheless,

103. My thanks to Dr Timothy Hitchcock for these examples.

104. C.J. Lecour, *La Prostitution à Paris et à Londres, 1789–1870* (Paris, 1870), pp.269–70.

105. M.A. Waugh, 'Attitudes of hospitals in London to venereal disease in the 18th and 19th centuries', *British Journal of Venereal Disease*, 47, 2 (1971), pp.146–51; J. Bettley, 'Post voluptatem misericordia: the rise and fall of the London Lock Hospitals', *The London Journal*, 10, 2 (1984), pp.167–75.

106. Waugh, 'Attitudes of hospitals in London to venereal disease'; Bettley, 'Post voluptatem misericordia'; A. Highmore, *Pietas Londinensis: the History, Design, and Present State of the various Public Charities in and near London* (1810), pp.142–51; Anon., *An*

by 1791, the governors of the hospital claimed to have cured 22,475 patients since the Lock's founding in 1747, a number which had risen to 30,222 by 1808.[107] Prostitutes obviously ran a higher than average risk of contracting venereal disease. Fielding observed that many of the women he seized from the Hedge Lane bawdy houses in 1758 were currently infected and that some had already been salivated (that is, undergone mercury treatment, one of the effects of which was to cause the patient to produce excessive quantities of saliva).[108] John Poynder, clerk of the Bridewell and under sheriff of London, believed that almost all cases of venereal diseases among prisoners held in Newgate were contracted *within* the prison through contact with the many prostitutes who were allowed free access to the inmates.[109] Boswell's, in the event well-founded, fears on this subject have already been noted.

One way in which Boswell attempted to protect himself from the medical consequences of his encounters with streetwalkers was by using condoms.[110] Made of sheep's bladder and secured to the wearer by means of a silk ribbon tied around his scrotum, condoms had been available in London since the late seventeenth century. In the 1740s they were chiefly manufactured and sold by a Mrs Lewis from her shop in St. Martin's Lane, although Boswell purchased his from Mrs Phillips of Half Moon Street who appears to have acquired the monopoly sometime in the 1750s.[111] Boswell used condoms primarily, perhaps solely, from fear of venereal disease rather than as a means of preventing conception and Lawrence Stone is probably correct in believing this to have been their principal function throughout the eighteenth century.[112] In this context, it is interesting to note that few, if any, of the prostitutes Boswell encountered carried condoms themselves, despite the obvious threat that pregnancy and motherhood – let alone venereal infection – could pose to their health and ability to earn a living.[113]

Whether this apparent recklessness on the women's part was because condoms were too costly or, even in the metropolis, relatively difficult to procure, it is not possible to say. It may be that

---

Account of the Proceedings of the Governors of the Lock-Hospital, near Hyde-Park-Corner (1792).

107. *An Account of the Proceedings*, p.10; Highmore, *Pietas Londinensis*, p.150.

108. B.L. Add.Mss.27825, Place Papers. ff.240–45.

109. *P.P.* (1817), Vol.VII, Police Committee, 2nd report, pp.341–2, 347.

110. Pottle (ed.), *Boswell's London Journal*, pp.227, 231, 255, 262.

111. Stone, *Family, Sex and Marriage*, pp.422–3, 537.

112. Ibid., p.422.   113. Pottle (ed.), *Boswell's London Journal*, p.49.

many concurred with those medical men who held that, for one reason or another, prostitutes were liable to be rendered barren by the practice of their trade. In 1758, Saunders Welch gave the relatively low figure of 3,000 prostitutes working within the area covered by the London Bills of Mortality, of whom he estimated 2,500 to be incapable of conceiving children.[114] The pseudonymous M. Ludovicus gave it as his opinion that if

> a woman has to do with a Variety of Men, one upon the Back of another, then and in that case she cannot conceive, by reason she engrates various and opposite Qualities of Blood, some of which being much contaminated by excessive Repetitions, imbecilitates the feminary Parts, and renders the Act of none Effect.[115]

While it true that the more virulent strains of veneral disease – if not 'excessive repetition' – do indeed have an adverse effect on the fertility of the sufferer, the risk of pregnancy must have existed for the majority of London's prostitutes and they, in turn, presumably took measures to guard against it.

While the contraceptive practice most commonly used in the eighteenth century – coitus interruptus – was clearly not a realistic option for prostitutes, other methods were available to them. We have already seen how non-penetrative sexual techniques were sometimes used to lessen the danger of venereal infection and it goes without saying that these would have been equally effective in forestalling impregnation, as would oral and anal sex. Should vaginal intercourse take place a variety of methods could be employed in an effort to prevent – or abort – fertilisation. These ranged from the use of vaginal douches, through medicinal preparations such as 'Hoopers Female Pills' advertised in the press and offered for sale at numerous outlets in London, to self-induced abortions.[116] Possibly the most effective action, although almost certainly the most dangerous to the woman's health, was to resort to an abortionist – one of the 'Persons of their own Sex, who live about Ludgate-Hill, and St. Martin's Lane, and put out Hand-Bills for the Cure of all Disorders incident to Women'.[117]

Of course, prostitutes were not alone in making use of these methods of birth control, although it may be reasonable to suggest

114. S. Welch, *A Proposal to Render Effectual a Plan, to Remove the Nuisance of Common Prostitution from the Streets of the Metropolis* (1758), p.13.

115. M. Ludovicus [pseud], *A Particular but Melancholy Account of the Great Hardships, Difficulties and Miseries, that those Unhappy and Much-to-be-Pitied Creatures, the Common Women of the Town, are plunged into at this Juncture* (1752), p.5.

116. Stone, *Family, Sex and Marriage*, pp.422–3.   117. *Low Life*, p.88.

that as a group they were likely to have a greater familiarity with them than the majority of women. And this raises a broader question which has underlain much of what has been said so far in this chapter; that is, how far (if at all) can the streetwalkers and brothel inmates of the eighteenth and early nineteenth century be described as a group, distinct and separate from the rest of plebeian London?

The prostitute as outcast?

In his work on Tyburn executions in the eighteenth century, Peter Linebaugh has written that he found it difficult to distinguish within his sources between criminals and the London poor in general and that 'that is why we can say of the hanged that they belonged to the *poor*'. He adds that 'the hanged, like the labouring people in London as a whole, worked with their hands and expended the energies of their bodies to make the civilisation of the eighteenth century ... [and] ... that is why we can say that they were of the *labouring poor*'.[118] Such arguments – assertions, rather – are clearly as applicable to London's prostitutes as they are to its executed felons, and yet even Linebaugh – anxious though he is to demonstrate the unity of the capital's poor – finds himself describing East End prostitutes as thriving *upon*, rather than alongside, their neighbours.[119]

Certainly, the majority of contemporary commentators preferred to see prostitutes as a distinct group – 'the frail sisterhood' – separate from the majority of labouring people either because they formed part of the idle and undeserving poor (referred to with increasing frequency as the criminal or 'dangerous' classes) or because they came originally from respectable, if impoverished, families and retained many middle-class virtues even in the midst of their degradation. For our present purposes, however, the views of such commentators are of less importance than those of the poor themselves. The attitudes adopted by such people towards their prostitute neighbours are, of course, difficult to disinter, given the inevitable dearth of documented testimony. Nevertheless, it is possible to piece together enough evidence to suggest that the depiction of a discrete and generally despised community of prostitutes and their hangers-on was and is, at the very least, overdrawn and

118. P. Linebaugh, *The London Hanged: Crime and Civil Society in the Eighteenth Century* (1991), p.xxi.
119. Ibid., p.434.

that, on the contrary, prostitutes, both individually and collectively, were perhaps as much an accepted part of plebeian London as any other identifiable group.

We have already seen that prostitution drew the great majority of its recruits from amongst the daughters of the poor and that the non-prostitute occupations entered by these women were little different from those of their sisters – domestic service, the clothing trade and the like. Further examples only serve to strengthen this picture of women who, as Defoe maintained, moved with relative ease between prostitution and various other kinds of low-status employment. Elizabeth Lancaster, aged twenty-seven when examined by the Overseers of the Poor for St. Martin Vintry in 1815, parted from her mother at the relatively late age of twenty-two. She had then entered domestic service – holding two separate positions in the space of some eight or nine months – before turning to prostitution, by which she managed to earn a living for four and a half years. The overseers placed her in the workhouse from where, suffering from venereal disease, she was sent to Guy's Hospital. She returned to the parish authorities within two years, having in the meantime moved to Braintree in Essex and become engaged to be married to one Leonard Allingford of the parish of Leigh, and asked, as a former pauper of St. Martin, for a marriage dowry. The request was refused by the churchwarden but within the year she again returned, this time accompanied by Allingford and a copy of their marriage certificate, whereupon the parish awarded the couple 25s. towards the cost of furnishing their intended home.[120] Elizabeth Lively, examined by the same parish in 1818, had 'lived in sundry places at weekly wages' for around two years. Aged eighteen, she had worked as a prostitute for just two months before she was arrested in a house of ill fame in St. Mary Newington and passed to her parish of settlement. Diseased, she was admitted to Showell's workhouse in Bear Lane 'until she is cured, and can get a place of service'. Five months later, she was clothed and discharged into the care of her father. In 1820, she had resort once again to the parish, having left a full-time position at a respectable boarding school in order to live with a young man in Westminster. Once more suffering from venereal disease she was placed in Guy's to be cured. From there we must assume she returned to prostitution, for

---

120. This and the following examination are taken from GL St. Martin Vintry, Examinations of the Poor, 1815–29, cited in J.S. Taylor, *Poverty, Migration, and Settlement in the Industrial Revolution* (Palo Alto, Calif., 1989), pp.122–3.

in September 1821 she successfully applied to enter the Magdalen Hospital for Penitent Prostitutes.[121]

There is no reason to suppose that these more than usually detailed biographies are in any way untypical of the lives of hundreds of others of London's prostitutes. Neither woman would have experienced any difficulty in finding a lodging house keeper prepared to let her accommodation for the purpose of carrying on her trade. Mrs Murphy, for example, who kept such a house in Blue Anchor Court in the 1790s, was well known to the court of the Old Bailey as one who specialised in providing rooms where out-of-place servants could receive men.[122]

Blue Anchor Court was situated off Cable Street in the centre of the expanding slum districts of London's East End. A full discussion of the geographical spread of prostitution in the capital is contained in the following chapter; it is sufficient here to note that although some districts clearly possessed greater concentrations of prostitutes than others, very few, if any, were exclusively given over to the trade. Prostitutes were not geographically segregated from the mass of the population but rather lived and, perhaps to a lesser degree, worked alongside them, sharing the same areas, the same streets, and frequently the same houses.[123] More specifically, prostitutes were regular patrons of those essential centres of plebeian leisure and entertainment, the gin-shops and public houses. The magistrate William Fielding reminded the 1816 Select Committee on the Police of houses such as the Dog and Duck and the Temple of Flora which had, until their demolition, been 'the resorts of women, not only of the lowest species of prostitution, but even of the middle classes . . . [and] . . . as well of apprentices as of every sort of dissolute, profligate, and abandoned young men'.[124] The beadles' report books for the Westminster parish of St. James contain numerous examples of public houses complained of on account of the disorderly behaviour of their customers and the habitual presence of prostitutes.[125]

121. Ibid., pp.123–4.

122. *OBSP*, 7 Jul. 1790, pp.677–9, trial of Mary Walker and Hannah Lout.

123. See, for example, *OBSP*, 27 Oct. 1790, pp.897–8, trial of Sarah Dagley, where 'a boy', 'an elderly gentlewoman', Dagley (described as being 'on the Town'), the landlady and her husband each occupy a separate room or set of rooms within the same house.

124. *P.P.* (1816), Vol.V, Police Committee, p.129.

125. WCA D2095 & D2096, Beadles' reports on activities during night patrol with the constables and at the watch houses, 1 Jul. 1815–31 Mar. 1819 and 1 Apr. 1819–31 May 1823.

Many publicans presumably welcomed the custom of prostitutes, both on account of the money they themselves spent on drink and because they attracted male customers. For example, a number of the houses in Billingsgate ward in the City, such as James Ogden's Dark House in Dark House Lane which regularly let rooms to prostitutes and which had 'a considerable connextion (sic) among the Shipping attending at the Port of London' were clearly reliant on the patronage of streetwalkers and their clients to get a living.[126] The Rose and Crown, owned by Hoare, the brewers, who placed six successive tenants in the house in the space of four years, was not the only struggling licensed house that would have gone under had it not acted as 'a receptacle for Prostitutes'.[127]

The attitude of local residents to these houses and to the prostitutes who frequented them cannot easily be summarised. Against the complaints and petitions drawn up by some calling for the closure of such places and the removal of prostitutes from the streets, one has to set the authorities' belief that 'it seldom happens that individuals trouble their heads about [the presence of brothels], except where they are particularly annoyed by the nuisance'.[128] Indeed, acknowledged prostitutes and keepers of 'irregular taverns' often appear to have had little difficulty in finding respectable local inhabitants to speak up on their behalf. Ogden's petition to have the licence of the Dark House renewed in a friend's name while he sought a buyer for the house was supported by the signatures of at least two, and possibly three, Commissioners of the Court of Requests as well as two members of the ward's inquest court.[129] When Mary Parker was charged with soliciting in Fleet Street in May of 1762, Michael Hudson, a carpenter of Lincoln's Inn Fields, not only gave her a good character before the court but was prepared to stand surety for her appearance at the next quarter sessions to the amount of £40.[130] Thomas Kew, prosecuted at the Old Bailey for bigamy, brought witnesses to his character who described him as always behaving as a gentleman; 'the prisoner always bore a very good character', said one, 'he kept a tavern in

126. GMR Ms.51/1 Billingsgate wardmote court minute book 1809–22: meetings 2 Oct. 1810, 14 Feb. 1811, 13 Feb. 1812 and 2 Feb. 1813.

127. GMR Ms.51/2 Billingsgate wardmote court minute book 1821–82: meeting 9 Feb. 1830.

128. *P.P.* (1816), Vol.V, Police Committee, p.49.

129. GMR Ms.51/1 Billingsgate wardmote court minute book 1809–22: meeting 14 Feb. 1811.

130. CLRO 204B GJR/M 3, sitting 3 May 1762.

our neighbourhood . . . where a man might have a girl if he thought proper'.[131]

Such sentiments were not expressed uniquely in the formal atmosphere of the courts. When Stephen Gathern snatched a watch from the prostitute Elizabeth Hammond, claiming that she had stolen it from his friend only moments before, passers-by urged her to charge him with street robbery.[132] Boswell's attempts to force himself upon a streetwalker who had taken his money but refused his advances led to his being rapidly surrounded by a hostile crowd, although to be sure he claimed to have soon persuaded them to his side.[133] The freeing of arrested prostitutes by crowds who challenged the right of watchmen and constables to take up the women was a commonplace. One reason for such behaviour may be found in the case of George Dorvel. Dorvel, of St. Paul's Shadwell, arrested a prostitute outside the Duke of York public house and carried her protesting to the watch house; there he was confronted by one of his neighbours, the wife of a baker, who demanded that he 'be very lenient with the person' for, she explained, 'you know we all get our living by these persons'.[134]

Leaving prostitution

How long were 'these persons' likely either to remain in the trade full-time or continue to move in and out of it as circumstances warranted? Commentators generally saw a prostitute's career as lasting no more than four or perhaps at most five years: 'High authorities give four years as the average period of a prostitute's life; not above one in eleven attains the age of twenty-five.' Indeed, many contemporary writers considered that most prostitutes quit not just their trade but life itself at the end of a few years.[135] The histories of

131. *OBSP*, 2–7 May 1753, pp.131–2, trial of Thomas Kew. Kew's witnesses argued that the prosecution was malicious, undertaken as a result of disagreements over the restructuring of the local vestry. Kew was found guilty and branded.
132. *OBSP*, 23–28 Oct. 1754, pp.308–9, trial of Elizabeth Hammond.
133. Pottle (ed.), *Boswell's London Journal*, pp.272–3.
134. *P.P.* (1817), Vol.VII, Police Committee, 1st report, p.149. See also A. Clark, 'Whores and gossips: sexual reputation in London, 1770–1825', in A. Angerman *et al.* (eds.), *Current Issues in Women's History* (1989), pp.231–48: Clark argues that 'the rules of plebeian sociability allowed an easy intercourse between respectable and "fallen" women' (p.235).
135. J. Edgar DD, *Female Virtue – Its Enemies and Friends: a Discourse on the Statistics, Evils and Cure of Prostitution* (1841), p.15; see also Anon., *An Address to the Benevolent Public in Behalf of the London Female Penitentiary* (1807), p.12; *P.P.* (1817), Vol.VII, Police Committee, 2nd report, pp.365 and 459.

those few women whose records of arrests can with some certainty be reconstructed continuously over a period of time suggest that this was an underestimate, but not by much. Jane Beckett, alias Taylor, appeared before the Westminster justices of the peace at least twenty-one times on various charges between October 1773 and May 1779.[136] Sarah Jones was first brought before the magistrate in Southwark in January 1816 aged about nineteen, she faced eight further charges over the next five years (in which time she progressed from being described as merely 'bad' to an 'incorrigible character') before disappearing from the records following a final appearance at the January 1821 sitting.[137] Bathia Atkinson was known to the aldermen presiding at the Guildhall Justice Room over a period of almost eight years from 1788 onwards, during which time she was charged with a variety of offences including picking up men, being loose, idle and disorderly, theft from the person of a client (this at the Old Bailey, for which she was found not guilty), resisting arrest, crying murder in the street for no reason (to which charge she responded by charging the constable with tearing her clothes), assaulting passers-by and being drunk. This impressive catalogue of wrongdoing led to her being variously discharged (once as a result of the intervention of some 'respectable gentlemen' who had objected to the arresting constable's ill-treatment of her), cautioned, passed to Stepney parish, and committed to Bridewell.[138]

Attempting to discover what these and other women did once they quit prostitution permanently is extremely difficult. Sarah Jones was still in her early twenties when she made her last appearance in the Southwark court records. As we have seen, the number of prostitutes found guilty at the Old Bailey who were older than this is relatively small, indicating that most women had left the trade by the time they reached their early to mid-twenties. As the age at first marriage for women during the eighteenth and early nineteenth centuries stood at around the mid- to late twenties prostitutes were thus unlikely to be handicapped by reason of age alone should they seek out a marriage partner at this time.[139] Unfortunately, with the exception of one or two individual examples like that of Elizabeth

---

136. WCA D2105–D2108 Charge books of the parish of St. James, Piccadilly, 1773–9, *passsim.*

137. CLRO 225E SC1/8 (Southwark compter). Commitments for trial at the sessions, Jul. 1814–Oct. 1842, sittings for Jan., Jun. and Oct. 1816, Mar. and Oct. 1818, Jan., Jun. and Sep. 1820 and Jan. 1821.

138. CLRO 204B GJR/M 38, 43, 46, 48, 50, 51, 53, 54 and 55.

139. B. Hill, 'The marriage age of women and the demographers', *History Workshop Journal,* 28 (1989), pp.129–47.

Lancaster who, as we saw above, worked as a prostitute for four and a half years before marrying, and the testimony of those such as Thomas Furley Forster, a member of the managing committee of the Refuge for the Destitute, who informed the 1816 Select Committee on the Police that a number of women who had left the Refuge the previous year and who had formerly been 'prostitutes of the lowest order' had since returned to display certificates showing they were now married 'and married well, and settled with families, and had children', we have little direct evidence as to the probability of other prostitutes entering wedlock.[140]

Forster would doubtless have claimed that these women's ability to contract successful marriages or find gainful employment was a direct result of their having been inmates of the Refuge for the Destitute which, he pointed out, trained such women in 'washing, needlework, and all kinds of housework; I mean, cleaning rooms, and those things which will make them good servants'.[141] Similar activities were undertaken by the Magdalen Hospital for the Reception of Penitent Prostitutes, the London Female Penitentiary, and the Guardian Society. All claimed to have permanently 'reclaimed' about one-half to two-thirds of the women who had passed through their doors;[142] most would argue that institutions such as theirs offered the only path by which prostitutes desiring to quit the trade could do so with any hope of success. Yet the numbers entering the asylums were small. The Female Penitentiary took in fewer than sixty women a year from the time of its foundation in 1807.[143] Although the Magdalen Hospital managed the higher figure of around ninety per year between 1758 and 1817, many of these were not in fact former prostitutes but rather women whom the directors of the Hospital considered at risk of so becoming.[144] Forster similarly admitted that the majority of the female inmates of the Refuge for the Destitute were not prostitutes but 'criminal destitutes'.[145] That prostitutes themselves did not consider the various refuges the best route to a life away from the streets is suggested both by the fact that many who entered them did so only at the behest of the courts and by the evidence of Dadson Coates, one of the secretaries to the Guardian Society, who came to believe that

---

140. *P.P.* (1816), Vol.V, Police Committee, p.168.   141. Ibid., p.169.
142. *P.P.* (1817), Vol.VII, Police Committee, 2nd report, (484), p.332.
143. Ibid., p.332.
144. Ibid., p.332; S. Nash, 'Prostitution and charity: The Magdalen Hospital, a case study', *Journal of Social History*, 17 (1984), pp.617–28.
145. *P.P.* (1817), Vol.VII, Police Committee, 2nd report, p.451.

'prostitutes generally are disinclined voluntarily to quit their present course of life' after finding so few willing to take up the Society's offer of asylum.[146] The Guardian Society had first made its offer to the 130 prostitutes confined in the Bridewell in February 1816 at the request of the City authorities. Of that number, just forty-five agreed to meet with the Society's representatives. Twenty-one were willing to enter the Society's refuge rather than remain in the Bridewell. Similar approaches made to 128 women over the course of the following year led to just fifteen acceptances.[147]

On the basis of the meagre evidence it is possible to collect, it seems most probable that the majority of women, on leaving prostitution, turned – or returned – to various forms of low-status, relatively badly paid employment, frequently in combination with or as a prelude to marriage. Most of the women who spoke to the representatives of the Guardian Society at the beginning of 1816 rejected the latters' offer on the grounds that they had work to go to on their release from the Bridewell and we have already noted that many prostitutes possessed experience of such work either prior to, or alongside, their career on the streets. Mary Maschal, a former streetwalker who went on to keep a house of ill fame in the notorious Hedge Lane district near Charing Cross, was one of the small number of women who instead of abandoning the trade, chose to advance within it.[148]

Conclusion

This chapter has attempted not only to describe the women who walked the streets of eighteenth- and early nineteenth-century London, but also to place them within a particular social context. Born into poverty, more often than not outside London, frequently orphaned or deserted by their parents, trained (if at all) only for the most menial and ill-rewarded employment, these women chose – or were forced by economic need – either to enter prostitution on a full-time basis or to engage in acts of prostitution as circumstances demanded or allowed. In the relatively short time that they spent in the trade, most were able to avoid the petty tyranny of pimps and bawds. Houses where the clients were brought to the

146. Ibid., p.459; see also *P.P.* (1818), Vol.VIII, First Report from the Select Committee on the Prisons within the City of London and Borough of Southwark, p.375.
147. Ibid., p.375.
148. *OBSP*, 28 Feb.–7 Mar. 1750, trial of Mary Maschal.

women were in any case rare. Most prostitutes preferred the relative independence of streetwalking where, often operating in pairs or larger groups, they were able to retain a greater proportion of their earnings for their own use, more easily refuse clients who seemed dangerous and come to each other's aid if necessary. Hazards, of course, remained, most especially the risk of infection with venereal disease. Nevertheless, in this as in much else, prostitutes were not alone. The attitude of their plebeian neighbours was as likely to be tolerant – and on occasion supportive – as it was to be hostile. On leaving the trade, prostitute women seem to have experienced little difficulty in reintegrating into a part of society which the great majority of them had never really left.

CHAPTER THREE

The Geography of Prostitution in London

O! may thy Virtue guard thee through the Roads,
Of *Drury's* mazy Courts, and dark Abodes,
The Harlots' guileful paths, who nightly stand,
Where *Katherine-street* descends into the *Strand*...[1]

John Gay's singling out of the neighbourhood around Drury Lane as one in which virtue was subjected to particular temptation reflected a common preoccupation among commentators with the trade's apparent predominance in that district. But there were many areas of the capital which were at one time or another perceived as especially vice-ridden. Hyde Park, Charing Cross, the Strand, Fleet Street, Holborn and Chick Lane, Cheap and Leadenhall Streets, East Smithfield, Petticoat Lane and Whitechapel, Vauxhall Gardens and Southwark were all denounced as nests of bawdy houses and the crowded haunts of low streetwalkers. It is the purpose of this chapter to locate more precisely the geography of prostitution in the capital and to examine those changes that took place over the course of the eighteenth and early nineteenth centuries.

The evidence of the Old Bailey

Given the physical spread of the city during this period, it would be strange if the areas favoured by prostitutes did not also change. The means by which any shifts in these areas can be mapped are the records of trials of prostitutes at the Old Bailey, as published in the *Printed Proceedings of Trials at the Old Bailey*, commonly referred

---

1. J. Gay, *Trivia: or the Art of Walking the Streets of London* (1716), in V.A. Dearing (ed.), *John Gay: Poetry and Prose* (Oxford, 1974), Vol.I, p.167.

to as the *Old Bailey Sessions Papers* or *OBSP*. Prostitutes brought before the Old Bailey were charged not with streetwalking, soliciting or being disorderly women (such offences being dealt with lower down the criminal justice system) but with theft from, occasionally combined with assault on, their clients, and it is this which gives the Old Bailey records their peculiar usefulness. Women were arrested and charged with being streetwalking prostitutes in almost all cases by officers of the local watch forces and the varying locations of those arrests are likely to reflect changing policing priorities as much as – if not more than – actual shifts in areas worked by prostitutes. Cases arriving at the Old Bailey, on the other hand, resulted primarily from decisions to prosecute made individually by aggrieved clients. As such, the greater vigilance of one parish's watch force than another's, or the decision to police, for example, Pall Mall more strictly than Oxford Street can have no effect on the overall distribution of places of solicitation between prostitutes and customers as recorded in the narratives of the Old Bailey trials. Such narratives thus give a more usefully random spread of soliciting locations from which to map the streetwalking districts of Georgian London.

Figures 3.1 to 3.3 are based upon three discrete ten-year samples. These contain all *OBSP* cases involving prostitutes for the years 1750–59, 1790–99 and 1820–29 respectively. The most outstanding feature of this evidence is the precipitate decline in the relative number of commercial sexual transactions being initiated within the boundaries of the old City of London. Of 93 cases whose locations can be mapped with confidence between 1750 and 1759 (Figure 3.1) 34 (36.55 per cent) occur within the City and 59 (63.44 per cent) without. By 1790–99 (Figure 3.2) while the overall number of locatable cases has increased to 127, the number taking place within the City has fallen in absolute terms to 21, making for an even greater relative decline to 16.53 per cent. Fully 83.46 per cent (106) of solicitations occur beyond the City boundaries. The trend continues, although it is less marked, in the final decade sampled (Figure 3.3). 26 (15.2 per cent) of 171 mapped encounters took place in the City, with 145 (84.79 per cent) outside.

A number of factors contributed to this dramatic fall in the relative numbers of prostitute/client meetings occurring within the City boundaries over the course of the eighteenth and early nineteenth centuries. Foremost amongst these was simply the growth and development of the rest of the metropolis, in Westminster and urban Middlesex. The period which witnessed a near doubling of

FIG. 3.1 *Sites of first contact between prostitutes and clients, 1750–59*

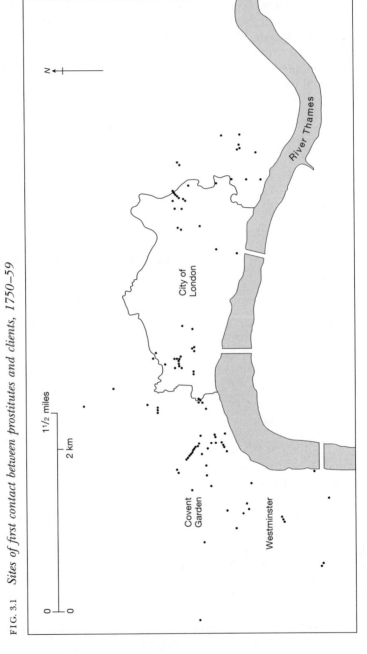

Source: OBSP

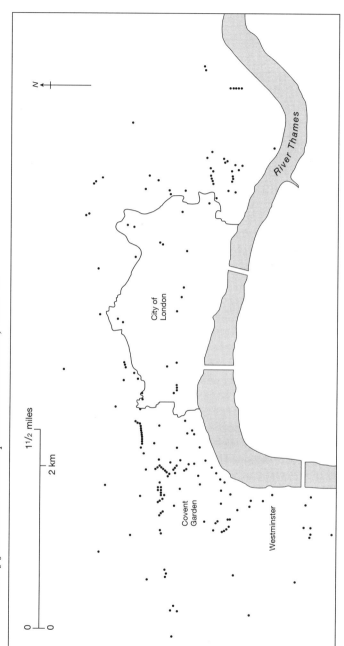

FIG. 3.2   *Sites of first contact between prostitutes and clients, 1790–99*

Source: OBSP

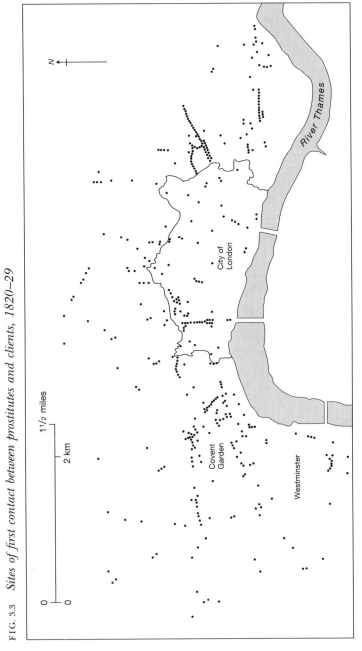

FIG. 3.3   *Sites of first contact between prostitutes and clients, 1820–29*

Source: OBSP

the population of the capital as a whole almost certainly saw an absolute decline in the numbers resident in the City.[2] Although Dorothy George states that 'the custom of living at a distance from the place of work was introduced by the City merchants', quoting Archenholz (writing in the 1780s) to the effect that '. . . there has been within the space of twenty years truly a migration from the east end of London to the west, thousands passing from that part of the City, where new buildings are no longer carried on, to this end . . .', she also makes it clear that from the 1720s at least the poorer inhabitants were likewise quitting the centre as, 'helped by the poor-law policy of its tiny parishes', the City chipped away at the more notorious districts and the old crowded tenements gave way to warehouses and offices.[3]

Some commentators, perceiving a general decline in the amount of crime and prostitution taking place within the City boundaries, contrasted it favourably with Westminster's apparently rising tide of lawlessness. They attributed this to the City's stricter enforcement of the watch regulations. In 1816, Sir Nathaniel Conant praised the City's greater ability to remove prostitutes from its streets, while deploring one consequence of the policy, which was to drive the women into Westminster.[4] The 1822 Select Committee on the Police laid the blame on Westminster's want of a central authority, without which 'there is not that unity of action upon which the maintenance of public order so much depends'.[5] The City's supplementing of its individually organised ward forces by a general police under the control of the Lord Mayor and aldermen was held to account for the more orderly condition of the streets within its jurisdiction and the shrinking number of prostitutes seen soliciting there.

Areas of particular concentration

Although streetwalkers were entirely absent from only very few areas of the capital, prostitution did not expand uniformly across London but rather became concentrated in specific districts. As elegant squares and thoroughfares arose in Westminster, so the eastern parishes built over their remaining vacant land. Figures 3.1 to 3.3 show a distinct rise in the proportion of soliciting occurring

---

2. M.D. George, *London Life in the Eighteenth Century* (1925; all citations refer to the 1985 edition), pp.37–8.

3. Ibid., pp.104, 93 and 40.   4. *P.P.* (1816), Vol.V, Police Committee, p.24.

5. *P.P.* (1822), Vol.IV, Police Committee, p.6.

to the east of the City, particularly around East Smithfield, Rosemary Lane, Whitechapel and at Shadwell, hard by the river. Many of these areas already possessed venerable reputations as centres of prostitution and criminality. The Spitalfields–Whitechapel district, extending in an arc from Bishopsgate in the north to Aldgate in the south, was a desperately poor area notorious for its 'open prostitution and gambling' in the sixteenth and seventeenth centuries, by which time Rosemary Lane also was home to a considerable population of prostitutes.[6] Such areas confirmed their status during the eighteenth and well into the nineteenth centuries, while other localities further east, such as Shadwell, gained theirs with the increase in the amount of shipping putting in downriver and the covering over of fields and commons by cheap and crowded housing. By 1817, Joseph Fletcher, churchwarden of St. Paul, Shadwell, was complaining to the Select Committee on the State of Police of the Metropolis that the public houses of the parish 'for a long time past have been the constant resort of the most abandoned and profligate women; and being in a situation affording peculiar convenience for their evil practices . . . they have occasioned an increase of the worst kind of houses of ill fame [while] prostitutes and procuresses filled the streets both night and day'.[7] Fletcher blamed the increase in the numbers of prostitutes in the parish on the poverty of its inhabitants, the 'superabundance of public houses', and its location on the banks of the Thames which resulted in the presence of a great number of cheap lodging houses for the reception of foreign seamen.[8]

Although there is a strong congruence between renowned 'criminal territories' and many of the concentrations of streetwalking as mapped via the Old Bailey samples, prostitutes did not work such areas exclusively. As Judith Walkowitz has pointed out in her study of nineteenth-century prostitution, the establishment of new entertainment centres often attracted prostitutes to districts where male customers could be found.[9] Certainly, it seems likely that the building in 1728 of a theatre in Goodmans Fields, in the southern half of the Spitalfields–Whitechapel arc, helped further to establish

6. J.L. McMullan, *The Canting Crew: London's Criminal Underworld, 1550–1700* (New Jersey, 1984), p.60; George, *London Life*, p.92. Ian Archer has mapped the locations of bawdy houses in London from 1575 to 1578 – the areas stressed by Archer largely conform to those described by McMullan: I.W. Archer, *The Pursuit of Stability: Social Relations in Elizabethan London* (Cambridge, 1991), p.212.

7. *P.P.* (1817), Vol.VII, Police Committee, 1st report, p.130.   8. Ibid., p.130.

9. J.R. Walkowitz, *Prostitution and Victorian Society* (1980), p.25.

prostitution in the area. Indeed, Thomas Penant spoke of 'a halo of brothels' encircling the East End theatre.[10]

Penant argued that all theatres tended to draw crowds of prostitutes to them. In the burgeoning West End, denunciations of the links between streetwalkers and playhouses were commonplace. *The Times* regularly criticised the managements of the West End theatres for allowing prostitutes to solicit in their lobbies and auditoria. The boxes at Drury Lane were, it declared, 'licensed stews for the abandoned and profligate to meet and pair off from'.[11] If the women of the town could not be barred altogether from the theatres then could they not at least, the paper asked, 'be confined to a less glaring spot' than the front rows of the boxes?[12]

Drury Lane, nearby Covent Garden, and the Strand were all recognised as districts where streetwalkers congregated and the areas are well represented in all three *OBSP* samples. John Fielding reckoned that of London's 'brothels and irregular (that is, unlicensed) taverns' most were situated around Covent Garden, with perhaps another thirty in St. Mary le Strand, twelve in St. Clement, five or six at Charing Cross and around twenty in nearby Hedge Lane, with others scattered about Westminster and the East End.[13] Boswell regularly sought out prostitutes along the Strand in the 1760s,[14] while the 1816 Select Commitee on the Police held that the area around Covent Garden and Drury Lane was nightly witness to the greatest debaucheries, although the chief clerk at Bow Street police office would only admit to the district having more 'bustle' than other parts of the town.[15] As with Goodmans Fields, so the theatres were held to be a great draw for prostitutes. James Bartlett, a Queen's Square police office patrol who had formerly been attached to Bow Street, believed that 'it is on account of the parish [that is, St. Paul, Soho] being so near the theatres that the girls lodge round there: Drury-lane, and the parts adjoining it, are quite full of them; it is quite handy for them to go on with their purposes'.[16] Fielding's 'irregular taverns' and a proliferation of cheap, unlicensed coffee shops, their close proximity to the market and the theatres allowing them to remain open beyond the conventional

---

10. Penant, *Some Account of London* (1813), p.374.　　11. *The Times*, 8 Oct. 1785.
12. *The Times*, 2 Nov. 1786.
13. *C.J.* (1770), Vol.XXXII, Report from the Select Committee to enquire into the Several Burglaries and Robberies that of late have been committed in and about the Cities of London and Westminster, p.881.
14. Pottle (ed.), *Boswell's London Journal, 1762–1763* (Yale, 1950), *passim*.
15. *P.P.* (1816), Vol.V, Police Committee, p.39.　　16. Ibid., p.150.

shutting-up time of eleven o'clock, were also cited as causes of the growing popularity of the area with streetwalkers.[17]

The apparent deepening impoverishment of the inhabitants was a further cause for concern. Covent Garden had begun to lose its position as a fashionable district by the early years of the eighteenth century as the wealthier residents moved westwards, to be replaced by the less prosperous.[18] John Fielding blamed the short time left on the leases of many of the houses in the area, believing this led directly to an increase in bawdy houses:

> . . . there having been several Estates in the Courts and contiguous Streets where the Leases of the Houses were so near expiring, that it was not worth while to repair them till they were out, by which means they were let for almost anything to the lowest of Wretches, who hired three or four of them and filled them with common Prostitutes . . .[19]

He singled out Exeter Street, Change Court, Eagle Court and Little Catherine Street off the Strand as especially infamous and pointed out that as the bawdy houses provided good custom for the local publicans and shopkeepers, there could be little hope of their laying information to allow prosecutions to be made. Drury Lane ran north from the Strand deep into the St. Giles rookery. The rookery, which was to become notorious during the eighteenth and nineteenth centuries for the squalor in which its inhabitants lived, had been marked from its inception in the early seventeenth century as a place of poverty and low social status. The early presence of a large Catholic Irish immigrant colony (nicknames for the area included 'The Holy Land' and 'Little Dublin') added to the rookery's reputation for vice and wrongdoing.[20] John Smith, beadle of St. Giles' parish in the early nineteenth century, blamed the inflated incidence of theft and prostitution in the district on the growing distress of the inhabitants, adding that the job of the watchmen and constables of the parish was made all the more difficult by the ease with which miscreants could escape into the maze of courts and alleys at the heart of the rookery.[21] Certainly, the district fell

---

17. *P.P.* (1817), Vol.VII, Police Committee, 1st report, pp.151 & 161–3.

18. George, *London Life*, p.92.

19. J. Fielding, *Extracts from such of the Penal Laws, as particularly relate to the Peace and Good Order of this Metropolis: with Observations for the Better Execution of Some, and on the Defects of Others* (1768), p.67.

20. D.R. Green, *People of the Rookery: a Pauper Community in Victorian London* (occasional paper no.26, King's College, University of London, Dept. of Geography, 1986), p.6.

21. *P.P.* (1817), Vol.VII, Police Committee, 1st report, p.154.

into increasing decay during the eighteenth century. By 1750 perhaps one quarter of the houses were gin-shops and many of even the larger buildings had been converted into collections of tiny apartments and lodging houses.[22] The proliferation of common lodging houses providing cheap accommodation attracted large numbers of prostitutes into the area and all three maps based on the Old Bailey samples show an increasingly dense concentration of solicitations within the rookery's borders.

Of the various witnesses brought before the parliamentary Committees into the State of the Police of the Metropolis in the 1810s and 1820s, officers and former officers of the united parishes of St. Giles and St. George, Bloomsbury, were the most eloquent in stating their belief that the amount of prostitution in the capital had increased in recent years. Samuel Furzman, the roundhouse keeper for the two parishes, told the 1817 Select Committee that he had recently arrested as many as forty-two prostitutes in the space of fifteen or twenty minutes on a Saturday night. John Fellows, a former constable of St. Giles and St. George, guessed that there might be a thousand prostitutes resident in the combined parishes.[23]

It seems clear that over the course of the eighteenth and early nineteenth centuries streetwalking spread out across the capital, largely following the general expansion of the built-up area both east and west of the City. Within this overall pattern another development is discernible. By the close of the eighteenth century streetwalking prostitutes were beginning to desert many of the major streets for the lanes and courts of the poorer quarters leading off them. Drury Lane itself, although continuing throughout this period to be the site of much soliciting, had lost out by the last quarter of the eighteenth century to the much narrower Parkers Lane, running east off Drury Lane, parallel to and slightly north of Great Queen Street. This lane became notorious enough for presiding judges at the Old Bailey routinely to assume that any male prosecutor claiming to have been robbed there had been visiting a prostitute. Other cases included within the Old Bailey sample decades point by the end of the century towards the commonest places of solicitation being narrow alleys and courts rather than London's main thoroughfares: Barrow's Court, for example, rather than Oxford Street; Angel Alley in place of Bishopsgate Street. Such a move was most probably the result of a combination of two factors: a growing number of parish

22. Green, *People of the Rookery*, p.6.
23. *P.P.* (1817), Vol.VII, Police Committee, 2nd report, pp.361–2.

officers, watchmen and patrols on the streets, and the progressive introduction and distribution of efficient street-lighting. Although the City was more rigorously policed than either Westminster or Middlesex in this period, all parishes in the capital increased the size of their watch forces over the course of the eighteenth and early nineteenth centuries, introducing patrols and paid inspectors and tightening up the regulations governing their officers' duties. Paving and Lighting Acts began to be introduced from the 1730s, often including enhanced watch provisions in the same act, and by the early years of the nineteenth century gas lamps had been installed along many of the major streets of the City and the West End. The common streets of the capital were not lit for many years. Thus, as a result of the concentration of police and the new improved illumination in the larger streets, prostitutes operating in many parts of London were compelled to move into the darkness and relative safety of the city's many narrow passages and yards.

Disorderly houses in the City

Despite the decline in the numbers of prostitutes soliciting within the City, houses for the reception of prostitutes continued to operate throughout this period. Unfortunately, no source exists comparable to the *Old Bailey Sessions Papers* that allows the locations of such houses to be plotted with confidence. There is, however, a very full collection of the annual presentments of the City of London wardmote inquest juries, with 3,336 presentments surviving out of a potential total of 3,380 between 1700 and 1830.[24]

In addition to its division into parishes, the City was also divided for many administrative and regulatory functions into twenty-six wards. Besides its role in the election of Aldermen and Common Councillors, the ward was principally responsible for preservation of the peace, the supervision of trading and sanitation, and ensuring that repairs and maintenance were undertaken to the physical fabric of the area. Each ward meeting (or wardmote) would annually elect from among its members an inquest jury, whose task it was to regulate trading standards and to enquire into all public nuisances within the ward, from dangerous chimneys to 'suspicious' houses. The jury would each year make its findings known to the Court of Aldermen in the shape of a formal presentment, in the

24. CLRO 242–246 A–E Ward presentments, 1668–present date.

hope that in cases where it had itself proved incapable of getting the nuisance abated, the latter might be prevailed upon to take action. Houses for the reception of prostitutes formed a considerable part of such presentments and these have been used as the basis for Table 3.1 (see page 65).

Before discussing the distribution of such houses as reflected in the presentments, it is necessary to note two difficulties arising from the use of these records. The first lies in the fact that although most of those accused are charged with 'keeping bawdy-houses' or 'houses of ill fame', or 'harbouring and entertaining lewd and disorderly women' and other equally unambiguous offences, many are complained against for running 'disorderly' or simply 'suspicious' houses and it is not immediately apparent that such houses were necessarily used by prostitutes. They have, nevertheless, been included in this analysis for the following reasons. Firstly, many of the houses so described are arraigned under one or other of the more explicit terms in previous and/or subsequent presentments. Secondly, inquest juries almost never presented separate lists of, for example, disorderly and bawdy houses, which would imply the existence of a distinction between the two types of establishment. And finally, just as streetwalking prostitutes were almost invariably referred to within the policing system as 'disorderly women', so much of the available evidence suggests that the regular presence of prostitutes within a house was a necessary condition of its being dubbed 'disorderly'. 'What in your opinion should constitute a disorderly house?' Patrick Colquhoun was asked: 'The evidence of men entering the house with women known to be common prostitutes; and the general character of the house being proved to be a house of evil fame by the neighbours, should be considered as sufficient evidence', he answered. William Newman, the City of London solicitor, agreed.[25]

The second problem has already been referred to above in the discussion of the *Old Bailey Sessions Papers*. It is that, unlike the *OBSP*, the majority of such records generated within the policing system, including the presentments used here, are more likely to reveal shifts in regulatory policy than any 'real' changes in incidence when used to map the numbers or locations of specific offences. A number of responses may be made to such an objection. The most obvious point to make is that the chronicling of such administrative currents provides a useful indication of regulatory

---

25. *P.P.* (1816), Vol.V, Police Committee, p.51, and *P.P.* (1817), Vol.VII, Police Committee, 2nd report, p.456.

policy, and is therefore worthy of analysis in itself. It is possible to go further in the case of the inquest presentments, however, and argue on a number of grounds that the figures derived from them actually bear a reasonably close relationship to the real distribution of bawdy houses across the City. Firstly, there is the general point that there exists an essentially reciprocal character to the association between the policer and the policed. It is the progress of that association that the documents record. To presume that figures derived from those documents represent only the activities of the policing agency is as untenable as to suggest that they reveal an untainted and unmediated reality. Secondly, there are more detailed reasons, specific to this undertaking, for believing that what is revealed by the presentment records is, in effect, a composite picture both of those districts in which houses for the reception of prostitutes were to be found and of the districts to which the inquest juries paid particular attention. A comparison of the distribution of disorderly houses as revealed in the inquest presentments with Figures 3.1, 3.2 and 3.3 derived from the *OBSP* shows a significant degree of congruence between the two groupings of offences. Furthermore, some of the concentrations of disorderly houses spill across the boundaries of two or more wards. As there is no evidence to suggest that neighbouring City wards jointly developed their regulatory policies regarding such houses (quite the opposite in fact) and the concentrations are therefore unlikely to reflect coordinated actions by the wards, it is reasonable to believe that the evidence of the presentments reveals the locations – if not the true extent – of genuine centres of prostitution.

Such evidence can therefore be used with tolerable confidence. Table 3.1 gives the relative numbers of houses presented by each City ward between 1710 and 1829, broken down into three equal periods. Houses or housekeepers presented two or more times within each period have only been counted once, unless it is clear in the case of the latter that they have moved premises and set up a separate establishment.

In the first period, between 1710 and 1749, the great majority of houses were found in the ward of Farringdon Without, which alone accounted for seventy of the total of 110 presented. The remaining forty were fairly evenly distributed across fifteen other wards, while ten wards made no presentments at all. Between 1750 and 1789, Farringdon Without ward again supplied the largest number of houses at forty-four out of eighty-two, with Aldgate presenting a further twelve houses. The number of wards making no presentments

TABLE 3.1   *Location of disorderly/bawdy/suspect houses by City ward,*
*1710–1829 (actual numbers)**

Ward	1710–49	1750–89	1790–1829
1. Aldersgate	–	–	10
2. Aldgate	1	12	26
3. Bassishaw	–	–	–
4. Billingsgate	2	2	–
5. Bishopsgate	5	3	–
6. Bread Street	1	–	–
7. Bridge within	1	–	–
8. Broad Street	1	1	7
9. Candlewick	–	1	–
10. Castlebaynard	–	–	3
11. Cheap	–	–	–
12. Coleman Street	2	7	3
13. Cordwainer	1	1	3
14. Cornhill	3	–	–
15. Cripplegate within	–	1	–
16. Cripplegate without	7	–	–
17. Dowgate	–	–	2
18. Farringdon within	3	4	–
19. Farringdon without	70	44	48
20. Langbourn	–	–	–
21. Lime Street	1	1	–
22. Portsoken	5	4	2
23. Queenhithe	–	–	6
24. Tower	5	–	–
25. Vintry	2	–	3
26. Walbrook	–	–	–
Total numbers	110	82	113

* *Source:* CLRO 242–246 A–E, Ward presentments, 1668–date

had grown to fourteen, leaving the remaining twenty-six presentments to be drawn from just ten wards. By contrast, from 1790 to
1829 Farringdon Without, although still accounting for the largest single group of presentments with forty-eight out of a total of
113 houses, had clearly lost something of its former pre-eminence.
It was not the case, however, that the remaining houses were distributed evenly throughout the rest of the City's wards. Of sixty-five
houses outside Farringdon Without, fully thirty-six are presented by
the two wards of Aldgate and Aldersgate. The number of wards
making no presentments had again grown, this time to fifteen, with

the final twenty-nine houses being presented by the eight remaining wards.

The steady decline in the proportion of houses presented by Farringdon Without, from almost 64 per cent in the first half of the eighteenth century to under 43 per cent by the early nineteenth, might be taken to imply that disorderly and bawdy houses gradually became more widely dispersed across the City. Yet a closer examination of the figures suggests that in fact the opposite was occurring. The total number of wards presenting such houses stood at sixteen between 1710 and 1749, fell to twelve between 1750 and 1789, and further declined to eleven between 1790 and 1829. The total number of houses being presented was much the same at the beginning and end of the period, implying an increasing density of houses in those wards that continued to make presentments. Moreover, this increased density was not experienced uniformly throughout these wards, but was concentrated within a small number. In the first sample period, Farringdon Without stands alone with almost 64 per cent of the total, by the second period it has been joined as a ward making a substantial number of presentments by Aldgate and together they account for nearly 69 per cent of the whole. By the third period, Aldersgate ward has come to rival these two, the three wards combined providing almost three-quarters of all presented houses. Such figures indicate that, rather than dispersing across the City, disorderly houses were becoming more densely concentrated into a small number of well-defined districts.

Farringdon Without contained the most substantial of these districts and the evidence shows clearly the changing distribution of bawdy houses within this particular ward. A large ward situated on the western edge of the City, Farringdon Without stretched down to the river from Holborn and West Smithfield Market in the north, while running east from Temple Bar as far as Ludgate Hill and the Old Bailey. It encompassed the great thoroughfares of Holborn and Fleet Street, in addition to Fleet Market and the Ditch. Running off these relatively wide highways were smaller streets like Shoe Lane and Fetter Lane, Snow Hill and Water Lane as well as innumerable narrow alleys, courts and yards.

Fleet Street and its immediate environs had long been recognised as a popular area for streetwalkers. It is not, therefore, surprising to find that many of the houses presented between 1710 and 1749 occupied sites in the lanes and courts running off Fleet Street to north and south, such as Apollo Court at the Temple Bar end, Ram Alley leading to King's Bench Walk, Red Lion Court,

Hanging Sword Alley and Sword and Buckler Court by Fleet Market. Two further concentrations of disorderly or bawdy houses occur along Fetter Lane and Shoe Lane, which linked Fleet Street to Holborn in the north of the ward, and the smaller streets alongside. A third clustering may be found beyond Fleet Bridge, in the alleyways of St. Martin's precinct immediately south-east of the Fleet Prison, itself later described in 1815 by the prison's own deputy warden as 'the largest bawdy house in London'.[26] The distribution of presented houses between 1750 and 1789 illustrates the remarkable degree of continuity in the locations of those districts most favoured by bawdy house keepers. Close proximity to Fleet Street remained an important factor in the siting of such houses, while the area behind Fleet Prison was also virtually unchanged. The principal alterations were the apparent decline of Fetter Lane as a centre of vice and the concentration of Shoe Lane's establishments in the northernmost part of that street. Presentments for the period 1790–1829 show the continuing absence of houses of ill fame from Fetter Lane together with a similar falling away around Shoe Lane. Fleet Street, however, retained its attraction, with Lombard and Silver Streets becoming particularly important districts on its south side. To the east of Fleet Market and the bridge, the houses adjacent to Fleet Prison were no longer presented. Most strikingly, a new zone had developed in the vicinity of Snow Hill, along Seacoal Lane and Cock Court.

In the absence of any detailed histories of particular streets and neighbourhoods, it is difficult to know precisely why shifts in the locations of prostitution districts occurred within the relatively small geographical area covered by a single City ward – even one the size of Farringdon Without. Gradual alterations in the social and economic structure of specific localities probably accounted for some of the changes, while spasmodically applied prosecutions of houses in streets felt to be especially scandalous were also important. The St. Sepulchre precinct of the ward, for example, set up a committee in 1825 to root out those 'houses for the reception of prostitutes' which had become established in the Snow Hill area. Within eighteen months the committee was claiming to have brought about their complete removal.[27] At the same time, it is not difficult

26. *P.P.* (1814–15), Vol.IV, Report from the Select Committee on the King's Bench, Fleet and Marshalsea Prisons, etc. p.149.
27. GMR Ms.3189 Parish of St. Sepulchre, Farringdon Without, Vestry Committee Appointed to Enquire into the Most Efficient Means of Removing Brothels, Disorderly Houses, which Exist in this Parish, Minutes 28 Jun. 1825–20 Oct. 1826.

to explain why so many neighbourhoods retained their share of the trade throughout the century and beyond. Farringdon Without ward occupied a prominent position at the very heart of the metropolis, one that could only be strengthened by the growth of the nearby West End, emphasising the importance of Fleet Street and Holborn as the main routes carrying citizens between the two halves of London as well as those coming into the capital from the west and south-west. Moreover, the area around Fleet Street in particular appears to have undergone very little structural redevelopment over the period. A comparison of Roque's map of 1747 with Horwood's of 1799 reveals the continued existence of a network of tiny courts and alleys to the north and south of the main thoroughfare.[28] The sweeping away of such mean districts was an acknowledged – and to the authorities, very welcome – byproduct of urban development schemes and the absence of such schemes in and around Fleet Street is of great importance in explaining the tenacity with which prostitution clung to the area.[29]

Streetwalking in Westminster

The parish of St. James, Westminster was carved out of that of St. Martin-in-the-Fields in 1685. It was bounded on its south side by the tree-lined avenues of St. James' Park and Green Park, to the north by Oxford Street, to the east by the crowded streets of St. Anne, Soho, and to the west by the great Berkeley and Grosvenor estates of the parish of St. George, Hanover Square. In contrast to London's out-parishes, St. James' population of at most 30,000 changed little over the course of the eighteenth century.[30] By the second half of the century, however, the parish's social composition had begun to alter. Golden Square, created in 1699 and originally every bit as aristocratic as St. James's Square itself, was an unfashionable address by the 1770s. By this time the parish had come to be roughly divided into a poorer, relatively insalubrious northern zone centred on the streets around Carnaby Market, and a southern district that had largely retained its high status and voguish popularity with society's elite, with Piccadilly forming the approximate boundary between the two halves.

28. Both these maps are available in modern editions published by the London Topographical Society: Roque's map as R. Hyde (ed.), *The A to Z of Georgian London* (1982), and Horwood's as P. Laxton and J. Wisdom (eds.), *The A to Z of Regency London* (1985).
29. G.E. Mingay, *Georgian London* (1975), p.124.   30. George, *London Life*, p.410.

In common with Westminster's other parishes, enforcing the law and keeping public order in the streets and squares of St. James was largely the responsibility of the parish watch committee, which was charged under the provisions of various Watch Acts with raising and maintaining a force of patrolling watchmen, in addition to the parish constables and beadles. In 1772, this force stood at fifty-six men, and was added to over the course of the eighteenth century.[31] By 1796, it consisted of sixty-four watchmen, six beadles and two inspectors as well as the body of constables, the whole being augmented by an extra eight sergeant watchmen and thirty-two additional or patrol watchmen during the winter months. The latter traversed the entire parish, while the watchmen themselves were assigned short beats of between 350 and 400 yards.[32] Women arrested for streetwalking and connected offences were conveyed to the parish's watch house where the charge against them (generally consisting of the single word 'disorderly' but occasionally 'picking up men' or 'a common prostitute'), together with their name, the date, time and place of the offence and the name of the arresting officer would be entered into the charge book. A number of such books have survived from the mid 1770s and it is these that have been used as the basis of Figure 3.4.[33]

A number of advantages accrue from the use of these charge books. The first is that they represent the 'lowest' official level at which any record survives – or, indeed, at which any record was made. As such the charge books are likely to give a truer picture of what was actually occurring on the streets than can be obtained elsewhere and information derived from them has been subject to less of the 'filtering out' process than those records originating at a more rarified level of the legal heirarchy. Secondly, there is every evidence to suggest that the charge books were kept with strict punctiliousness. Very few days are obviously missing from the surviving books. Each book was prefaced with a dire warning as to the consequences of writing charges anywhere other than within its pages or of removing said pages 'on any pretence'. The books were regularly inspected by the constable and the chairman of the parish watch committee. There is no reason to suppose that the practice in St.

31. C.J. (1772), Vol.XXXIII, Report from the Select Committee to Enquire into the State of the Nightly Watch within the City and Liberty of Westminster, p.761.
32. WCA D2075 Rules, orders and regulations for the better management of the nightly watch and beadles in the parish of St. James, Westminster, 1796.
33. WCA D2105–D2108 Charge books of the parish of St. James, Piccadilly, 1773–79.

FIG. 3.4   *Arrests for streetwalking-linked offences in St. James, Piccadilly, 1774–79*

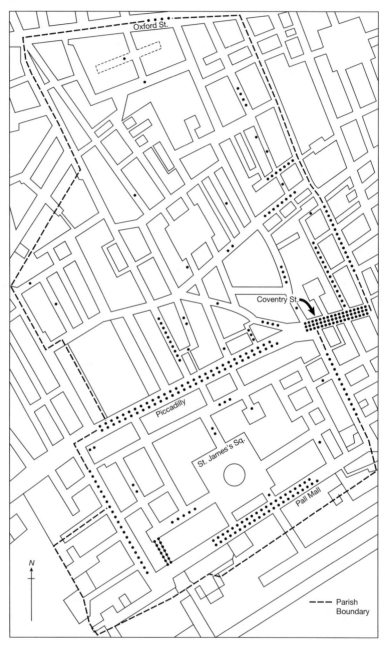

Source: WCA D2105–D2108. (Base map redrawn from Bowles' London, 1770.)

James was any different from that of St. Paul, Covent Garden, whose watch house keeper assured the 1816 Select Committee on the Police that all charges were invariably entered into the charge books.[34] The problems associated with the historian's use of such books are those encountered when using any records generated within the policing system in order to look at the activities of those being policed. The most important of these is that it is principally the actions of the authorities that are being measured rather than those of the objects of their attentions. The pros and cons of this argument have largely been rehearsed above, but there remain a number of points specific to the present use of the St. James charge books which should be dealt with here. To argue that the numbers of streetwalkers arrested in the parish mainly reflect shifting policing priorities is entirely valid, particularly if seasonal or yearly variations are being sought, and internal evidence suggests that, in the case of St. James at least, this is almost certainly true.[35] Equally, it can be pointed out that as it is known from other sources that many streetwalkers were simply required to move on rather than being arrested and charged, then any figures taken from the charge books are dangerously flawed by the absence of this sizeable group of women. Finally, it is possible to maintain that apparent concentrations of arrests for prostitution in particular geographical locations within the parish reveal less about the actual areas favoured by streetwalkers than about the concerns of the parish authorities to keep some, and not other, districts free of the trade.

Each of these criticisms can be addressed in turn. The first falls as it is not the fluctuating numbers of prostitutes that are being measured here but their preferred sites for soliciting custom. The second point (concerning the 'moving on' of groups of prostitutes) is subject to the same objection and is further invalidated in that an examination of other records produced by the parish watch, the beadles' report books for example, indicates that the streets from which groups of streetwalking prostitutes were dispersed coincided with those in which they were arrested.[36] The final point (that it is police rather prostitutes' activity that is being measured) is the most cogent of the three. It would have greater force were St. James

---

34. *P.P.* (1816), Vol.V, Police Committee, p.149.
35. A day or two of particularly zealous policing could cause a surge in the arrest rates that affected an entire month's figures.
36. WCA D2092–D2096 St. James, Piccadilly, Beadles' reports on activities during the night patrol with the constables and at the watch houses, 1739–1823 (a broken series with, unfortunately, many years missing).

subject to a divided jurisdiction, where the officers of one district could be shown to be more actively engaged against vice than those of another. The parish, however, possessed but one watch authority and there is no evidence to suggest that it concentrated its forces in one neighbourhood as opposed to another. Here it can be contrasted with St. Paul, Covent Garden, for example, which in response to repeated complaints clearly did reinforce its patrols in the vicinity of the piazza.[37]

Accepting, then, that the locations of arrests within St. James's borders give some indication, however imperfect, of the actual sites most commonly worked by the parish's streetwalkers, it is possible to make some observations as to where those sites were and why they were favoured over others. The most striking thing to note is the concentration of streetwalking sites in the southern and, although to a lesser extent, the eastern districts of the parish. That rough parallelogram of streets surrounding St. James's Square, comprising Pall Mall, the Haymarket, Piccadilly and St. James's Street, accounted, together with the smaller streets running off, for the great majority of the parish's arrests for prostitution in this period. Just to the east, Princes Street, Rupert Street, Knaves Acre and Peter Street are also well represented while Coventry Street alone supplied something over 17.5 per cent or fifty-seven out of a total of 324 arrests.

The most obvious circumstance shared by most if not all of these streets, from fashionable Piccadilly down to the narrow course of Paved Alley with its victuallers', small chandlers' and greengrocers' shops, was that they either were themselves, or stood in close proximity to, centres of leisure and entertainment. The wide and elegant Pall Mall was a popular place of resort for strolling Londoners. It was as well celebrated for its coffee houses as for its expensive shops and grand residences. Piccadilly, fronted to the north for part of its way by Burlington House, was similarly situated. The Haymarket, a renowned red-light district in the later nineteenth century, was a spacious thoroughfare lined by inns and houses of entertainment including, most famously, the Theatre Royal. It had the additional advantage, from the point of view of streetwalkers, of being no more than a stone's throw from the brothels and common lodg-

37. WCA H891 St. Paul, Covent Garden, Minutes of vestry meetings to consider the watch and watch trustees' or commissioners' minutes, meetings 3 Nov. 1783, 7 Apr. 1792, 20 Sep. 1793. See also WCA H889, meetings 12 Oct. 1799, 10 Oct. 1800, 3 Nov. 1807, 3 Nov. 1809 and 28 Nov. 1809.

ing houses of Hedge Lane.[38] Coventry Street had been recognised almost from its building in 1681 as a place of recreation rather than a residential street, with cheap taverns and gaming houses predominating well into the nineteenth century.[39] In this context, it is significant that of the four arrests made along the largely residential Oxford Street on the northern perimeter of the parish, two occurred in the entrance to James Wyatt's Pantheon, opened in 1772 to host masquerades, fêtes and concerts.

It was principally the role of these streets as sites of amusement, and hence places where male customers might be found, that attracted streetwalking prostitutes to them. Some among them offered an additional advantage in that they were, as the map makes clear, bisected by parish boundaries. This enabled women threatened with arrest under one jurisdiction to avoid being taken up by simply crossing the street into another. Parish authorities, and more especially their watchmen, were notoriously reluctant to take notice of offences committed beyond their borders. As Emmanuel Allen, vestryman of St. Anne, Soho, told the 1817 Select Committee on the Police, no watchman in the parish considered it his duty to assist the officers of a neighbouring parish – even in the case of a felony or a breach of the peace. If a disturbance was to occur in the same street, but out of the parish, the watchman would most likely, thought Allen, 'stand and look on'.[40] Indeed, men were liable to be reprimanded for leaving their beats in order to assist the watch of a neighbouring parish.[41] The exact location of parish boundaries was a matter of considerable importance. The parishes of St. Paul, Covent Garden and St. Martin-in-the-Fields, for example, were particularly handicapped in policing the women who solicited for business in and near the Theatre Royal, Drury Lane, in that the boundary between the two parishes ran through the centre of the theatre's lobby.[42]

That the capital's streetwalkers knew of and exploited such difficulties is confirmed by the evidence given to the 1822 Committee on the State of the Police by Sir Richard Birnie, the then Head Magistrate at Bow Street Police Office. Not only did the watchmen of adjoining parishes never come to each other's assistance, said

38. In 1770, John Fielding thought there to be about twenty such houses in Hedge Lane: *C.J.* (1770), Vol.XXXII, Committee to Enquire into the Several Burglaries and Robberies, p.881.

39. B. Weinreb and C. Webb (eds.), *The London Encyclopaedia* (1983), pp.205–6.

40. *P.P.* (1817), Vol.VII, Police Committee, 2nd report, p.475.

41. WCA H889 St. Paul, Covent Garden, Watch trustees' minutes, 3 May 1794–14 Oct. 1820, meeting 18 Aug. 1808.

42. *P.P.* (1816), Vol.V, Police Committee, p.149.

Birnie, but 'the disorderly women know it; they cross the street if it divides the parishes, and then make use of very awkward language to the watchmen'.[43] The problem along the St. James/St. Anne border became such that in later years the watch committees of the two parishes were forced to collaborate in discovering the best means of 'preventing the nightly assemblage of prostitutes and other disorderly persons' along Princes Street. They eventually agreed to fund jointly the employment of a temporary watchman to keep order at the point where Princes Street met Knaves Acre and Old Compton Street.[44]

Conclusion

Over the course of the eighteenth century the majority of prostitutes abandoned the old City of London in favour of the rapidly expanding areas in the east and, more especially, the west of the metropolis. This abandonment proceeded at an even greater pace than the parallel shift that took place amongst the population at large. That this was so is perhaps best explained by the more rigorous style of policing preferred by the City authorities. This suggestion is supported by the claims made in the 1830s that the number of streetwalkers in the City had once again overtaken that to be found elsewhere and that the reason for this was the City's retention of the old-style watchmen against the recent adoption by the rest of the capital of the sterner – if less numerous – New Police.[45]

Once outside the old City boundaries, prostitution did not spread uniformly across the entire urban sprawl but became increasingly concentrated in specific districts. Most commonly, it was those areas which offered the combination of an abundance of cheap lodging houses together with a plentiful supply of male customers which proved most attractive to prostitutes. The parishes of St. Giles and St. James in Westminster are good examples of this, with slum housing existing in close proximity to the public houses, theatres and parks of the burgeoning West End. To the east lay the newly built London, West and East India Dock systems (joined in 1825 by

43. *P.P.* (1822), Vol.IV, Police Committee, p.20.
44. WCA A2053 St. Anne, Soho, Minute book of the committee for regulating the nightly watch and beadles, 16 Jun. 1803–1 Apr. 1819, meetings 5 Oct., 2 Nov., 7 Dec. 1815.
45. M. Ryan, *Prostitution in London, with a Comparative View of Paris and New York* (1839), p.89.

the St. Katherine's Docks at Tower Bridge), the communities that grew up around them adding both to the need for, and the supply of, cheap accommodation and 'unrespectable' drinking places. The thousands of sailors, often with an entire voyage's pay on them and, for those in the West India Docks, prohibited by law from remaining aboard their ships overnight, were an obvious draw for prostitutes.[46] The trend towards greater concentration in relatively small areas is confirmed by the evidence for the shifting locations of brothels and disorderly houses inside the City walls, where over the course of the century an increasing percentage was found within the three wards of Farringdon Without, Aldgate and Aldersgate.

As London changed, so prostitution in the capital changed with it. While some older areas confirmed their status as centres of vice, nevertheless, prostitutes took advantage of the opportunities presented by an increasingly wealthy and populous city successfully to establish themselves amid the 'bustle' and confusion of newer districts. That they were able to do so was due in part to the ambiguous legal position enjoyed by the trade. The next chapter examines that position.

46. *P.P.* (1817), Vol.VII, Police Committee, 1st report, pp.48–51, 133, 149, 195; *P.P.* (1823), Vol.IV, Report from the Select Committee Appointed to Consider the Means of Improving and Maintaining the Foreign Trade of the Country: West India Docks, p.496.

CHAPTER FOUR

Prostitution and the Law

Those in the eighteenth century who pointed to deficiencies in the legal system to explain the apparent openness of prostitution in London frequently looked to past laws for inspiration. The severity with which the Anglo-Saxon and medieval kings had, it was supposed, treated prostitutes and brothel keepers was applauded, as was the seeming pragmatism that had allowed the licensed bawdy houses of pre-Reformation Southwark. Such good sense, some argued, compared favourably with the harsh, but unjust because incoherent, policing of contemporary vice.[1]

Part of the problem lay in the fact that almost none of the laws under which prostitutes were most commonly arrested in the eighteenth century referred to their offence by name. Rather, prostitutes were charged for violating laws whose architects had had much broader, and often very different, aims in mind. Laws against night-walking had originally been intended to enforce a dusk-to-dawn curfew in medieval towns; the numerous vagrancy laws were designed to enable the nation's rulers to regulate the movements and activities of the mass of the poor. Prostitution fitted precariously into laws aimed at 'Roberdesmen, Wastors, and Draw-latches' (varieties of thief), 'Rogues, Vagabonds and Sturdy Beggars'.[2]

Eighteenth-century reformers cited legal precedents that were centuries old. The agents of the law relied on tradition, custom and a set of laws which remained largely silent on prostitution. Where the subject was touched upon, there existed the long-standing and notorious problem of the ambiguity of legal terminology with regard to sexual offences. For these reasons, any examination of the

---

1. See, for example, Anon., *Some Considerations upon Streetwalkers with a Proposal for Lessening the Present Number of them* (c.1735), pp.4–5, 9–15.
2. 5 Edw.III c.14; 7 Jac.I c.4.

legal position of prostitution in the eighteenth century must begin by describing the thousand-year-old basis of that position.

Sometime between 921 and 939 the English and Danish kings Edward and Guthrum decreed that wizards, sorcerers, perjurers, conspirators to murder and 'vile, polluted, notorious *horcwenan*' were to be banished or 'utterly destroyed in the land' should they refuse to stop their practices and 'make amends to the utmost of their ability'.[3] *Horcwenan* is a key word. It is usually taken to mean prostitutes, but it has been pointed out that the translation is by no means so straightforward and the decree may refer to 'whores', 'prostitutes', 'fornicators' or 'adulterers', the only certainty being that the word has a feminine construction.[4] Whichever was the correct rendering, the difficulty of executing such a wide-ranging piece of legislation must have been acute and, the driving off of a few unlucky or unpopular individuals from some towns and villages apart, it seems unlikely to have had a significant impact. The decree, however, had a long life, and it was re-enacted by Æthelred II between 1008 and 1009 and again by Canute a few years later.[5]

Prostitution and brothel keeping, as offences affecting public order, continued to receive the particular attention of the secular authorities.[6] Although the Conquest and the Gregorian reforms of the late eleventh century extended the power of the church in matters of sexual morality, thereafter such offences as prostitution, procurement and keeping a bawdy house were presentable before borough and manor courts. These evolved their own punitive systems, and the medieval period saw a steady trickle of fines and other punishments meted out to convicted procurers (*Communis Lena*), keepers of brothels (*Communen Domum Lenocinii*) and prostitutes (*prostibula* or *meretricula*).[7] The courts appear to have made little distinction between prostitution and fornication or adultery and the Latin terms (with the probable exception of *prostibula* and, less certainly, *meretricula*) could also be used to refer to pre-marital liaisons and adulterous relationships.[8]

3. F.L. Attenborough (ed.), *The Laws of the Earliest English Kings* (Cambridge, 1922): Edward & Guthrum cap.11.

4. C. Fell, *Women in Anglo-Saxon England* (1984), p.66.

5. A.J. Robertson (ed.), *The Laws of the Kings of England from Edmund to Henry I* (Cambridge, 1925), VI Æthelred II cap.7 and II Canute cap.4a.

6. Fell, *Women in Anglo-Saxon England*, p.152; R.M. Karras, 'The regulation of brothels in later medieval England', *Signs: Journal of Women in Culture and Society*, 14, 21 (1989), p.406.

7. Karras, 'The regulation of brothels', p.406; W. Nelson, *The Office and Authority of a Justice of the Peace* (1718), p.88.

8. Karras, 'Regulation of brothels', pp.406–7.

In London and the larger towns, however, a series of local and royal ordinances made explicit reference to prostitution. Most English towns technically outlawed the trade, although in the majority of places such a ban seems to have developed early on into a system of regulation, with repeated fines for brothel keeping taking on the character of *de facto* licensing fees.[9] Nevertheless, spasmodic attempts were made throughout the period at least to push prostitution beyond the city walls. Henry III, for example, had ordered the expulsion of all prostitutes from Oxford in 1234, and in the late thirteenth century Edward I prohibited any *femme coursable* from residing within the City of London.[10] City customs already barred prostitutes from remaining within the walls on pain of sentence to forty days' imprisonment[11] and soon after Edward's declaration a succession of harsh by-laws were enacted for the further punishment of prostitutes, bawds, adulterers and fornicating clergymen.[12] The impact of these measures can perhaps best be judged by the fact that in 1310 Edward II felt it necessary to issue a further decree ordering the closure of all brothels in the capital.[13]

This indicated that prostitution was viewed as a specific legal offence. In addition, prostitutes were also subject to sumptuary laws.[14] Attempts to regulate the types of clothing worn by different social groups were a common feature of medieval legislation. The majority of such laws were the result of a desire to make visible the social and economic distinctions between society's ranks, combined with the need to protect English manufacturers against the importation of foreign cloths and finished goods.[15] Local sumptuary orders aimed at prostitutes, such as the London ordinance of 1351, were, however, motivated more by the wish to deny to the practitioners of vice one of its few benefits (and thus lessen its attractions for others) and to ensure that prostitutes were not mistaken for 'honest' women.[16]

9. Ibid., p.407.
10. F. Pollock and F.W. Maitland, *The History of the English Law before the Time of Edward I* (Cambridge, 2nd edn. 1911), vol.2, p.543.
11. Karras, 'Regulation of brothels', p.408.
12. Pollock and Maitland, *History of English Law*, p.543.
13. Karras, 'Regulation of brothels', p.408. Karras cites similar attempts to expel prostitutes and brothels from Bristol, Coventry in 1445, Leicester in 1467 and London (again) in 1459.
14. F. Henriques, *Prostitution and Society, Vol.II: Prostitution in Europe and the New World* (1963), p.61; Karras, 'Regulation of brothels', p.421.
15. N.B. Harte, 'State control of dress and social change in pre-industrial England', in D.C. Coleman and A.H. John (eds.), *Trade, Government and Economy in Pre-industrial England: Essays presented to F.J. Fisher* (1976), pp.132–65.
16. Such legislation was equally common in other countries: see J. Harsin, *Policing Prostitution in Nineteenth-Century Paris* (Princeton, 1985), pp.60–2; M.E. Perry,

Edward's decree of 1310 appears to have had some effect, for by the late fourteenth century brothels were permitted in just one part of the City, in Cock's Lane.[17] The only other major exception lay outside the City's jurisdiction, over the river in Southwark. The Southwark brothels – known as stews or bathhouses from their original function as public baths – provided an alternative model of the control and regulation of prostitution which some eighteenth-century commentators were keen to follow.

The Southwark stews

Much of Southwark came under the authority of the bishops of Winchester[18] and it was here – paradoxically enough – on church lands, that the only officially recognised brothels in England were situated.[19] When brothels first became established in Southwark is not known. The earliest known reference to the stews occurs under Henry II in 1162 when it was declared that 'divers constitutions for ever should be kept within that lordship or franchise, (that is, the liberty of the bishop of Winchester) according to the old customs that had been there used time out of mind' and a series of regulations were laid down concerning the management and day-to-day running of the stews.[20]

Officially condoned and policed brothels were widespread in other European countries and the rules governing the Southwark stews had much in common with those found elsewhere, being designed both to restrict the exploitation of prostitutes by the stew keepers and to limit the disruption to public order threatened by the presence, just outside the city walls, of brothels and of sexually active single women. The stew holders, who had to be men, were forbidden to keep women in the houses against their will; indeed,

---

'Deviant insiders: legalised prostitution and a consciousness of women in early modern Seville', *Comparative Studies in Society and History*, 27, 1 (1985), p.141; L. Roper, 'Discipline and respectability: prostitution and reformation in Augsberg', *History Workshop Journal*, 19 (1985), p.8.

17. Karras, 'Regulation of brothels', p.408.

18. See D.J. Johnson, *Southwark and the City* (1969).

19. Sandwich in Kent ran a solitary municipal brothel for much of this period but the operation was clearly on a far smaller scale than that in Southwark, see Karras, 'Regulation of brothels', p.411.

20. John Stow, *A Survey of London Written in the Year 1598* (W.J. Thomas, ed., 1842), p.151.

prostitutes were not allowed to board in the stews at all.[21] An upper limit of 14d. per week was placed on the rent a woman could be charged for her room in the house – this was high but probably represented the stew holders' only legitimate source of income as there is no indication that they took money from the men visiting the prostitutes and they were prohibited from selling 'bread, ale, flesh, fish, wood, coal, or any victuals, etc'.[22] The stews were to be closed during holy days and at night when parliament was sitting; this and other rules to be enforced by regular searches made by the liberty's officials. No prostitute was to take money from a client without spending the entire night with him.

This last regulation was probably intended to ensure that over-night the streets around the stews remained fairly free both of women and their male clients.[23] It is indicative of the way in which the Southwark stews, as potential disturbers of the peace, were tolerated but not encouraged.

Prostitution might be inevitable and even, it was argued, neces-sary, but it was to be contained as far as possible and the authorities in London issued a number of orders in repeated attempts to limit the impact of the trade on the city. The confining of brothels and prostitutes to Southwark and Cock's Lane has already been noted. London customs had long prohibited the Thames boatmen from taking men or women across the river to the stews at night[24] and in 1417 the City forbade all stews from operating within its jurisdiction on the grounds that their harbouring of lewd men and women led to unrest, murders and multiple other crimes.[25] Within Southwark, the visibility of the stews was limited by a ban on overt soliciting – no man was 'to be drawn or enticed into any stew-house'.[26]

Despite the severity of many of the regulations governing the conduct of the Southwark stew keepers, the profits to be made from the trade appear to have been considerable. In the fifteenth century, many stew keepers were wealthy enough to be called to sit on assize juries for Surrey. A statute of 1433 attests to the authorit-ies' alarm that

21. For the regulations governing the Southwark stews, see Karras, 'Regulation of brothels', pp.399–433; Stow, *Survey of London*, p.151 and Henriques, *Prostitution and Society, Vol.II*, p.59.

22. Stow, *Survey of London*, p.151.   23. Karras, 'Regulation of brothels', p.422.

24. Ibid., p.408.

25. The ruling was revised in 1428 to allow those free of the City to keep stews, Ibid., p.409.

26. Stow, *Survey of London*, p.151.

divers Persons of great Poverty, without Conscience and of an evil Governance, now and late dwelling in a Place suspected, called the Stews ... as well by the Receipt of common Women, Thieves, Mankillers, and Adulterers, as by Murders and privy Robberies, as well by themselves as by many other there harboured without Pity Loyalty and good Conscience there done, have suddenly come to great Riches, by which they have purchased great Livings of Land and Tenements, to great yearly Values.[27]

Thenceforth, the Sheriff of Surrey was forbidden to call any South-wark stew keeper to jury service. The same statute also barred any person who had lived within the stews from keeping a tavern else-where 'to avoid Murders, Robberies, and Adulteries that might by likelyhood happen'.

In 1506, the stews were ordered to be shut up temporarily, and, on reopening, the eighteen houses previously allowed were cut to twelve.[28] The last Southwark bathhouses were finally closed, prob-ably as part of an effort to combat the spread of syphilis, by order of Henry VIII in 1546.[29]

The church courts

Although the stews at Southwark had operated on land governed by the bishops of Winchester, this did not imply that the church – then or later – looked favourably on prostitution. While working in the stews, women were forbidden the religious rites. If they had not quit the trade, when they died they were refused burial in consecrated ground, being buried instead in the specially set aside 'single women's graveyard'.[30] Men who frequented the stews were liable to prosecution in the church's own courts.[31]

These courts were responsible for the maintenance of accept-able standards of Christian behaviour from soon after the Conquest to their decline in the late seventeenth century.[32] Before the arch-deaconry courts, the lowest in the church's juridical hierarchy, were presented cases of drunkenness, slander and defamation, generally disruptive disorderly behaviour and, perhaps most prominently, sexual immorality of one kind or another.

27. 11 Hen.VI c.1.   28. Stow, *Survey of London*, p.151.
29. Henriques, *Prostitution and Society, Vol.II*, p.62.
30. Stow, *Survey of London*, p.151.   31. Karras, 'Regulation of brothels', p.411.
32. M. Ingram, *Church Courts, Sex and Marriage in England, 1570–1640* (Cambridge, 1987); P.E.H. Hair (ed.), *Before the Bawdy Court, 1300–1800* (1972); C. Hill, *Society and Puritanism in Pre-revolutionary England* (1964), pp.298–343.

In 1286, the church courts' powers to punish fornication, adultery and similar offences had been recognised by statute.[33] The courts were not empowered, however, to try those whose crimes were cognisable at common law, therefore brothel keeping, indictable under the common law as a public nuisance, fell largely outside their jurisdiction.[34] Similarly the chastisement of prostitutes, as first and foremost offenders against public order, was usually the business of the secular courts.[35] Nevertheless, the 'vaguely defined but immensely wide jurisdiction'[36] of the church's canon law and the absence of a strict dividing line between the ecclesiastical and secular domains meant that many prostitution-related offences were tried before the church courts.

The church's attitude toward prostitution was deeply ambivalent.[37] The urge to sexual gratification was recognised to be strong and at times overwhelming in both sexes. The sole legitimate avenue of expression for this urge was within Christian marriage. All sexual relationships outside marriage were condemned as necessarily involving the sin of fornication. Fornication was, however, reluctantly acknowledged to be very common, though this did not lessen, indeed, rather strengthened, its infamy. Prostitution, as the embodiment of extra-marital, non-procreative, indiscriminate and, in all probability, excessive sexual activity stood doubly condemned and medieval canonists were able to justify that condemnation by referring not just to Scripture, but to natural and Roman law. Yet the response of churchmen was not simply one of attempting to eradicate prostitution. Many within the church, despite the repugnance with which they viewed prostitution, were prepared to tolerate the trade and argue that it had an essential role to play in Christian society. In doing so, they based themselves on the fifth-century teachings of St. Augustine. Augustine taught that prostitution was a necessary evil; if prostitutes (for all their wickedness) were not tolerated, men would turn to sodomy, bestiality and the corruption of respectable women – leading to the utter destruction

33. 13 Edw.I (*Circumspecte agatis*); Ingram, *Church Courts*, p.150.

34. H. Fielding, *A Charge delivered to the Grand Jury, at the Sessions of the Peace held for the City and Liberty of Westminster* (1749), p.46; J.H. Baker, 'Criminal courts and procedure at common law 1550–1800' in J.S. Cockburn (ed.), *Crime in England, 1550–1800* (1977), p.32; Karras, 'Regulation of brothels', p.406.

35. Karras, 'Regulation of brothels', p.406.

36. Ingram, *Church Courts*, p.150.

37. This summary of the church's attitude towards prostitution draws heavily on the work of J.A. Brundage, 'Prostitution in the medieval canon law', *Signs: Journal of Women in Culture and Society*, 1, 4 (1976), pp.825–45.

of established sexual and social patterns of behaviour. Prostitution was to be preferred as both a lesser sin and, if rigorously controlled, a smaller threat to the social order.

Acknowledgement of a sexual impulse in both men and women did not imply that the sexes were to be treated equally. Women were possessed of naturally warmer, more passionate, constitutions than men. Moreover, they were easily led astray, were more sensitive to physical arousal and were likelier to surrender to momentary sexual whims. For all this, a higher standard of sexual morality was demanded of women with a modest, but unassailable, chastity being the ideal state to which all women should aspire. It is surprising, therefore, to find that the church appeared little concerned with the punishments to be meted out to prostitutes. The answer probably lies in a combination of reason and practicality. To punish a prostitute severely when she was, after all, undertaking a necessary – albeit a wicked – task, would be impolitic. In addition, it was plausible to argue that her guilt, though great, was mitigated by the fact that she had been acting in accord with her sexual nature. The practical effect of such reasoning was that the church courts devoted greater efforts to penalising those who facilitated prostitution – procurers, panders and brothel keepers – than to disciplining actual prostitutes.[38]

The church courts suffered some loss of influence in the immediate aftermath of the Reformation but had largely regained their previous vigour by the end of the sixteenth and the opening years of the seventeenth century.[39] Their powers were increased, a regular system of more frequent visitations and presentments evolved, and they showed an increasing tendency to encroach on areas of common-law jurisdiction.[40] The growing importance attached to controlling personal behaviour and the zealotry of the Puritan reformation of manners helped to produce a doubling of prosecutions for sexual immorality of all kinds between 1595 and 1635.[41] The Puritan emphasis on the individual's responsibility for their sins no doubt hardened the attitude of the courts towards women suspected of prostitution.

38. Brundage, 'Prostitution in canon law', p.835; Karras, 'Regulation of brothels', p.413.
39. K. Wrightson, *English Society, 1580–1680* (1982), p.209.
40. Hill, *Society and Puritanism*, p.290.
41. J.A. Sharpe, *Crime in Early Modern England, 1550–1750* (1984), p.171; L. Stone, *The Family, Sex and Marriage in England, 1500–1800* (1977), p.631; Hill, *Society and Puritanism*, p.296.

Under article 109 of the revised canon law of 1604, church-wardens were obliged to present to the courts 'all persons who offended their brethren by committing adultery, whoredom, incest or any other uncleanness or wickedness of life'.[42] Fornication was one of the most common accusations made and it is probable that, in the larger towns at least, prostitutes, as repeated offenders, could be found among those accused.[43] The penalty for fornication had origin-ally entailed being whipped while processing around the wrong-doer's parish church or market, although by the fifteenth century this form of punishment had disappeared in all but the northern dioceses. Thenceforth, convicted fornicators were to be shamed in front of their neighbours by being sentenced to walk in the par-ish procession on successive Sundays, clad in the white sheet of penitence and carrying a candle.[44] The courts were, in theory, disallowed from imposing fines or imprisonment on malefactors, though examples of the latter can be found and the growing tend-ency for the performing of penance to be commuted to a cash payment made it all but indistinguishable from a fine.[45]

Despite the greater engagement of the church courts in the polic-ing of sexual offences in the first half of the seventeenth century, it was the inadequacy of the penalties inflicted on the guilty that most agitated contemporary moral reformers.[46] The 'toyish censures' of the ecclesiastical courts had been criticised as useless since the middle of the sixteenth century. Attempts to set down harsher punishments for adultery, incest and fornication had come to nothing until 'by 1640 the soft treatment of sexual offenders had become one of the leading charges against the bishops'.[47] Growing Puritan disbelief in the ability of the established church to reform itself in this or in other matters was fuelled by the appearance of histories that looked back to the fierce decrees of Æthelred and Canute. Had the church not wrested jurisdiction over sexual morality from the Prince follow-ing the Norman Conquest, the full power of the state might have been brought to bear on the adulterous and the incontinent.[48]

42. G.R. Quaife, *Wanton Wenches and Wayward Wives: Peasants and Illicit Sex in Early Seventeenth-century Somerset* (1979), p.39.

43. Ingram, *Church Courts*, p.268.

44. R.H. Helmholz, *Marriage Litigation in Medieval England* (Cambridge, 1974), p.182.

45. Hill, *Society and Puritanism*, pp.301–2.

46. K. Thomas, 'Puritans and adultery: The Act of 1650 re-considered', in D.H. Pennington and K. Thorras (eds), *Puritans and Revolutionaries: Essays in Seventeenth-Century History Presented to Christopher Hill* (Oxford, 1978), pp.263–4.

47. Ibid., p.264.   48. Ibid., p.265.

The conviction that the secular authorities would prove more effectual in the struggle against vice was at least partly responsible for the suppression of the church courts in 1646. Henceforth 'all issues triable by the ordinary or bishop shall be tried by jury in the usual course'.[49] Four years later, in 1650, the Rump Parliament passed an act formally bringing all sexual misdemeanours under secular jurisdiction. Incest and adultery were declared felonious and punishable by death. Fornicators were to be imprisoned for three months and then give surety for their good behaviour. Brothel keeping carried a penalty of whipping, branding on the forehead with the letter B, followed by three years' imprisonment. A second conviction brought death.[50]

The act of 1650 proved unenforceable. Adultery was rarely prosecuted and there is no record of any of the few convicted being hanged. In the ten years of the act's operation, the Middlesex Quarter Sessions saw twenty-three women and fourteen men tried for the offence;[51] the various assizes covering the West Country heard just eight cases.[52] Fornication was more commonly prosecuted (generally at sessions as a misdemeanour)[53] but, owing to the extreme difficulty of proving the crime unless the couple were taken in the act, those most at risk from the courts were unmarried pregnant women and 'bastardy' and 'fornication' were used indiscriminately with reference to offenders.[54] As with the prosecution of fornication by the church courts, it is highly likely that numbers of prostitutes were taken up under the act of 1650. No figures are available for prosecutions of brothel keepers under the act and so little can be said about its effect on this aspect of the trade. Bawdy house keepers were, besides, already liable to presentment before the secular courts as common law nuisances and the act's only departure from past practice was to bring the offence within statute law and make more severe the penalties. The act was evidently unpopular and, despite Cromwell's efforts to secure stricter enforcement in 1655, it lapsed in 1660.[55]

The full panoply of the ecclesiastical courts had been revived on the restoration of the monarchy in 1660, but the courts were never

49. Ordinance of 9 Oct. 1646 abolishing episcopacy, quoted in Hill, *Society and Puritanism*, p.331.
50. Quaife, *Wanton Wenches*, p.41.   51. Stone, *Family, Sex and Marriage*, p.632.
52. S. Roberts, 'Fornication and bastardy in mid-seventeenth century Devon: how was the act of 1650 enforced?' in J. Rule (ed.), *Outside the Law: Studies in Crime and Order, 1650–1850* (Exeter, 1982), p.3.
53. Roberts, 'Fornication and bastardy', p.3.   54. Ibid., p.2.
55. Stone, *Family, Sex and Marriage*, p.632.

to regain the influence and power they had enjoyed before the revolution. The fact of Charles II reinstating the courts made plain the church's subordination to the civil power.[56] Other factors also worked to undermine the church courts. These included the steady expansion in the responsibilities of justices of the peace, the inadequacy of shame punishments (particularly in the relative anonymity of London) and the collapse – brought about by the growth of religious dissent – of the Protestant consensus.[57] These factors combined decisively to undermine the role of the church courts in the disciplining of illicit sexual activity. Henceforth, it was to the lay magistracy that moral reformers looked to enforce Christian standards of behaviour among the nation.

The secular law 1670s–1830

No large-scale reshaping of the law occurred. There was, rather, a series of lay initiatives. The increasing concern of some in the late seventeenth century that irreligion and vice were sweeping the country and, more particularly, London, prompted the formation of societies whose aim was the finding out and punishing of the sinful. The nation was to cleanse itself before the Almighty visited his displeasure upon it.[58]

The first of these societies was formed in 1690 by the parish officers and more substantial citizens of Tower Hamlets, a suburb to the east of London. The society expressed itself determined to suppress the bawdy houses for which the area had become notorious.[59] The movement spread rapidly with the formation of other societies, including one in the Strand and another in the City made up entirely of parish constables, and culminating in the setting up of the London Society for the Reformation of Manners in 1691.[60] A morals police emerged, with paid agents operating local offices. These were supplied with blank warrants which informers, of whom the Societies claimed to have between 150 and 200, would complete

56. 13 Car.II c.12, see Hill, *Society and Puritanism*, p.331.

57. Ingram, *Church Courts*, pp.372–3.

58. See R.B. Shoemaker, *Prosecution and Punishment: Petty Crime and the Law in London and rural Middlesex, c.1660–1725* (Cambridge, 1991), pp.238–72; E.J. Bristow, *Vice and Vigilance: Purity Movements in Britain since 1700* (1977), pp.11–31.

59. Anon., *Antimoixeia: or, the Honest and Joynt Design of the Tower Hamblets for the General Suppression of Bawdy Houses, as Encouraged by the Publick Magistrates* (1691).

60. Bristow, *Vice and Vigilance*, p.19; Shoemaker, *Prosecution and Punishment*, pp.238–72.

with details of a particular offence, take before a justice for his signature, and then present to a constable for serving on the malefactor.[61]

The suppression of streetwalking prostitutes was a central aim of the Societies and it was clearly important that their members were aware of the laws under which such women could be successfully prosecuted. In addition to relying on the standard works providing guidance to justices of the peace, the Societies printed their own handbooks detailing the laws governing lewd and disorderly practices, stating whether an offence was punishable by summary conviction or had to be prosecuted by indictment, and setting out the penalties to which the guilty were liable.[62] The confusion surrounding these laws, and the inconsistency with which many justices interpreted them, placed a considerable obstacle in the way of the success of the Societies' endeavours.

Justices of the peace had long involved themselves in the struggle against vice. Their jurisdiction was based principally on the doctrine that many sexual offences, including prostitution and its related activities, were breaches of the peace that it was their duty to prevent.[63] From 1635 onwards, Michael Dalton's influential handbook was available to advise justices that acting alone they might bind over to good behaviour all 'such as be of evil name and fame' but more especially those

> resorting to houses suspected to maintaine Adultery or Incontinency
> . . . Also against the maintainers of houses commonly suspected to be
> houses of common Bawdrie . . . Also against common whore-mongers,
> and common whores; for (by good opinion) Avowtry or Bawdry is
> an offence temporall, as well as spirituall, and is against the peace of
> the land.[64]

Whether the wrongdoer was to provide sureties or not was left to the discretion of the individual justice.[65]

A binding over order was also liable to be issued against prostitutes arrested as nightwalkers.[66] Nightwalking was held to be contrary

61. Bristow, *Vice and Vigilance*, p.18; Shoemaker, *Prosecution and Punishment*, p.242.

62. For example, Anon., *An Account of the Societies for the Reformation of Manners in England and Ireland* (1701).

63. See Thomas, 'Puritans and adultery', pp.265–7 for examples of sixteenth-century justice of the peace-led campaigns against vice.

64. M. Dalton, *The Countrey Justice, Containing the Practice of the Justices of the Peace out of their Sessions* (1635), p.189.

65. Nelson, *Office and Authority*, p.89.

66. Dalton, *Countrey Justice*, p.189; W. Nelson, *Office and Authority of a Justice of the Peace* (1718), p.90.

to the Statute of Winchester passed in 1285 which had provided for the setting of a night watch in towns and required the watchmen to arrest suspicious persons and deliver them to the magistrates.[67] What constituted 'suspicion' was open to doubt although in 1656 Lord Chief Justice Sir John Popham held that the fact of arrest in itself was sufficient to prove the accused a nightwalker.[68] Whether or not this opinion was universally shared, it was a measure of the breadth of interpretation given to nightwalking as an offence – and the use to which it was most commonly put – that when Statutes of the Realm were compiled under George III, the Winchester and two similar medieval statutes were indexed under 'Nightwalking' and, in one case, 'Street-walking', although none make any use of either term.[69]

Although prostitutes arrested for bawdry or nightwalking were, strictly speaking, subject to orders to keep the peace, justices interpreted their discretionary powers liberally. Dalton's handbook may have stipulated that it was 'reasonable, just, & expedient' that prostitutes be bound over to their good behaviour but it also recommended that 'the strumpet' was most fit to be committed to the house of correction.[70] The advantages that committal to a bridewell offered to a prosecutor lay in the immediacy of its punishment. Whipping and hard labour were held to give more discouragement to prostitution than a binding over order and the fact that the offender was removed from the streets meant that she was unable to repeat the offence for the period of her confinement.[71] Justices of the peace favoured such commitments because they allowed the individual justice to retain complete control over each case – deciding the duration and severity of the punishment – in contrast to binding over by recognisance which could only be terminated by justices sitting collectively at sessions.[72] For these reasons, and because it was necessary for a warrant to be issued before an individual could be bound over, commitments to bridewells were favoured by the agents of the Societies for the Reformation of Manners. Robert Shoemaker has in his study of the prosecution of petty crimes in the period found a trend toward such commitments and away from

---

67. 13 Edw.I Stat.Wynton, c.4.
68. *Reports and Cases Collected by the Learned Sir John Popham* (1656), p.208.
69. *Statutes of the Realm* (1810), Vol.2.
70. Dalton, *Country Justice*, p.190; J. Innes, 'Prisons for the poor: English bridewells, 1555–1800' in F. Snyder and D. Hay (eds.), *Land, Labour and Crime: an Historical Perspective* (1987), pp.70–1.
71. Shoemaker, *Prosecution and Punishment*, p.167.   72. Ibid., p.167.

binding over orders for offences such as prostitution over the course of the late seventeenth and early eighteenth centuries.[73]

The Reformation Societies faced considerable popular opposition. Their use of informers was widely criticised and on occasion hostile crowds rescued arrested prostitutes and attacked their captors. In a famous case of 1709, the reforming constable John Dent met his death at the hands of a group of soldiers when attempting to apprehend Ann Dickens as a known prostitute.[74] Nor was the judiciary uniformly supportive of the Societies' efforts to eradicate vice. Dent's killers were freed on what was effectively a number of technicalities by a jury under the firm guidance of the Lord Chief Justice Sir John Holt, who made no secret of his dislike of the reformers' methods.[75] And there were many other less celebrated instances of judicial resistance to the Societies' activities.[76] Ultimately, such opposition proved impossible to overcome and by the 1730s the Societies were in terminal decline. Their prosecutions for all offences, including prostitution and bawdy house keeping, fell away from a high point of 7,251 in 1722 to 734 in 1730. The last set of annual figures published by the Societies, for the year 1738, totalled just 545 prosecutions.[77]

The gradual disappearance of the Societies' agents left responsibility for the policing of London's prostitutes in the hands of the parish watch. These were forces that were more concerned with the maintenance of public order than with the suppression of irreligiosity and vice. In an attempt to make the watch more effective in that role, the forces run by the Westminster parishes and by the City of London were reorganised and placed on a more regular footing by a series of Watch Acts beginning in 1735 with 'An Act for the Better Regulating the Nightly Watch and Bedels [sic], Within the Two Parishes of Saint James and Saint George Hanover Square, Within the Liberties of the City of Westminster'.[78] This was followed within a year by acts applying to St. Martin in the Fields, St. Paul, Covent Garden, the combined parish of St. Margaret and St. John the Evangelist, St. Anne, and, in 1737, the City of London

73. Ibid., pp.177–8; See also Nelson, *Office and Authority*, p.91 for examples of warrants and recognisance for good behaviour.
74. Bray, *Tryals of Jeremy Tooley, William Arch and John Clauson, Three Private Soldiers for the Murder of Mr. John Dent, Constable, in the Parish of St. Paul's Covent Garden, March 18, 1708–9* (1732).
75. Ibid.   76. Shoemaker, *Prosecution and Punishment*, pp.252–72.
77. Langford, *A Polite and Commercial People: England 1727–83* (1989), p.129.
78. 8 Geo.II, c.15.

itself.[79] It was to these and later Watch Acts as well as to the several Vagrancy Acts (of which those of 1609 and 1744 were the most important) that the parish City ward watch committees looked for a legal basis on which to ground the arrest and prosecution of prostitutes – exercises which nevertheless in practice rested more on traditional usage and custom than on any clearly defined statutory footing.

The acts were often copied into the fronts of the watch books or pasted to the walls of the parish watch house.[80] The watchmen were frequently reminded of their duty, in the words of the City of London Watch Act, 'to apprehend all Nightwalkers, Malefactors, Rogues, Vagabonds, and all disorderly Persons whom they shall find disturbing the Publick Peace, or shall have just cause to suspect of any evil Designs'.[81] Those arrested were to be delivered to the Constable of the Night, who was to carry his prisoners before a justice of the peace as soon as was convenient, there 'to be examined and dealt with according to the Law'.[82]

In practice, however, prostitutes who were taken up by the watch were frequently expelled from the watch house after a few hours without seeing any magistrate. And even those kept overnight and taken before a justice in the morning stood a very good chance of being discharged.

Reformers were increasingly dissatisfied with such a state of affairs, perceiving myriad problems – most with lengthy historical antecedents. Above all, the lack of clarity in the laws regarding prostitution (not least in their failure to mention the trade by name) created confusion as to when, where and for what reason prostitutes could be arrested by the watch. Added to this, the readiness of the justices of the peace to discharge the great majority of women brought before them gave the law an air of futility, as did the failure of current sentencing policy to bring about any diminution in the numbers of women on the streets. Hence many commentators

79. 9 Geo.II, c.8; 9 Geo.II, c.13; 9 Geo.II, c.17; 9 Geo.II, c.19; 10 Geo.II, c.22. Most other parishes eventually received their own acts; those that did not were to be covered by 14 Geo.III, c.90.

80. See, among others WCA A2052a St. Anne, Soho, Minutes of the committee of evening patrol and names of subscribers thereto, Nov. 1792–Mar. 1793; WCA E2643 Minutes of the vestry of St. Margaret and St. John the Evangelist relating to the watch, 21 Jun. 1726–17 Oct. 1766.

81. 10 Geo.II, c.22 (1737) An Act for the Better Regulating the Nightly Watch and Bedels within the City of London, and Liberties thereof; and for Making more Effectual the Laws now in Being, for Paving and Cleansing the Streets and Sewers in and about the said City.

82. 10 Geo.II, c.22.

were encouraged to press for changes in the legislative framework within which prostitution operated. Some, such as Sir John Fielding, advocated bringing streetwalkers more clearly within the compass of the vagrancy laws.[83] Others considered that the problem could only properly be addressed by the suppression of the disorderly houses, alehouses and bawdy houses upon which the prostitutes apparently depended.[84]

Partly as a result of such pressures, some changes were enacted to the laws – albeit in a piecemeal fashion. The first important innovation in the laws surrounding prostitution was the Disorderly Houses Act of 1752.[85] Prior to this act, bawdy houses had been indictable as nuisances under the law. The legal basis was their perceived threat to the public peace and their 'tendency to corrupt the manners of both sexes'.[86] Offended parishioners were free to initiate a prosecution themselves or to attempt to persuade the parish authorities to do so – although the latter were under no obligation to act. In either case, prosecutions were liable to prove expensive and were often subject to lengthy delays. In 1695, the Tower Hamlets Society for the Reformation of Manners, for example, was forced to caution its members against prosecuting bawdy houses by indictment, such proceedings having cost the Society the then huge sum of £80 the previous year.[87] When the inquest jury of Bridge Ward in the City preferred a bill against William and Susanna Baker for keeping a disorderly house in Pudding Lane in 1705, the issuing of a warrant for the couple's arrest prompted the husband to abscond, defeating the ward's attempts to have him found and returned. Unusually in English law at this time, a married woman was indictable for keeping a bawdy house even if her husband was present during the commission of the offence. In most other types of offence the presence of the husband rendered her legally irresponsible as she was presumed to have committed any alleged crime under his direction. The legal basis in the case of bawdy house keeping was that 'this is an offence as to the government of the

---

83. *P.P.* (1812), Vol.II, Report from the Select Committee on the Nightly Watch and Police of the Metropolis, Appendix 8 quoting the testimony of Sir John Fielding to the 1770 Select Committee to enquire into the Several Burglaries and Robberies that of late have been committed in and about the Cities of London and Westminster.
84. *P.P.* (1817), Vol.VII, Police Committee, 2nd report, p.456.
85. 25 Geo.II, c.36 (1752), An Act for the Better Preventing Thefts and Robberies, and for Regulating Places of Public Entertainment, and Punishing Persons Keeping Disorderly Houses.
86. R. Burn, *The Justice of the Peace and Parish Officer* (2nd edn., 1756), Vol.I, p.132.
87. Shoemaker, *Prosecution and Punishment*, p.246.

house, in which the wife has a principal share; and also such an offence as may generally be presumed to be managed by the intrigues of her sex'. Thus Susanna Baker appeared at the Old Bailey, pleaded not guilty and was bailed to answer the charges the following month.[88] On the eve of the trial she succeeded in having the case removed by *certiorari* to the Queen's Bench for the Michaelmas Term, before which time she too fled the ward. The inconclusive case had taken at least six months and cost the ward £3 15s, which money it raised by levying 5s from each of the inquest jury's members.[89]

Although most prosecutions appear to have begun at the urging of aggravated parishioners, the authorities did not have to wait for complaints before moving against known or suspected bawdy houses. By the Vagrancy Act of 1609,[90] two justices of the peace acting in concert were able to issue privy search warrants requiring constables within their jurisdiction to seek out and bring before them 'rogues, vagabonds, and sturdy beggars, and all such persons as are suspected to keep bawdy houses, and the frequenters thereof, and also all disturbers of the peace'.[91] The Vagrancy Act of 1744 added the requirement that the privy searches be carried out at least four times a year.[92] Press articles rebuked the magistracy for its apparent reluctance to suppress brothels in the capital[93] – provoking the justices of St. James in Westminster to place notices reminding complainants that the bench sat in petty session thrice weekly to hear both written and oral informations against such houses in addition to regularly issuing general privy search warrants for the apprehension of all offending against the public peace 'that they may be dealt with according to law'.[94]

Once suspected bawdy house keepers were brought before the courts, the presiding justice had a relatively free hand in deciding what action to take against them. Those seized under a general warrant were liable to be temporarily discharged to await indictment

88. Burn, *Justice of the Peace*, p.132. See also Fielding, *Charge Delivered to the Grand Jury*, p.47.

89. GMR Ms.3461/3 Bridge ward within wardmote inquest minute Book, 1698–1747, p.120, meeting 21 Dec. 1705.

90. 7 Jac.I, c.4 (1609), An Act for the Due Execution of Divers Laws and Statutes heretofore made against Rogues, Vagabonds and other Idle and Disorderly Persons.

91. Anon., *The Complete Parish Officer* (1772), p.114.

92. 17 Geo.II, c.5 (1744), An Act to Amend and make more Effectual the Laws relating to Rogues, Vagabonds and other Idle and Disorderly Persons and to Houses of Correction.

93. *The Times*, 6 Nov. 1788.   94. Ibid., 8 Nov. 1788.

at a later date, the arresting constable or watchman giving recognisance to prosecute,[95] although it was within the justice's power simply to bind over the accused to good behaviour. Binding over orders had the advantage, from the point of view of the magistrate, of removing the necessity for a decision to be made as to the guilt or innocence of the party before him. Refusal to accept the order resulted in immediate commitment to gaol.[96] Those indicted and found guilty faced a variety of penalties. They could be bound over, fined, imprisoned with or without hard labour, pilloried and whipped – or any combination of these.[97]

It was generally agreed that successful prosecutions of bawdy houses under the common law were difficult to obtain for a number of reasons. Justices interpreted the law narrowly, requiring unambiguous proof that the house was used for 'acts of bawdry' and not that it was merely suspected of being so. Bawdy house keepers developed various strategies for evading prosecution, such as having cases removed to higher courts (hoping thereby to increase the costs in time and money faced by the prosecutor), or concealing the true identity of the owner of the house. In addition, houses run in a quiet and disciplined manner could not be charged as disorderly. Perhaps most importantly, the delays and expenses and the uncertainty of conviction to which cases were subject served to confirm the reluctance of parishes to initiate legal proceedings in response to residents' complaints when, as already noted, they were under no obligation to do so. It was to problems such as these that the Disorderly Houses Act of 1752 was largely addressed.

The act embodied several of the recommendations made by the House of Commons Committee on the Criminal Laws, set up in 1751 in response to what appeared to many to be the growing disorder and lawlessness of London.[98] Section two of the act declared that 'the multitude of places of entertainment for the lower sort of people is another great cause of thefts and robberies, as they are thereby tempted to spend their small substances in riotous pleasures' and that the purpose of the act was to prevent these temptations by ensuring that such places kept for public dancing, music or the like in London or its environs for twenty miles around were obliged to

95. GL SL71/061 Collection of newspaper cuttings relating to the City of London, 1771–1830, cutting dated 5 Mar. 1771; WCA F2028 St. Martin in the Fields vestry and watch committee minutes, 3 May 1736–6 Aug. 1754, vestry meeting 18 Apr. 1738.
96. Dalton, *Countrey Justice*, p.189; Nelson, *Office and Authority*, p.89.
97. Burn, *Justice of the Peace*, p.132.
98. J.M. Beattie, *Crime and the Courts in England, 1660–1800* (1986), pp.520–2.

be licensed at the discretion of the justices of the peace. Any such place not so licensed was, by definition, disorderly. Constables armed with a JP's warrant were then at liberty to enter and arrest all those within, including the keeper of the house. The latter was automatically to forfeit £100 and be otherwise punishable for keeping a disorderly house. Licensed houses were to proclaim their legality in large capital letters inscribed in some prominent place and were forbidden to open their doors for entertainment before five in the evening on pain of having their licence revoked.

It will be seen from these provisions that the act was not directed solely at the suppression of bawdy houses. Other clauses in the act were, however, aimed more directly at the keepers of brothels. Section five stated that, 'in order to encourage prosecutions against persons keeping bawdy-houses, gaming-houses or other disorderly houses', any two inhabitants of a parish 'paying scot and bearing lot therein' could give notice in writing to the constable of the existence of a house. The constable was then legally obliged to bring the complainants before a justice of the peace and on their entering into recognisances of £20 each to furnish evidence of their accusation, the constable was to be similarly bound (in his case, for £30) to prosecute the alleged offence. The justice was then to issue a warrant for the arrest of the accused, who was to be brought before him to be bound over to appear to answer the charge at the next sessions. The justice could also, if he thought the evidence of wrong-doing sufficiently strong, bind the accused over to be of good behaviour until the case came to court.

The constable's expenses in prosecuting a case were to be recoverable from the overseers of the poor of the parish. In an attempt to address the reluctance of parish authorities to follow up complaints about bawdy houses, constables who failed to act on such complaints were liable to forfeit £20 to each of the unsatisfied complainants. The unwillingness of parishioners to bring such houses to the attention of the authorities was to be overcome by the payment of a reward of £10 to each of the two inhabitants making the accusation, provided their evidence secured a conviction. The practice of delaying the outcome of a prosecution by having it removed by writ of *certiorari* into another court was to be forbidden. The act also attempted to deal with what were described as 'the many subtle and crafty contrivances of persons keeping bawdy-houses, gaming-houses or other disorderly houses [whereby] it is difficult to prove who is the real owner or keeper thereof, by which means many notorious offenders have escaped punishment'.

Henceforth, any person who behaved as, or merely appeared to be, the master or mistress of the house 'shall be deemed and taken to be the keeper thereof, and shall be liable to be prosecuted and punished as such, notwithstanding he or she shall not in fact be the real owner or keeper thereof'.

The comprehensive character of this clause is an indication of the determination of the 1752 act's framers to make it far easier than hitherto to prosecute bawdy and similar houses as disorderly and to obtain the conviction of the keepers. Certainly, parliament thought the act a success, praising its usefulness and making it perpetual in 1755.[99] Most of the available evidence suggests, however, that the new provisions made little or no difference to the numbers of prosecutions being undertaken.

The inquest juries of the twenty-six wards in the City of London were legally responsible for presenting to the Court of Aldermen any disorderly and bawdy houses found within the old City boundaries. While the number of such presentments cannot be exactly equated with that of subsequent prosecutions, it is reasonable to expect that a greater likelihood of successful prosecutions would be reflected in a rise in the number of presentments being made. In fact, although little consistent pattern emerges, it is possible to discern a steady decline in presentments after 1753 until a brief (and by the surviving sources inexplicable) flurry of activity in the early 1770s. It is not until the turn of the century that the number of presentments began to climb again, although even here there were some years in which no houses were named at all. The greatest number of presentments made in any one year actually occurred in 1742, before the passing of the act, when twenty-one houses were presented by the ward inquests to the Aldermanic Court.[100] The evidence suggests that while parish authorities could, perhaps, be somewhat more certain of gaining the conviction of those they indicted, the process of prosecution remained both expensive and time-consuming. For this reason it continued to be seen as a last resort, to be entered into only after all other possible means of suppressing a particular house had been exhausted. (See Chapter Six.)

99. 28 Geo.II, c.19 (1755), An Act for Making Perpetual an Act passed in the Twenty-Fifth Year of the Reign of his Present Majesty, for the Better Preventing Thefts and Robberies.
100. See CLRO 242–246A–E ward presentments, 1668–present date. All presentments from 1699 to 1830 were noted for the purpose of this study. Presentments were made annually and the survival rate is extremely high – of a possible total of 3,380 ward-years, only forty-four are missing.

No significant changes were made to the laws affecting street-walking until 1822. Sir John Fielding's opinion, given to the House of Commons committee on burglaries in 1770, that streetwalking prostitutes were 'scarce, if at all, within the description of any Statute now in being' came to be widely held over the following decades.[101] Complaints made to the watch commissioners of St. Paul in 1799 about the failure of the parish watch force to arrest prostitutes congregating in and around the Covent Garden piazzas led to the drafting of new regulations setting out the duties of the force in apprehending such offenders.[102] The 1812 Committee on the Police quoted approvingly Fielding's comments of 1770 in their report.[103] One witness to the 1816 Committee on the Police spoke of the lenity of the English law and the consequent inability to suppress open streetwalking.[104] Another, when asked if he considered it the duty of the Bow Street patrol to clear the streets of the disorderly people, replied that the term 'disorderly people' was so general that he scarce knew how to answer – he took it that a specific offence had to be committed before an arrest could be made.[105]

These views were part of a large body of evidence presented to the members of the committee. Patrick Colquhoun told the committee that in his view, too, the recent claimed increase in the numbers of prostitutes on the streets derived from the deficiency of the law.[106] William Fielding, a magistrate at Queen's Square police office, agreed with the Police Committee of 1817 that the streets could be cleared of prostitutes but admitted he had no notion as to how it might be accomplished.[107] A second witness produced the considered opinions of the Guardians of the Poor of St. Luke, Middlesex, the Churchwardens of St. Botolph without Aldgate, the committee of the Guardian Society and two 'eminent counsels' in order to bolster his assertion that streetwalkers stood at present outside the law and that 'some further legislative provisions, applicable to the appearance and conduct of prostitutes in the streets, is

101. *P.P.* (1812), Vol.II, Police Committee, Appendix 8, quoting the testimony of Sir John Fielding to the 1770 Select Committee to enquire into the Several Burglaries and Robberies that of late have been committed in and about the Cities of London and Westminster.
102. WCA H889 St. Paul, Covent Garden, watch trustees' minutes, 3 May 1794–14 Oct. 1820, meeting 12 Oct. 1799.
103. *P.P.* (1812), Vol.II, Police Committee, Appendix 8.
104. *P.P.* (1816), Vol.V, Police Committee, p.23: evidence of Sir Nathaniel Conant, chief magistrate at Bow Street.
105. Ibid., p.39: evidence of John Stafford, chief clerk at Bow Street and clerk of indictments on the Home Circuit and Middlesex sessions.
106. Ibid., p.50.   107. *P.P.* (1817), Vol.VII, Police Committee, 2nd report, p.405.

required'.[108] The City of London added its influential voice to the calls for a change in the laws, having been provoked by public pressure in 1814 into forming its own committee to deal specifically with prostitution in the City.[109]

The Police Committee of 1816 was moved by the weight of opinion to include in its report a recommendation that alterations be made in the laws regarding streetwalking, although it felt obliged to remark that stricter enforcement of the current regulations (and greater vigilance in supervising the conduct of the parish watchmen) would prevent 'nine-tenths of the nuisances complained of'.[110]

The committee's recommendations were taken up and embodied in the Vagrancy Act of 1822.[111] This act was of some historic importance in that it was the first to use the term 'prostitutes' and to include provisions directed specifically at them. It declared that

> all common Prostitutes or Night Walkers wandering in the public Streets or public Highways, not giving a satisfactory account of themselves, shall be deemed idle and disorderly Persons; and it shall and may be lawful for any Justice of the Peace to commit such Offenders (being thereof convicted before him, by his own View, or his, her or their own Confession, or by the Oath of One or more credible Witness or Witnesses,) to the House of Correction, there to be kept to hard Labour for any Time not exceeding one Calendar Month.

By replacing what was generally accepted to have been the previous requirement for the conviction of a prostitute – that she had to be proven to have been committing a specifically offensive act at the time of her arrest – with the requirement that she simply be a known prostitute unable to give a 'satisfactory account' of herself, the 1822 statute appears to signal a fundamental change in legal thinking on the matter.

In theory, at least, reputed streetwalkers were now required to prove their innocence. In practice, there was little change in the numbers of women suffering arrest and prosecution, although a slightly larger proportion of these were subsequently sentenced

108. Ibid., pp.462–3: evidence of Dadson Coates, secretary to the Guardian Society.
109. The Corporation formed the 'Committee to Consider the Petition of Inhabitants of the City Complaining of Prostitutes Frequenting the Streets' in December, 1813 (CLRO Misc.Mss 283.4 Committee Papers, 1814–25); for the petition and the reports of the committee, see GL Co.Co. Reports 1816–21 nos.1 and 3. Through this committee the City was closely involved in attempts to bring new laws on prostitution to the statute book.
110. *P.P.* (1818), Vol.VIII, Police Committee, 3rd report, pp.29–30.
111. 3 Geo.IV, c.40 (1822), An Act for Consolidating into one Act and Amending the Laws relating to Idle and Disorderly Persons, Rogues and Vagabonds.

to brief terms of imprisonment. The parish watch of St. James, Piccadilly apprehended 166 'disorderly women' in 1821, the last full year before the introduction of the 1822 act. Ninety-one per cent (152) of these were discharged upon facing the magistrate the morning after their arrest. 1823 – the only full year in which the new act applied – saw a slight rise in arrests to 175, while the proportion being discharged fell to a little over 75 per cent (132). The act was repealed in 1824. During 1825, the number of women arrested and charged as disorderly in St. James fell back to 148, while the proportion securing a discharge approached the pre-1822 act figures at almost 82 per cent (121).[112]

Prior to 1822, the very vagueness of the various legal formulae under which streetwalkers were arrested had allowed for the taking up of relatively large numbers of women. The almost universal discharges that followed such arrests were of little concern to the parish watches. The pattern of arrests in both the City of London and the Westminster parish of St. James suggest that the watch combined casual harassment of streetwalkers with the short-term clearing of specific locations where the numbers of women – and possibly the openness of their soliciting – had exceeded 'acceptable' levels. Neither task necessitated the conviction of the women.[113]

Nevertheless, either because the provisions of the 1822 act shifted the burden of proof onto the accused to an unacceptable degree or because they failed to achieve any real diminution in the incidence of prostitution, these new provisions were discarded just two years later on the introduction of a new Vagrancy Act in 1824.[114] By this act the pre-1822 position was, in effect, restored, the key phrase demanding that known streetwalkers 'give a satisfactory account of themselves' being replaced by the requirement that they be 'wandering and behaving in a riotous and indecent manner'.[115]

112. WCA D2116–D2123 Charge books of the parish of St. James, Piccadilly, 30 Jan. 1821–7 Mar. 1826. Actual percentages of discharges were: 1821 = 91.56%; 1823 = 75.42%; 1825 = 81.75%.

113. These conclusions are principally based on an examination of CLRO 204B Guildhall Justice Room Minute Books of Proceedings, 1752–96 (henceforward CLRO GMR/M); and WCA D215-D2108 Charge books of the parish of St. James, Piccadilly, 1773–9. They are discussed at length in Chapter Five.

114. 5 Geo.IV, c.83 (1824), An Act for the Punishment of Idle and Disorderly Persons, and Rogues and Vagabonds in that part of Gt. Britain called England. M.J.D. Roberts, 'Public and private in early nineteenth-century London: the Vagrant Act of 1822 and its enforcement', *Social History*, 13, 3 (1988), pp.273–94, deals with the debates that erupted around the operation of the act but says little about its effect on the capital's streetwalkers.

115. 5 Geo.IV, c.83, sec.3.

Throughout this period, the apparent inability of the authorities to suppress prostitution, whether by arresting streetwalkers or by closing brothels and disreputable lodging houses, ensured that there were continual proposals for changes to the legal position of what was seen as an ever-growing problem of prostitution.

Some such propositions were fairly eccentric. Between 1780 and 1781 the Reverend Martin Madan addressed himself, over three volumes, to the subject of prostitution. He concluded that the only viable remedy was the introduction of an act to legalise polygamy. This, Madan felt, would go a long way to eradicating the cause of prostitution, which cause he identified as the male's incorrigible need for sexual variety.[116] The only substantial results of Madan's proposals were the ignition of a monumental pamphlet war and his consequent ejection from the post of chaplain to the London Lock Hospital.[117] The anonymous author of a pamphlet published in 1756 entitled *Reflections Arising from the Immorality of the Present Age* suggested that the medieval sumptuary laws might be profitably revived, with prostitutes being required to wear some item of distinctive clothing or other distinguishing mark. Further on in the work, however, he tentatively withdrew the idea, with the comment that fashionable women were certain to imitate any such apparel.[118]

Not all the proposed legislation was quite so fantastic. Indeed, the author of the above work, having similarly considered and then dismissed branding and transportation as possible answers to the problem of prostitution, concluded that the best solution lay in the setting up of government-run bawdy houses in one small part of the capital – the already less-than-respectable Cupers Gardens being the ideal location. Trading justices would be compensated for the financial loss legalisation would inflict on them by being given the task of ensuring that private enterprise did not attempt to regain a foothold in the trade.[119] The possible benefits to society of legalising prostitution – preferably in imitation of the Southwark stews with a small number of strictly policed brothels being confined to a single district – had, for example, long been discussed: 'for surely it would be more agreeable to have them orderly with law, than disorderly and licentious without it'.[120] Bernard Mandeville's

116. M. Madan, *Thelyphthora* (1780/81).
117. For Madan's sacking, see J. Bettley, 'Post Volupatem Misericordia: the rise and fall of the London Lock Hospitals', *The London Journal*, 10, 2 (1984), p.169; at least thirty pamphlets were published in reply to Madan, both critical and supportive of his ideas.
118. Anon., *Reflections Arising from the Immorality of the Present Age* (1756), *passim.*
119. Ibid.   120. *The Times*, 29 Aug. 1787.

Modest Defence of Public Stews published in 1724 was, and remains, the best known of the calls for legally accepted bawdy houses. Mandeville proposed the setting up of around one hundred brothels in London (and a proportionate number in each county town) each governed by a 'matron' and staffed by twenty young women, divided by 'beauty or other qualifications' into four differently priced classes. Within easy reach of the houses was to be established an infirmary employing two physicians and four surgeons who would treat infected inmates of the brothels free of charge. The whole would be overseen and regulated by three commissioners.[121] Mandeville's plan was bitterly criticised by, among others, the Societies for the Reformation of Manners (to whom he had had the effrontery to dedicate the work) but was defended by those who keenly felt the sinfulness of such a design but suggested that 'tolerating Fornication and restraining the Irregularities of Harlots' might be a more successful policy than that adopted by 'Street-Reformers, who are inclined to make human Weakness no Allowances [and] think of no Cure for Lewdness, but Amputation'.[122]

Mandeville had proposed that the brothels be limited to 'some convenient Quarter of the City' and, as noted above, similar suggestions occurred throughout the century, often drawing on the example of other European cities.[123] The reformer Jonas Hanway, for one, while principally concerned in his pamphlet of 1758 with demonstrating the desirability of establishing a place of refuge for 'repenting Prostitutes', allowed himself a digression on the subject of licensed prostitution. If brothels were confined to a certain spot, wrote Hanway, then not only might many men be kept on the path of virtue for shame of being seen to search out vice, but the women too would benefit from the provision of speedier and more certain medical care.[124]

The overwhelming majority of calls for the reform of the laws dealing with prostitution urged not toleration, however, but greater severity. Demands that unlicensed premises such as coffee shops and lodging houses be somehow brought within the power of licensing authorities were common. Faced, for example, with a house

121. B. Mandeville, *A Modest Defence of Public Stews: Or an Essay upon Whoring, as it is now Practis'd in these Kingdoms* (1724), pp.12–15.

122. Anon., *Some Considerations upon Streetwalkers* (c.1735), pp.4–5.

123. Classical Rome was also cited in support of the argument: see for example, *The Times*, 19 Jul. 1788.

124. J. Hanway, *Letter V to Robert Dingley, Esq; Being a Proposal for the Relief and Employment of Friendless Girls and Repenting Prostitutes* (1758), pp.18–19.

such as the Union Hotel in Dean Street which sold no liquor, and so required no licence, which conducted itself with outward decorum, and so could not be indicted disorderly, and yet as a parliamentary committee was told, caused the surrounding streets to be filled with prostitutes, the authorities considered themselves legally powerless.[125] Robert Baker, a stipendiary magistrate at Great Marlborough Street police office, suggested that a coffee shop's failing to close at a reasonable hour of the night should automatically be considered an act of disorder, though he was concerned at the difficulties that would arise in attempting 'to draw a line between houses of that description and houses for the reception of higher company'.[126] Patrick Colquhoun thought that such a problem might be overcome by the institution of a register only of those lodging houses 'not paying above a certain rent', overlooking the fact that the keepers of many houses letting rooms to prostitutes paid higher than average rents.[127]

That bawdy and disorderly house keepers were able and willing to pay relatively inflated rents made them understandably attractive tenants to many landlords. The churchwardens of Aldgate parish believed that if landlords could be compelled to use legal means of evicting their tenants, on receiving notice from the parish officers that the house was being used to harbour prostitutes, then they would be more cautious in letting.[128] The Guardian Society went further, proposing to the 1817 Select Committee on the Police that landlords should be held legally responsible for the behaviour of their tenants and be equally if not more liable to the penalties for any offence committed in the running of the house.[129]

At the same time, the Society called for the removal of the right to trial by jury for those accused of keeping a bawdy or disorderly house. A suspected keeper should in the first instance be tried by a summary proceeding before a magistrate and only be allowed resort to the sessions on appeal. This, the Society argued, would 'remove the obstructions which are often thrown in the way by traversing immaterial facts, quashing indictments for informalities, by permitting delay upon fictitious or insufficient ground, and removals by *certiorari* without just causes'. To be absolutely sure that

125. *P.P.* (1817), Vol. VII, Police Committee, 2nd report, p.478.
126. *P.P.* (1816), Vol.V, Police Committee, p.79.
127. Ibid., p.48 and see above, Chapter Two.
128. *P.P.* (1817), Vol.VII, Police Committee, 1st report, p.55.
129. *P.P.* (1817), Vol.VII, Police Committee, 2nd report, p.463.

this speedier, cheaper and less cumbersome procedure would also result in more certain conviction, keepers of brothels were to be deemed 'infamous persons' incapable of giving evidence in court.[130]

The demand that the offence of keeping a bawdy house should be made subject to summary jurisdiction was a perennial favourite. In 1768 John Fielding suggested that 'if a Power was given to two or more Justices of the Peace to enquire into these offences in a summary Way, and on the Conviction of such Bawds, to commit them for three months and make them pay a penalty of £10 it would suppress the Evil to a desirable degree'.[131] Colquhoun's *Treatise on the Police of the Metropolis* of 1796 proposed that any two magistrates should be given the power to try, convict and sentence keepers to terms of between three and six months.[132] He repeated his idea before the Police Committee of 1816, where it found considerable favour.[133] The Police Committee of 1818 adopted the plan as their own.[134]

Conclusion

Just as Bernard Mandeville was able to look to the example of the medieval stews of Southwark for support, so the advocates of a more authoritarian approach could – and did – point to the supposed severity of ancient legislation with regard to prostitution.[135] With equal facility, those arguing against (or at the least uneasy with) any substantial alteration in the laws were able to draw their justification from the past. For not only would it prove extremely difficult in practice to implement more draconian measures but attempts, for example, to add brothel keeping to the range of offences subject to summary jurisdiction, were indisputably, as William Newman, the City solicitor, told the 1817 Committee on the Police, 'in derogation of the common law of the land and liberty of the subject'.[136]

130. Ibid., pp.463–4.

131. Fielding, *Extracts from Such of the Penal Laws, as Particularly Relate to the Peace and Good Order of this Metropolis: with Observations for the Better Execution of Some, and on the Defects of Others* (1768), p.67.

132. P. Colquhoun, *A Treatise on the Police of the Metropolis: Containing a Detail of the Various Crimes and Misdemeanours by which Public and Private Property and Security are, at Present, Injured and Endangered: and Suggesting Remedies for their Prevention* (1796).

133. *P.P.* (1816), Vol.V, Police Committee, p.51.

134. *P.P.* (1818), Vol.VIII, Police Committee, 3rd report, p.31.

135. Mandeville, *Modest Defence of Public Stews*, pp.74–8.

136. *P.P.* (1817), Vol.VII, Police Committee, 2nd report, p.455.

It is an indication of the confusion surrounding the subject that some were able to hold a number of apparently conflicting points of view simultaneously. In the same pamphlet in which John Fielding proposed the extension of summary jurisdiction to the keepers of bawdy houses, he also praised the efficacy of the Disorderly House Act of 1752. He went on to blame the profusion of brothels around Covent Garden in part on the lack of clarity in the law, to argue that 'the Police in arbitrary Government' might easily eradicate brothels but that 'the Laws of England are not to be executed on Caprice or Fancy', and suggest that to suppress prostitution altogether would only give rise to a 'worse vice, already too common', before calling for the 'humane' deportation of prostitutes to the Americas.[137] Two years later Fielding was pressing the case for prostitutes to be automatically considered vagrants and to be punished as such.[138]

Such confusion, with reformers and the authorities able with ease to pick and choose the appropriate historical precedents with which to defend their respective proposals, and – more importantly – the legislation itself being imprecise and to a considerable extent grounded in such precedents, helped make for equal incoherence in the everyday execution of the law. The following two chapters examine that execution in greater depth.

137. Fielding, *Penal Laws*, pp.63–9; 184–5.
138. *P.P.* (1812), Vol.II, Police Committee, Appendix 8, quoting the testimony of Sir John Fielding to the 1770 Select Committee to enquire into the Several Burglaries and Robberies that of late have been committed in and about the Cities of London and Westminster.

CHAPTER FIVE

Policing the Streets

They would do as they please whether or no in spite of the watchman in the execution of his duty.

> *Katherine Green and Mary Forbes on being arrested as*
> *disorderly women, 25 April 1774.*[1]

Be Sober, Be Vigilant.

> *Motto commonly inscribed on first page of*
> *St. James Watch charge books.*[2]

Lane Watchman Drunk and asleep in his Box, and a Woman with
him.

> *Complaint laid against a member of the Watch of*
> *St Margaret and St John the Evangelist.*[3]

Throughout the eighteenth and early nineteenth centuries, the
policing of London's streetwalkers and disorderly houses was the
responsibility not of the godly few of the Reformation Societies but
of the more numerous, if less fervent, agents of the many local
bodies empowered to enforce and maintain public order and the
rule of law in the capital. In the absence of any centrally directed
approach to prostitution, the imprecise tenets of the laws were
applied unevenly and spasmodically from parish to parish. Lengthy
periods of apparent toleration in one parish or ward would be accompanied by efforts to clear entire streets of the trade in a neighbouring area. Disagreements among those in authority, whether

1. WCA D2105, Charge book of the parish of St. James, Piccadilly, 11 Aug. 1773–
4 Oct. 1774.
2. For example, WCA D2107, Charge book of the parish of St. James, Piccadilly,
28 Jul. 1776–1 Oct. 1777.
3. WCA E2648, Minutes of the Proceedings of the Comity of the Watch of the
Vestry of St. Margaret and St. John the Evangelist, 7 Sep. 1791–3 May 1808; complaint heard 3 Jun. 1795.

between individual watchmen and their superiors or, for example, that between the City and the governors of Bridewell which threatened to blight the former's attempts to control street soliciting in 1814, weakened the authorities' endeavours both to maintain some degree of day-to-day control over prostitution and periodically to intensify the struggle against it. This chapter will describe and evaluate the operation of this heterogeneous system of policing and the responses of the women who were subject to it.

The role of the watch

Responsibility for maintaining order on the crowded streets of the capital lay first and foremost with the constables, beadles, patrols and watchmen of the local watch committees. In Westminster since 1735, a series of Watch Acts, applicable either to individual parishes or to the City and Liberty as a whole, had given each parish the right and duty to establish a parochial watch, under the general supervision of the Middlesex justices of the peace.[4] In the City, the system was subject to a greater degree of centralisation.[5] There existed both a general police force consisting of upper and under marshals, marshalmen, day and night patrols and a special patrol for the Smithfield area, whose authority extended over the whole City, while each of the City's twenty-six wards also possessed its own force of constables, beadles and watchmen authorised to act principally within the ward, although ultimate responsibility for the direction of these ward forces lay with the Lord Mayor, Aldermen and Common Council of the City. Although the City day patrol was formed in 1784 and, in Westminster, a small Bow Street day patrol in 1822, 'before 1828 no parish anywhere in London had considered it either necessary or desirable to provide . . . intensive daylight patrols'.[6] Most of the available resources were devoted to the nightly watch.

Of the various officers employed by the parish and ward watch committees, probably the most important from the point of view of

4. S. & B. Webb, *English Local Government: the Manor and the Borough*, I (1924), pp.226–7. For the Acts, see L. Radzinowicz, *A History of English Criminal Law and its Administration from 1750, II* (1956), p.185.

5. The whole of the City was covered by 10 Geo.II, c.22 (1737) and 14 Geo.III, c.90 (1774).

6. Paley, 'An imperfect, inadequate and wretched system? Policing London before Peel', *Criminal Justice History*, 10 (1989), p.118.

London's prostitutes – because the most intrusive – were the watchmen. Local Watch Acts had reduced the importance of the constables. Elected within the parish vestry and confirmed in office by the justices, the constable, usually in company with the beadle, was supposed to patrol the streets of the parish at frequent and regular intervals throughout the night. In practice, with some exceptions, much of their time was spent in the more congenial surroundings of the watch house, while many failed to turn up for duty at all. Watchmen, on the other hand, were expected to be on the streets from the setting of the watch in early evening till dawn. In 1796, an extensive parish such as St. James, Westminster was employing sixty-four watchmen, six beadles and two inspectors as well as its body of constables, the whole being augmented by an extra eight sergeant watchmen and thirty-two additional or patrol watchmen in the months from October to March.[7] Even the smaller parishes maintained relatively large forces. St. Paul, Soho, deployed sixteen watchmen in 1760, a number which had risen to nineteen watchmen, four patrols and two beadles by 1794.[8] Each of the watchmen was assigned a regular beat of, in St. James, around 350 yards and, in St. Pauls, considerably less.[9] Within the confines of his beat each watchman was expected to deal with drunkenness, soliciting and petty tumult, ensure the safety of the parishioners' lives and property from burglary and street theft, question and, if necessary, detain suspicious characters and, in general, enforce conformity to a standard of acceptable public behaviour that grew decreasingly permissive over the course of the eighteenth century.

Accommodation and compromise

Of course, watchmen were not alone in having the public thoroughfares as their place of work. Most of the hours a prostitute spent working would also be passed on the street. For the great majority of women involved in the trade, at any level except the most remunerative, this was where first contact would be made with a potential customer, regardless of whether the sexual act then

7. WCA D2075 Rules, orders and regulations for the better management of the nightly watch and beadles in the parish of St. James, Westminster, 1796.
8. WCA H891 St. Paul, Covent Garden, Minutes of vestry meetings to consider the watch, 10 Nov. 1757–21 Apr. 1791, meeting 30 Jan. 1760.
9. WCA D2075 Rules, orders and regulations; WCA H889 St Paul, Covent Garden, Watch trustees' minutes, 3 May 1794–14 Oct. 1820, meeting 3 Nov. 1794.

took place in a court or a park, the woman's lodgings, a bagnio or the back room of a public house. Even those, relatively few, women who operated out of organised brothels touted for custom, for the most part, in bawdy house doorways and the adjacent streets. Soliciting for clients appears to have been a boisterous and noisy affair and the large numbers of prostitutes lining many of the principal streets of the city almost inevitably came into conflict with other individuals and groups using London's often narrow and crowded thoroughfares. Shopkeepers complained that the activities of prostitutes and their bullies along Fleet Street and Ludgate Hill adversely affected their business.[10] The residents of fashionable Leicester Fields were upbraided for their failure to demand that a stop be put to the 'effrontery and frequent disturbance' displayed by the nightly assemblage of prostitutes in the square.[11] The housekeepers of Oxford Street showed less tolerance in complaining to the parish authorities of St. Anne, Soho, of the 'behaviour and language' of the 'prostitutes of the very lowest class' who gathered in front of their houses each evening and who were 'so extremely profligate and indecent that the Persons passing and repassing were insulted and that their Families within doors were disturbed'. The watch committee responded by ordering the beadles to patrol the area at the close of every evening and by replacing the watchman with a younger man.[12] The anonymous author of *Some Considerations upon Streetwalkers* was indignant at being 'put to the Halt; sometimes by the full Encounter of an audacious Harlot' while 'in full Speed upon important Business'. He complained about the 'Twitches on the Sleeve, lewd and ogling Salutations' and 'the more profligate Impudence of some Jades, who boldly dare to seize a Man by the Elbow, and make insolent Demands of Wine and Treats before they let him go'. The writer went on to compare London unfavourably with other European cities such as Paris which was 'as debauch'd a place to the full as London' but where 'Men meet no Temptations in the Streets, tho' every one knows where he may repair when Frailty comes upon him'. 'We are', he wrote, 'more scandalously lewd, tho' they may be as sinfully so.'[13]

10. J. Innes, 'William Payne of Bell Yard, Carpenter c.1718–1782: the life and times of a London reforming constable' (Unpublished typescript, circulated by author, p.36).

11. *The Times*, 25 Oct. 1786.

12. WCA A2053 St. Anne, Soho, Minute book of the committee for regulating the nightly watch and beadles, 16 Jun. 1803–1 Apr. 1819, meeting dated 3 Dec. 1818.

13. Anon., *Some Considerations upon Streetwalkers, with a Proposal for Lessening the Present Number of them, in two Letters to a Member of Parliament* (c.1735), pp.2–4.

There can be little doubt that it was the very public nature of prostitution in the capital that caused most disquiet to the authorities. The author of the above complaints emphasised the disruption caused to business by the numbers of prostitutes that congregated in Fleet Street. Later in the century, the emphasis lay most often on the danger the women represented both to the purses and the delicate sensibilities of passers-by. The groups of women who crowded the city's newly-established pavements were a 'horrid nuisance' and an 'evil . . . justly complained of'.[14] They were 'the shame and reproach of the Magistracy', spreading 'blasphemies and infection' and were 'one of the principal causes of the increase of thieves'.[15] 'The indecencies practised by the crowds of prostitutes before Somerset-House, every night, not only put modesty to the blush, but absolutely render it dangerous to pass.'[16] Behind these and innumerable similar complaints can be seen a direct conflict of interest between the prostitutes and other users of the streets and pavements over the appropriate function of such public spaces. To the latter, the public streets were places wherein one might 'take the air', view the sights of the great city and be seen doing so. Most importantly, they were passageways, necessary conduits for the movement of vehicles and pedestrians about their business.

To the prostitutes, however, the streets and squares of London were a workplace, essential points of contact between prostitute and client. Success necessitated relative immobility (at most 'wandering back and forward')[17] within a restricted area – whether it be Fleet Street, Leicester Fields, the frontage of Somerset House or another recognised place. That confrontations between prostitutes and individual passers-by were in the main short-lived and non-violent was probably due in part to the latters' willingness to abide by the growing 'etiquette of acceptable street behaviour [that] seems to have been in gradual process of definition' over the century.[18] It owed something more, perhaps, to the fact that such passers-by were, by definition, no more than temporary trespassers upon the women's precariously held territory. As we have seen, there was, however, another group – the men of the watch – for whom the street was a place of work and whose principal task was to impose

14. *The Times*, 27 Oct. 1787; GMR Ms. 1428/1 Bishopsgate wardmote court minute book, 1737–1839, meeting 23 Dec. 1814.
15. *The Times*, 17 Oct. and 29 Aug. 1787; 26 Jul. 1785.   16. Ibid., 2 Jun. 1787.
17. WCA D2107, Charge book of the parish of St. James, Piccadilly, 25 Sep. 1777.
18. Corfield, 'Walking the city streets: the urban odyssey in eighteenth-century England', *Journal of Urban History*, 16, 2 (1990), p.154.

and maintain those very conventions of behaviour that prostitutes violated.

The various Watch Acts which regulated the nightly watch of Westminster and the City frequently included specific instructions as to the nature of the watchmen's role. The act of 1737, for example, regulating the nightly watch for the City, stated that watchmen were to 'apprehend all Night-walkers, Malefactors, Rogues, Vagabonds, and all disorderly Persons whom they shall find disturbing the publick Peace, or shall have just cause to suspect of any evil Designs'.[19] That of 1774 for Westminster repeated the formula, adding that they should also arrest 'all Persons lying or loitering in any Square, Street, Court, Lane, Mews, Yard, Alley, Passage, or Place'.[20] The watch committees of the various parishes were keen to ensure that their watchmen were aware of their duties as laid down in the statutes, hanging the relevant sections of the acts on the wall of the watchhouse and regularly issuing stern reminders to the men.[21] These were reinforced by locally devised rules for the conduct of the watchmen and patrols which, by the turn of the century, frequently singled out prostitutes for especial attention. St. Paul, Covent Garden, reminded its constables, beadles and watchmen in 1799 of 'their Duty from time to time in apprehending . . . Common Prostitutes, Pickpockets and other Offenders'.[22] In 1800, the watch trustees of the tiny St. Mary le Strand advised their lone patrol to be 'more diligent in keeping Clear the Streets etc. within this Parish from the Nusance [sic] of Women of the Town'.[23] The regulations governing the parish's watchmen stated that they were not to 'permit Prostitutes or any suspicious Person or Persons to loiter in the Streets' and required the watchmen to report any public house allowing prostitutes or suspicious persons to drink after 11 p.m.[24] The parishes of St. Bride and St. Martin, Ludgate, required their patrols 'to inspect properly the Public Streets, Courts and Alleys, to see if there are any Common Prostitutes, or other noisy persons or Suspicious Characters committing a breach of the Peace'; any so

19. 10 Geo.II, c.22 (1737).

20. 14 Geo.III, c.90 (1774).

21. See, e.g., WCA H891 St. Paul, Covent Garden, Minutes of vestry meetings to consider the watch, 10 Nov. 1757–21 Apr. 1791 and watch trustees' or commissioners' minutes, 3 May 1791–4 Apr. 1794, entries for 9 Oct. 1782 and 20 Sep. 1793.

22. WCA H889 St. Paul, Covent Garden, Watch trustees' minutes, 3 May 1794–14 Oct. 1820, meeting 12 Oct. 1799.

23. WCA G1044 St. Mary le Strand, Watch trustees' minutes, 29 Jun. 1774–1 Oct. 1829, meeting 13 Nov. 1800.

24. Ibid., meeting 11 Nov. 1819.

discovered were to be held overnight in the City compter and brought before the justices in the morning.[25]

All encounters between prostitute and watchman thus contained the potential for conflict, which could lead, ultimately, to the arrest and detention of the woman. And yet, clearly, not all contact between the two led to such an outcome. In practice, the watch conceded a privileged use of the streets to the women, allowing them to gather and solicit for custom, provoking outraged complaints at the watchmen's apparent reluctance – or inability – to enforce the law: 'Why are these women permitted to carry on this infamous trade? Why are they not apprehended and brought before justice to answer for their offences?', demanded *The Times* in 1786.[26]

The minute books of the various wardmote courts, parish vestries and committees for the watch are filled with complaints against watchmen and other officers of the law for overlooking the activities of the prostitutes who shared their walk. A few examples must stand proxy for the whole:

Thos. Savage Patrole for Neglect of Duty Harbouring a bad Woman in Blue Ball Yard St. James's Street at 3 o'Clock in the Morning;

Wm. Capwell on 28 Beat Sackville St. for harbering [sic] women of the Town to stand and talk with him;

Watchman Clarke No.13 with setting [sic] with a Woman upon his Beat and neglecting his duty at 1/2 past 4 o'clock;

Caslake Watchman Parliament St. for harbering [sic] bad Women on his beat at 1/2 Past 2 O Clock;

Danks Watchman in Parliament St. for Been [sic] with a Disorderly woman on his Beat near 12 o Clock ye 14;

Evans reported . . . by Mears and Westerbe Patroles for abusing them and harbouring disorderly Women on his Beat;

Gibson Watchman in Tothill Street reported by Lee & Lennard Patroles for neglect of Duty in not dispersing some disorderly People at 1 o'Clock 2 August last;

Dawson a Supernumery Watchman for harbouring loose Women in and about his Box or Stand;

25. CLRO Mss.113.1 Returns of the wards to the committee re. prostitutes of their systems of watchmen and patroles, 1818, no.2 return of St. Bride's and St. Martin's, Ludgate, parishes, 17 Sep. 1818.

26. *The Times*, 10 May 1786.

McDonald one of the Supernumerary Watchmen of this parish for suffering Disorderly Women to be Cursing and Swearing in the Street and making a Riot and he in his box and took no notice of them;

Fitzgibbon one of the Watchmen of this parish for being in Liquor at a publick House and Suffering improper Women to be about the Door.[27]

Constables and watchmen alike refused to arrest or take charge of prostitutes. When Hunter and Witherall, two patrol officers of St. Margaret, Westminster, arrested a woman they recognised as a prostitute at the corner of King Street and took her to the watch house, they later reported the constable of the night for refusing to enter her name in the charge book or detain her.[28] Watchmen Cockburn and Burton of St. Anne, Soho, were reported by the beadle of the parish for refusing to comply with the constable's order that.they carry a disorderly woman to the watch house.[29] Watchman Samuel Sheepard was given a similar order by the constable of St. James. Awoken from his sleep and told to take to the watch house a woman who had been standing behind his box, Sheepard refused and 'a Buse him verey Grosley by Call in him Rascal and . . . severel out Dayshious wordes' [sic passim].[30]

There is no evidence that explains directly what lay behind such refusals and the watch's evidently more common habit of simply turning a blind eye to much street soliciting. Joseph Thomas, constable of St Paul's, Covent Garden, told the 1828 Select Committee on the State of Police of the Metropolis that 'it was mortifying to see a party of officers standing at one end of the street, and night after night a throng of prostitutes and well-known thieves, congregating at the other end of the street, and no steps taken to remove them'. He was referring here to the Bow Street patrols and other special forces but he went on to make it clear that the parish watchmen were equally inactive.[31] Many of the reasons for this can probably be found in the quotation with which this chapter opens. When Katherine Green and Mary Forbes told the constable of St. James

27. WCA D2096, 11 Oct. 1819 and 14 Jun. 1822; WCA A2053, 2 Jan. 1806; WCA E3048, 20 Aug. 1785; WCA E3050, 15 Mar. 1791; WCA E2649, 1 Aug. 1815 and 3 Oct. 1815; WCA, 30 Jul. 1784 and F2282, 29 Sep. 1791 and 21 Jun. 1792.
28. WCA E3047 St. Margaret, Westminster, Beadles' report book, 1 Aug. 1781–29 Nov. 1783, entry 22 Aug. 1782.
29. WCA A2053 St. Anne, Soho, Minute book of the committee for regulating the nightly watch and beadles, 16 Jun. 1803–1 Apr. 1819, meeting 6 Apr., 1809.
30. WCA D2093 St. James, Westminster, Beadles' reports, 26 Dec. 1749–20 Apr. 1752, entry 15 Aug. 1751.
31. *P.P.* (1828), Vol.VI, Police Committee, p.74.

that 'they would do as they please whether or no in spite of the watchman' they were, on one level, doing no more than expressing the truth of the situation. Evidence of the obstacles put in the way of watchmen attempting to move on or apprehend prostitutes is patchy and difficult to interpret. The surviving watchhouse charge books record, by definition, examples of unsuccessful attempts to defy the watch or avoid arrest. Watch committee minute books testify only to those cases that came to the attention of the parish authorities.

The sometimes terse and formulaic entries are, nevertheless, suggestive. A variety of incidents illustrates the informality that surrounded watch/prostitute encounters. John Pearce of St. James complained that Martha Land (described as 'a common street-walker') 'always abuses me and calls me several ill names and will not let me do my duty';[32] Jane Beckett and a Miss Gordon were accused by Edward Sutherland of assaulting and abusing him on his duty;[33] Margaret Green was charged with being disorderly and 'refusing to go away when ordered';[34] Caterine Jones, with being a 'loose and disorderly woman and abusing him [the watchman] on his duty'.[35] Two watchmen privately employed by the housekeepers of Coventry Street (an area where arrests of prostitutes were very common) were jointly set upon by Mary Bignall, Sarah Hallbuts and Ann Williams.[36] When John Joyce arrested Elizabeth Shage and Mary Loyde as disorderly women, Shage responded by striking him, Loyde by making off with his watchman's rattle.[37] Attempts were made to rescue women who had been arrested. Merrit Langton, a watchman of Drury Lane ward in St. Martin in the Fields, excused his failure to carry a woman prisoner to the watch house by explaining that 'she was rescued from him by several women at the end of Exeter Street'.[38] One William Smith was charged with attempting to free 'a disorderly woman' from the St. James's watch.[39] Jacob and Elizabeth Levy were charged at the Guildhall with striking a watchman in St. Paul's churchyard as he was taking up 'unfortunate girls'.[40]

32. WCA D2105, Charge book of the parish of St. James, Piccadilly, 1 Jul. 1774.
33. Ibid., 2 Sep. 1774.
34. WCA D2106, Charge book of the parish of St. James, Piccadilly, 6 Sep. 1775.
35. Ibid., 19 Sep. 1775.   36. Ibid., 4 Nov. 1775.
37. WCA D2108, Charge book of the parish of St. James, Piccadilly, 9 May 1778.
38. WCA F2028, St. Martin in the Fields, Vestry and watch committee minutes 3 May 1736–6 Aug. 1754, meeting 23 Nov. 1739.
39. WCA D2105, Charge book of the parish of St. James, Piccadilly, 13 Nov. 1773.
40. GL SL71/061 Collection of newspaper cuttings relating to the City of London 1771–1830, 13 Aug. 1807. The Levys were well known for keeping 'a house of ill-fame' in King's Head Court in nearby St Martin's-le-Grand.

Watchmen who successfully effected an arrest then had to leave their stand in order to convey their prisoner, if taken in Westminster, to the parish watch house, or, in the City, the greater distance to the City compter, leaving their beats unpoliced the while. The problem in the City was seen as acute enough to merit the attention of the Lord Mayor, who suggested in 1815 that the City wards build strongrooms attached to their watch houses to avoid the necessity of removing watchmen from their patrols in order to accompany disorderly persons to the compter.[41]

If the effort involved in making an arrest and laying a charge was enough to discourage some members of the parish watch from such activities, it is also the case that having to press the charge before a justice of the peace the following morning acted as a further disincentive to watchmen and constables alike. The charge books of St. James, Westminster, and the Guildhall Justice Room records for the City both contain numerous examples of prostitutes freed by the justices owing to the non-appearance of the prosecuting officer. The 1817 Committee on the Police heard a plea from a former constable of St. Giles for greater financial compensation for time lost to parish constables in attending court, agreeing with the committee's suggestion that 'offenders often escape on account of the inconvenience and expence that would attend their prosecution'.[42] The former constable of St. Anne, Soho, told the committee that the effect of obliging the constable to attend the magistrates in the morning was that 'many persons are discharged who ought not to be'.[43]

Active parish officers were vulnerable to being prosecuted for false arrest and imprisonment. Constable Prince of St. Clement Danes was threatened with an action against him by one of two women he arrested as disorderly under a general search warrant. The governors of the parish watch agreed to defend him against any subsequent prosecution.[44] A Mrs Brimer of Little Bedford Street brought an action against Moses Lany, a laceman who was serving as the constable of St. Paul, Covent Garden, after he had apprehended her as a disorderly woman in King Street.[45] Samuel Trafford,

---

41. GMR Ms. 4069/4 Cornhill wardmote court and inquest minute book: 1801–1833, letter from Lord Mayor read out at meeting held probably Dec. 1815.
42. *P.P.* (1817), Vol.VII, Police Committee, 2nd report, p.362.
43. Ibid., p.397.
44. WCA B1292, St. Clement Danes, Governor's of the nightly watch and beadles' minutes 7 Nov. 1768–11 Jul. 1785, meeting 11 Oct. 1784.
45. WCA H891, St. Paul, Covent Garden, Minutes of vestry meetings to consider the watch, 10 Nov. 1757–21 Apr. 1791, meeting 29 Sep. 1778.

roundhouse keeper for the same parish, was similarly indicted by Lucy McDonald and one other for imprisoning them after they had been delivered to him by constables acting under a general search warrant. Trafford was defended by the parish but a subsequent decision was taken not to receive prisoners into custody from other parishes (as evidently had been the case here) unless they were charged with a serious offence such as robbery or grievous assault.[46]

That not even the authority conferred by the possession of a general search warrant protected members of the parish watch forces from prosecution for false arrest underlines what many contemporaries thought to be the inadequacy of the laws regarding street-walkers. Sir John Fielding protested to a committee of the House of Commons in 1770 at 'the great difficulty, as the law now stands, to punish those offenders, they being, as common prostitutes, scarce, if at all, within the description of any Statute now in being'.[47] The 1816 Committee on the Police asked Sir Nathaniel Conant, the Chief Magistrate at Bow Street, if he was aware that London was unique among the great European cities for tolerating such open soliciting by prostitutes. He replied that the adoption of continental policing methods would in all probability lead to the suppression of streetwalking in London, but 'the lenity of the English law does not allow it [that is, policing] to be carried to the full extent that it is in those countries'.[48] Conant's belief was shared by the members of the vestry of St Botolph without Aldgate, who replied to a request for information on the matter from the Guardian Society for the Preservation of Public Morals that in their opinion the present laws were insufficient to clear the streets of prostitutes, the reason being that 'even where prostitutes are walking the streets and using the most obnoxious and obscene language, they are not cognizable to the law, without an actual breach of the peace'.[49] Similar replies from other parishes circulated by the Society led it to seek the advice of two eminent counsels, one of whom gave it as his opinion that no woman could legally be apprehended solely because 'her gestures and demeanour' indicated that she was a prostitute. Even open soliciting was not an offence, nor could she

46. Ibid., meetings 13 Feb. and 4 Mar. 1765.

47. *P.P.* (1812), Vol.II, Police Committee, Appendix 8, quoting the testimony of Sir John Fielding to the 1770 Select Committee to enquire into the Several Burglaries and Robberies that of late have been committed in and about the Cities of London and Westminster.

48. *P.P.* (1816), Vol.V, Police Committee, p.23.

49. *P.P.* (1817), Vol.VII, Police Committee, 1st report, p.55.

be committed on reputation alone. The other went further, stating that prostitutes also stood outside the provisions of the Vagrancy Acts of 1609 and 1744 (7 Jac.I, c.4 and 17 Geo.II, c.5). The Society's response was to press parliament to bring in new laws, thereby removing 'all doubts and uncertainties' on the matter.[50]

And yet there is no doubt that throughout this period many women were arrested and charged with simple soliciting and were frequently convicted on the grounds that they were known to be prostitutes. Many commentators felt that any fault lay not in the inadequacy of the legal provisions but rather in the reluctance of the watch to apply the law. 'We want no new laws to prevent these evils', *The Times* declared, 'we only want those we have to be enforced.'[51] In the opening remarks to its third report, the 1818 Committee on the State of the Police began by saying that some alteration in the existing laws governing female prostitution appeared necessary but they went on, somewhat inconsistently, to stress that 'a greater degree of vigilance on the part of the watchmen . . . would operate as a more effectual check to it, than any alteration of the existing laws, to which they feel inclined to object'.[52]

The Select Committee felt that the watchmen were demonstrably failing in their duty to impose order on the public streets.[53] Some part of that failure has been seen above. Occasionally, the reports of the parish and ward watch authorities suggest that numbers of watchmen not only neglected to arrest or move on the city's streetwalkers, but actively colluded with the women on their beats. Watchman Lane, mentioned at the start of this chapter, was not alone in being found in his box in company with a woman. Others were accused of frequenting public and bawdy houses with prostitutes, lighting them home, harbouring them in their apartments, and paying their recognisances in court. Joseph Thomas, constable of St. Paul, Covent Garden, bemoaned the tendency of the parish's watchmen to spend much of the time between walking their rounds, loitering 'under the Piazzas, and round the coffee stands . . . they are there nearly all night in conversation with the prostitutes . . . except when disturbed by the superior officers of the parish'.[54] Thomas attributed the watchmen's familiarity with such 'bad characters' in part to the fact that both watchmen and offenders were liable to be Irish.[55] The *Morning Chronicle* reporter, Edward Edmonds, agreed

50. *P.P.* (1817), Vol.VII, Police Committee, 2nd Report, pp.462–3.
51. *The Times*, 14 Oct. 1789.
52. *P.P.* (1818), Vol.VIII, Police Committee, 3rd report, pp.29–30.
53. Ibid., p.30.   54. *P.P.* (1828), Vol.VI, Police Committee, p.25.   55. Ibid., p.25.

but added that the watchmen were also ill-paid and, in consequence, generally in the pay of the prostitutes whom they were employed by the parish to control.[56] Edmonds' belief in the widespread venality of parish watchmen was a commonplace, with bribes being referred to as 'hush-money' by the parish authorities and 'gin-money' by the prostitutes.[57] A comic pamphlet of 1764 told of 'Common Whores telling their lamentable Cases to Watchmen on their Stands, and treating them with Geneva and Tobacco, for the Liberty of walking about their respective Beats'.[58] The anonymous author of *Thoughts on the Means of Alleviating the Miseries Attendant Upon Common Prostitution* quoted one woman to the effect that, 'not content with receiving from us outlaws of society a brutal gratification gratuitously, as a privilege of office, they [that is, the watchmen] extort a tithe of prostitution'.[59] The watchmen along the Strand looked benignly upon open soliciting as they had 'so much per head from every couple that make up matters'.[60] Between prostitutes and watchmen there existed 'a grand chain of connection, bribery producing permission of guilt'.[61] If some women were arrested, 'the only means to save them from the watch house . . . is a fee to the patrole'.[62]

Similar claims of extensive corruption among the watch forces were made to the House of Commons Committees on the Police,[63] but many vestries and watch committees were extremely sensitive about such matters and while prepared to admit the force of these charges in general were less ready to accept that they applied to their particular parishes or wards. Even Sir Nathaniel Conant downplayed the extent of bribe-taking, agreeing that the low pay of the watchmen must leave them open to temptation but suggesting that the practice was 'less than one might reasonably expect'.[64]

56. Ibid., p.269.

57. *P.P.* (1818), Vol.VIII, Police Committee, 3rd report, p.137.

58. Anon., *Low Life: Or One Half of the World Knows not How the Other Half Lives, Being a Critical Account of What is Transacted . . . in the Twenty-Four Hours between Saturday Night and Monday Morning as It Is Usually Spent within the Bills of Mortality* (3rd edition, 1764), pp.4–5.

59. Anon., *Thoughts on the Means of Alleviating the Miseries Attendant upon Common Prostitution* (1799), p.21, whether the quotation is genuine or not matters less here than that it reveals the beliefs of the pamphlet's author.

60. *The Times*, 14 Oct. 1788.   61. Ibid., 22 Sep. 1788.

62. Ibid., 11 Sep. 1788.

63. See, e.g., *P.P.* (1816), Vol.V, Police Committee, pp.148, 229, 266; *P.P.* (1817), Vol.VII, Police Committee, 2nd report, p.398; *P.P.* (1818), Vol.VIII, Police Committee, 3rd report, pp.134, 137; *P.P.* (1822), Vol.IV, Police Committee, pp.92–3; and *P.P.* (1828), Vol.VI, Police Committee, p.269.

64. *P.P.* (1816), Vol.V, Police Committee, pp.22–3.

Thus, for example, the watch house keeper of St. Paul, Covent Garden, denied the 1816 committee's claim that the parish's watchmen commonly received money from the women on their beats, though he accepted that they often drank together and that 'an understanding' existed between the two groups.[65] William Hale, treasurer of Christ Church, Spitalfields, emphasised the strict moral probity of the men employed by his parish, reinforced by the threat of instant dismissal for any watchman allowing prostitutes to operate on his round.[66] Other parishes were similarly strict and although surviving records are few, they suggest that parish officers proven to have received or demanded bribes from prostitutes were, at the least, severely reprimanded and frequently discharged. The vestry of St. Martin in the Fields dismissed watchmen Thomas Wood and Robert Tucker in 1748 for each taking one shilling to release 'a disorderly Woman' whom the justice had already sentenced to the house of correction.[67] Thomas Cole, beadle of St. Mary, was threatened with dismissal and saw his salary cut from £30 to £27 per year after a number of women complained to Litchfield Street Rotation Office justices that he had extorted money, cloaks, rings and, in one case, a watch from them under pretence of taking bail for their appearance before the magistrates.[68] And while a promise of future good behaviour allowed St. Paul's standsman Andrew Gray to keep his post despite taking money to permit streetwalkers to solicit in Covent Garden piazza, James Talbot of St. Anne lost his after demanding twopence from Margaret Lane of Peter Street, St. James, in 1816.[69]

Despite such occasional severity – and the apparent confidence of the local authorities when questioned by the Commons committees – there can be little doubt but that the perceived readiness with which officers of the parish watch forces accepted (or extorted) bribes from the capital's prostitutes was seen as a serious obstacle to the removal of the trade from the streets. A former constable of St. Anne, Soho, told the 1817 committee that the

65. Ibid., pp.149–50.
66. *P.P.* (1817), Vol.VII, Police Committee, 1st report, pp.109–10.
67. WCA F2028 St. Martin in the Fields, Vestry and watch committee minutes, 3 May 1736–6 Aug. 1754, meeting 11 Nov. 1748.
68. WCA G10144 St. Mary le Strand, Watch trustees' minutes, 29 Jun. 1774–1 Oct. 1829, meeting 7 Oct. 1776.
69. WCA H891 St. Paul, Covent Garden, Minutes of vestry meetings to consider the watch, 10 Nov. 1757–21 Apr. 1791, meeting 27 May 1782; WCA A2053 St. Anne, Soho, Minute book of the committee for regulating the nightly watch and beadles, 16 Jun. 1803–1 Apr. 1819, meeting 3 Oct. 1816.

practice of watchmen 'levying contributions on the unfortunate women walking in their district' was made easier by the fact that 'each of [the women] has her proper beat, the same as the watchmen themselves have, and each watchman knows those who have given to him'.[70]

In 1801, St. Paul, Covent Garden, had attempted to solve this chronic problem by ordering that in future no watchman should be placed on the same beat for two successive nights.[71] Although eight years later St. Paul reverted to its original practice of assigning each watchman a permanent beat (in order that householders might more easily lay complaints against individual officers),[72] the new system appears to have been successful enough to prompt other parishes to emulate it. In 1816, the Corporation communicated to each of the City's twenty-six wards a number of suggestions for improving the efficiency of their watch forces. Among the points made was the recommendation that 'the several beats or rounds of the watchmen should be changed every night, so that no watchman shall know previously to what beat or round he may be appointed'.[73] The responses of Billingsgate and Cheap wards survive – both declaring that such was already their practice, the former adding that

> all Prostitutes if any are found in the Ward are immediately apprehended by the Watchmen or Patroles and that it would not be possible to bribe the Watchmen . . . The Beats of the Watchmen are changed every Night and however such corrupt practises may exist in Fleet Street or other Public Streets the Common Council of this Ward know nothing of them in theirs.[74]

Although both City and parish authorities no doubt felt that these and similar practices helped to lessen the problem of crowds of tolerated streetwalkers on the streets of the metropolis, from the perspective of the prostitutes and the watchmen such measures served primarily to disrupt a relationship which, by and large, served the interests of both parties in allowing the former to earn their living with a minimum of police interference and the latter to supplement their meagre incomes whilst avoiding the expense, trouble and risk involved in making arrests. The structured nature of such

70. *P.P.* (1817), Vol.VII, Police Committee, 2nd report, p.398.
71. WCA H891 St. Paul, Covent Garden, Vestry meetings, meeting 13 Oct. 1801.
72. Ibid., meeting 1 Feb. 1809.
73. *P.P.* (1822), Vol.VI, Police Committee, p.91.
74. GMR Ms. 51/1 Billingsgate wardmote court minute book, 1809–1822, meeting 14 Oct. 1816; see also GMR Ms. 3462 Cheap ward Common Council minute book, 1789–1821, meeting 31 Oct. 1816.

a relationship had the more general advantage of ensuring that a greater degree of stability and order prevailed than would otherwise have been the case.

Disruption

Despite such advantages, the relationship between the policeman and the policed was open to dislocation by either side. The policeman might attempt to change the largely implicit rules by which that relationship was governed (for example, by arresting women engaging in activities which had previously been tolerated). Equally, the prostitute might overstep the ill-defined but still tangible boundary between acceptable and inadmissible behaviour. The situation was a peculiarly complex one. Although the circumstances that allowed prostitutes privileged, but not entirely free, use of the streets were the result of a compromise between the essentially opposed claims of watch and prostitutes to control activity within a given public space, the terms of that compromise were never settled. Thus there existed stability, but not stasis, as first one side and then the other gained the ascendancy. If enough women, for example, successfully behaved in a way that had previously been considered unacceptable, then the watch would have little choice but to accede to this redrawing of the line dividing the tolerated from the intolerable. Major changes were rare, however, and it is not unreasonable to suppose that, on the whole, the rules under which both parties to the compromise operated were sufficiently unambiguous to allow experienced streetwalkers to predict what would – and what would not – be permitted by the watch.

The insistent nature of much soliciting has already been noted above, as have some of its effects on other users of the streets. For the most part, it appears to have been tolerated by the watchmen and patrols of the parishes but when it caused severe dislocation to the streets' primary function of allowing passengers to move freely about the city, the prostitutes involved rendered themselves liable to arrest. This was particularly so where solicitation had progressed to the abuse or assault of passers-by, as on occasion it seems to have done. Other women, perhaps mistaken for streetwalkers infringing upon the locals' territory, were frequent targets.

Again, a variety of examples illustrates the point. Two young women, together with their father, were 'saluted with a volley of indecent and blasphemous expressions' by a group of prostitutes in the Strand after an evening at the theatre.[75] In another incident, a young woman returning from the park with her brother, was 'attacked with a volley of oaths and indecencies'.[76] The watch occasionally took the part of the prostitutes in these confrontations, especially where the target of the abuse was male and had responded in kind. In 1818, Mr Horniman of Threadneedle Street was astounded to be arrested by the constable of Broad Street ward who encouraged one prostitute to charge him with abuse after he had called her 'an Evil B—' in response to her assault upon his shins with her boots.[77] It is unlikely that these were isolated incidents, although the nature of the watch records as sources does not permit certainty.

Witnesses testifying before the Police Committees in the 1810s were divided on the question of whether such occurrences were becoming more or less common. The 1816 committee asked Conant if he thought some means might be found whereby 'women of another description' (that is, *not* prostitutes) might be able to pass through the streets 'without the protection of men'. He replied that the magistrates had shown themselves to be so severe against the instigators of such confrontations that 'such insults are now unfrequent'.[78] His evidence was contradicted, however, by that of other witnesses called before the committee. Patrick Colquhoun informed the committee of his conviction that London's prostitutes were both more numerous and more 'profligate in manners' of late.[79] John Lavender, a Queen's Square police office patrol, reckoned that 'they have certainly got more depraved', although he denied the committee's suggestion that the number of streetwalkers had increased in recent years.[80] Samuel Furzman, constable of the united parishes of St. Giles in the Fields and St. George, Bloomsbury, agreed with Colquhoun that not only had the number of prostitutes grown but that they were 'a great deal worse' than they had been.[81]

Lavender told the committee that the women's increased depravity derived, in part, from the 'connexion and interest that subsists between them and those whose duty it is to keep the streets orderly'. Furzman also substantiated his claim that prostitutes had grown more numerous in recent years by pointing to the increased

75. *The Times*, 7 Jun. 1787.   76. Ibid., 19 Oct. 1787.
77. GMR Mss.1229/2 Broad Street wardmote court minute book, 1808–1831, meeting 13 Oct. 1828.
78. *P.P.* (1816), Vol.V, Police Committee, p.23.   79. Ibid., p.50.
80. Ibid., p.229.   81. *P.P.* (1817), Vol.VII, Police Committee, 2nd report, p.360.

number of arrests his men were making. And yet an enlarged arrest quota may reasonably be thought to indicate a breakdown in that very connection which the members of the Police Committees so deplored. Prostitutes who severed that connection by, for example, refusing to bribe the local watchman, rendered themselves more, and not less, likely to apprehension. Lavender, for one, believed that failure to make payment of half a crown to a watchman was enough to see a prostitute charged and lodged in the watch house.[82] Three gentlemen arraigned before the sitting Aldermen at the Guildhall Justice Room on 9 April 1793 on a charge of obstructing the watch in their duty by rescuing two prostitutes from custody saw the case against them abruptly dropped when witnesses claimed the arresting officers commonly allowed 'a constant set of Prostitutes' to work the alley in question and that the two who had been arrested were taken up simply because they were new to the area – clearly implying that the other women were tolerated because they had come to an arrangement of some kind with the officers.[83]

In his evidence to the committee, Lavender hinted at the two-way nature of such arrangements by commenting that he had seen watchmen not only abusing those women who had refused to pay bribes but also being insulted, attacked and beaten themselves by streetwalkers who had paid but whom they had subsequently failed to protect from arrest.[84]

Any short-term advantages that prostitutes were able to win by attempts to work outside the informal structure of co-existence that normally governed the conduct of watch/prostitute relations were outweighed by the risk that such defiance might provoke the watch into asserting their ability – and, in their view, their right – to determine the bounds of acceptable behaviour on the street. Prostitutes had more to lose in any major disruption of the fragile *modus vivendi*. Such breakdowns as did occur were most often the result of changes introduced by the watch. Should the authorities, or individual officers, decide that customarily tolerated behaviour by – or simply the continued presence of – streetwalkers was no longer acceptable, the impact on the working lives of the women could be immense.

Even a single officer could have a large effect. The best-known example is probably that of William Payne, whose career has been

82. *P.P.* (1816), Vol.V, Police Committee, p.148.
83. CLRO 204B GJR/M 51, 9 Apr. 1793.
84. *P.P.* (1816), Vol.V, Police Committee, p.148.

documented by Joanna Innes.[85] Payne was a 'reforming constable', active in the City of London from the early 1760s until his death in 1783. An enthusiastic member of the newly reformed Society for the Reformation of Manners, Payne concentrated his energies on the hounding of Catholics, Sabbath-breakers, and prostitutes – the latter so much so that by 1762 he was 'an acknowledged expert on the streetwalkers of the Fleet Street area'.[86] Payne refused to accept the attitude prevailing among his peers that prostitutes, particularly those willing to pay a bribe, were to be tolerated. On at least one occasion, Payne reported a fellow constable to the magistrate for having accepted gin and beer from a group of streetwalkers in exchange for releasing them from custody.[87] A pamphlet of 1808 looked back with nostalgia to the days when Payne was 'the terror of this abandoned class of society'.[88]

> He would not allow within the limits of the City any one known prostitute to loiter about the public streets; much less would he suffer any group of them to stand . . . either enticing or insulting every passenger. If they dared to attempt such a breach of public decorum, they were sure to find their way . . . to some neighbouring watch-house, and answer for it the next morning before some City magistrate.[89]

The anonymous author went on to claim that as a result of Payne's activities great numbers of prostitutes quit the City, those few remaining being forced into retirement.[90] That this remembered state of affairs was not entirely fanciful is suggested by the surviving records of the Guildhall Justice Room for the relevant period. Of 347 arrests of streetwalkers for soliciting between 1775 and 1780, fully three-quarters were made by Payne.[91]

Measures to suppress prostitution

Although Payne clearly saw the arrest and, if possible, conviction of prostitutes as the most effective way of suppressing the trade, other

---

85. Innes, 'William Payne of Bell Yard'.   86. Ibid., p.25.
87. GJR/M 17, sitting 19.8.82.
88. Anon., *Letter to the Right Rev. the Lord Bishop of London: Containing a Statement of the Immoral and Disgraceful Scenes which are Every Evening Exhibited in the Public Streets by Crowds of Half-naked and Unfortunate Prostitutes . . . by a Citizen* (1808), p.36.
89. Ibid., pp.35–6.   90. Ibid., p.36.
91. CLRO GJR/M 4–10: this must be taken as an absolute minimum as the records of many sittings have not survived.

methods were also advocated. In 1753, John and Henry Fielding had, on the occasion of John Fielding's assumption of Henry's position at Bow Street, compiled a list of six resolutions. The sixth stated their intention 'to prevent Street-walking, by keeping the Whores within Doors'.[92] Indeed, the most common way in which a watchman could enforce his claim to control of the streets involved neither detaining nor charging the women but simply ordering them to disperse. While considered novel, and much resented, when applied to working class men in the mid-nineteenth century,[93] 'moving on' groups of streetwalking prostitutes was routine practice in eighteenth-century London. As already noted, watch committee instructions enjoined watchmen to clear the streets of loitering prostitutes and as Sir Nathaniel Conant admitted, 'they do it more by driving them away than by taking them into custody'.[94] William Smith, the beadle of Broad Street ward, told the City of London's committee on prostitutes in 1818 that while he did not know if any prostitutes actually resided in the ward, 'when any of them are seen walking about they ordered [sic] to go out of the Ward'.[95] Such action was held to be a sufficient deterrent for the parish of St. Paul regularly to print handbills – to be pasted up around the parish – warning 'Prostitutes, pickpockets and other offenders' of a forthcoming sweep.[96] Although these sweeps were not daily affairs, that watchmen and patrols were expected routinely to break up groups of streetwalkers is further indicated by the reprimand handed out to two officers of St. James when they were seen by the parish's inspector of patrols to ignore a group of five or six women 'making a noise laughing and talking' in King Street. The inspector told the two men that he considered them to have failed in their duty and proceeded to disperse the women himself.[97]

As these examples suggest, periodic efforts to clear the streets of prostitutes were most likely to be undertaken not on the initiative of individual officers – with the exception of zealots like William

92. J. Fielding, *An Account of the Origin and Effect of the Police* (1758), p.18.

93 R.D. Storch, 'The Policeman as domestic missionary: urban discipline and popular culture in northern England, 1850–80', *Journal of Social History*, 4, 9 (1976), pp.481–509.

94. *P.P.* (1816), Vol.V, Police Committee, p.22.

95. CLRO Mss.113.1 Returns of the wards to the committee re. prostitutes of their systems of watchmen and patroles, 1818, Return of Broad Street ward, 17 Aug. 1818.

96. WCA H889, St. Paul, Covent Garden, Watch trustee minutes, 3 May 1794–14 Oct. 1820, meeting 12 Oct. 1799.

97. WCA D2096 St. James, Piccadilly, Beadles' reports, 1 Apr. 1819–31 May 1823, Inspector's Report for 10 Nov. 1821.

Payne – but rather at the prompting of higher authority. For example, in October 1787 the sitting magistrates at Bow Street began issuing a series of privy search warrants to the high constable, with the stated aim of entirely removing the prostitutes, pickpockets and other offenders who were said to prevail in the area between Temple Bar and Exeter Exchange.[98] The magistrates had acted after being confronted by a deputation of 'several respectable residents' of the Strand. That such action took place only after it was explicitly demanded by the inhabitants of a neighbourhood was not unusual. In November 1789, a number of the residents of Charing Cross attended the vestry meeting of St. Martin in the Fields parish in order to complain about the behaviour of 'improper women' in Johnsons Court, a narrow alleyway running alongside Northumberland House.[99] It was pointed out at the same time that robberies were 'daily Committed at Sunsett' [sic] on carriages passing Horseguards by numerous gangs of men. The vestry immediately set up a committee for the purpose of hiring twelve men, 'properly armed' to patrol the area from sunset till ten o'clock. Demonstrating a lively respect for the dangers presented by the robbery gangs at Horseguards, the vestry suggested that the patrol 'be particular in their Attention towards the removing the Nuisance in Johnsons Court'.

Not all demands for action met with such a prompt response from the authorities. In the 1810s – after receiving a petition signed by over 2,000 residents of the City of London – the Common Council of the City attempted to lessen the number of streetwalkers within its boundaries.[100] The attempt foundered in the face of the refusal by the Bridewell governors to set aside any further room to accommodate the expected increase in the number of convicted prostitutes. The affair rapidly degenerated into a power struggle between the two bodies. At one point the Common Council's committee obtained a leaked copy of an internal Bridewell report which, the committee maintained, showed that the Bridewell was both duty bound and perfectly able to provide more places for convicted prostitutes. That the Bridewell board of governors was so porous is

98. *The Times*, 27 Oct. 1787.
99. WCA F2282 St. Martin in the Fields, Draft vestry and watch committee minutes, 14 Nov. 1785–14 Feb. 1793, Vestry meeting 14 Nov. 1789.
100. For the work of the committee set up by the City in response to the petition see the published reports of the committee – GL, Common Council reports 1810–15, reports no.14 and 18; and Common Council reports 1816–21, reports no.1 and 3.

unsurprising given the presence on it of a number of City Aldermen and Common Councillors.[101]

Less ambitious efforts to clear the streets were frequently more successful. They employed a variety of methods to achieve their aims. The simplest was to remind the officers of the watch of their duty to enforce the law – and more especially those clauses in the Watch Acts and regulations that forbade 'loitering' by prostitutes and others in the streets. Indeed, this was the approach favoured by the Common Council in 1814. Apprehensive that 'many of the Patroles, Watchmen, and Night Officers of this City, execute their several Duties in a very negligent manner',[102] the Common Council urged the City magistrates to ensure that both they and the various officers under them administered the laws 'with more than ordinary Attention and Diligence'.[103]

When it was thought necessary – and the cost not too prohibitive – the parish and ward authorities deployed additional forces to patrol especially notorious areas. St. Paul, for example, in addition to pasting up warning notices, regularly requested the magistrates to swear in extra men as constables so that they might be employed in removing prostitutes from the piazzas and market place at Covent Garden.[104] In 1777, the watch trustees of St. Mary le Strand ordered that 'the two Constables of this Parish do alternately with the Beadle patrol the whole of this Parish every Night from the Dusk of the Evening till 10 o'Clock and do use their utmost endeavours to prevent the Women of the Town from parading the Streets . . . and picking up Men'. The constables were to be paid an additional half a guinea per week (to be divided between them) 'for such extraordinary trouble'.[105]

On New Year's Day, 1776, the governors of St. Clement Danes' nightly watch agreed that the parish's patrolmen should in future, and in addition to their regular duties, assist the constables in 'clearing the streets of bad Women and idel [sic] Persons' each evening. Two weeks later, the order was withdrawn. They were to return to

101. In addition to the printed reports, see also *P.P.* (1818), Vol.VIII, First report from the committee on the prisons within the City of London & borough of Southwark, pp.426–7, 437–43, where the argument is rehearsed to the committee.

102. GL, Co.Co. Repts. 1810–15, Report no.14.

103. Ibid.

104. WCA H891 St. Paul, Covent Garden, Vestry and watch trustees' Minutes, meetings 3 Nov. 1783, 20 Aug. 1785, 31 Aug. 1785 and 7 Apr. 1792; WCA H889 St. Paul, Covent Garden, Watch trustees' minutes, meetings 12 Oct. 1799, 10 Oct. 1800, 3 Nov. 1807, 3 Nov. 1809, 28 Nov. 1809, 12 Jan. 1810.

105. WCA G1044 St. Mary le Strand, Watch trustees' minutes, 29 Jun. 1774–1 Oct. 1829, meeting 23 Dec. 1777.

their normal hours except on 'Search Nights', when the patrols were again to give special aid to the constables.[106] 'Search Nights' took place as a result of the making out of search warrants by two or more justices of the peace. These were issued either on a regular basis – the Surrey magistrates sent out such warrants quarterly – or after some specific complaint had been laid, as in the example given above of the Bow Street justices ordering searches in response to the petitioning of residents of the Strand.[107] The words of the warrant, made out to the high constable of the county for transmission to the parish officers, commanded the latter to scour the streets under their jurisdiction, on a specified night, for 'rogues, vagabonds, and sturdy beggars, and all such persons as are suspected to keep bawdy-houses, and the frequenters thereof, and also all disturbers of the peace, &c'.[108] Those apprehended were to be taken before a magistrate by ten o'clock the next morning 'to be dealt with according to Law'.[109]

Over the short term, search nights could be immensely disruptive of prostitutes' ability to continue working. One reason for this lay in the vague and all-encompassing nature of the offences described in the warrant. Despite the supposedly landmark decision of 1709 – where the murder of the reforming constable Dent after he had arrested a well-known streetwalker had been adjudged justified because 'a light Woman hath a right of Liberty as well as another to walk about the Streets' – it is not difficult to find examples of women arrested because, in the words of one of Dent's colleagues when explaining the arrest to the Court, 'we knew her to be a very common Woman of the Town and in common plying Place for such People, therefore we took her up'.[110] Thus, large numbers of women could be arrested during one night under a single warrant. In December 1789, for example, one Saturday night sweep of the Strand resulted in the apprehension of over fifty streetwalkers.[111] A similar search by the City marshall in 1771 saw thirty-four 'disorderly persons' taken out of houses of ill fame and brought before the Lord Mayor, sitting at the Mansion House.[112] While the charge books of the parish of St. James do not record any sweeps on quite

106. WCXA B1292 St. Clement Danes, Governors' of the nightly watch and beadles' minutes, 7 Nov. 1768–11 Jul. 1785, meetings 1 Jan. and 15 Jan. 1776.

107. *P.P.* (1817), Vol.VII, Police Committee, 2nd report, p.470.

108. Anon., *The Complete Parish Officer* (1772), p.114.   109. Ibid., p.114.

110. Bray, *Tryals of Jeremy Tooley*, p.6.   111. *The Times*, 16 Dec. 1789.

112. GL SL71/061 Collection of newspaper cuttings relating to the City of London, 1771–1830, 4 May 1771.

the same scale, they nonetheless contain numerous examples of groups of between ten and twenty women being brought into the watch house at one time.[113] The admittedly partial description in *The Times* on 10 November 1785 of one such sweep is worth quoting at some length.

Last Monday evening was exhibited in the environs of St. Martin's-lane, a scene shocking to humanity. It was *search-night*, in the cant of the police: the *sharks* of the watch-house were abroad, aided by the *runners* of Justice, or rather those who *out-run* Justice; and the unhappy women of the town were the devoted victims. Of these the most youthful and best clad were selected. They were dragged away with all the insolence of brutal authority to St. Martin's watch-house; and that their wretchedness might be complete, imprisoned together in a confined cellar, an European Black-hole, where they lay till Tuesday forenoon.[114]

The author of the piece concluded with the supposition that those women who were unable to pay a bribe to gain their release would be later confined to the Bridewell.

Many of the ways in which prostitutes responded to the threat or the reality of apprehension by officers of the watch – including payments in cash or in kind, prosecution for false arrest, and more or less violent resistance – have already been detailed above. Given the fragmented structure of policing in the capital, an equally effective response to a wave of arrests taking place in a single parish or, at most, within the boundaries of the old City, was for the women temporarily to abandon the affected area for the duration of the authorities' campaign. It has already been seen that streetwalking prostitutes both knew about and made use of the officially encouraged reluctance of officers to operate outside their stated beats. The commencement of mass arrests in one area would frequently lead to the inundating of a neighbouring district with displaced prostitutes. In November 1785, for example, *The Times* remarked that the City magistrates having ordered their constables to drive the City's streetwalkers into Westminster, 'on the other side the Westminster justices have resolved to act with equal zeal, by driving the night walking fair in their districts, towards the City'.[115] A campaign against soliciting in the neighbourhood of Fleet Street in March 1788 saw the women deserting that area in favour of

---

113. Examples of arrests of large numbers of prostitutes on single nights can be found in the St. James charge books at D2105.
114. *The Times*, 10 Nov. 1785.   115. *The Times*, 7 Nov. 1785.

Duke's Place near the Houndsditch in the City. When the arrests spread to the Strand in the summer of that year, still larger numbers, as *The Times* put it, 'sheltered within the walls of the City'.[116]

The fate of those arrested

Despite such tactics many prostitutes were arrested. The surviving charge books for St. James show a total of 2,880 individuals being charged with offences of all kinds at the parish watchhouse between 1773 and 1779.[117] Of these, 1,407 (48.85 per cent) were women. Those women arrested and charged with a variety of soliciting offences totalled 1,028 – 35.69 per cent of the whole and almost three-quarters of all female charges. Whether arrest occurred as a result of the action of an individual officer or during a major sweep, it would be followed by the removal of the woman to the nearest watch house or compter. Here the constable of the night or the watch house keeper was required to enter into the charge book the name of the arresting officer, the date, time and location of the arrest, the charge against the woman, and her name. In practice, many of the arrested women refused to co-operate. The St. James's charge books, for example, make frequent reference to the arrest of such as 'Ann Nothing', 'Mrs No Name', 'Mrs Nothing at all', 'Mr and Mrs Nothing', 'Mrs Don't tell you', 'Mrs No Matter', 'My Name is Nothing', 'Mary Knowbody' [sic], 'Miss Nobody', the more imaginative 'I'll tell you my name tomorrow' and 'Kis my Comekel' [sic], or the blunt 'What's that to you?', 'Whyso?' and 'Won't tell you, damn my eyes'. None of this, of course, takes any account of the undoubted use of more plausible aliases.[118]

Conditions in the watch houses varied. Those held in the Wood Street compter in the City before the gaol's closure in 1791 were confined in a special section reserved for 'drunks, street-walkers, vagabonds, stray children and other nuisances picked up in the night'.[119] In 1792, the magistrates at the Queen's Square police office complained to the watch committee of the combined parish

116. Ibid., 15 Jul. 1788.
117. WCA D2105–D2108 Charge books of the parish of St. James, Piccadilly, 1773–9 (broken series).
118. WCA D2105–D2108 Charge books of the Parish of St. James, Piccadilly, *passim.*
119. Howson, *It Takes a Thief: The Life and Times of Jonathan Wild* (1987), p.15.

of St. Margaret and St. John the Evangelist about the conditions prevailing in the parish's watch house. The 'Cages or places of Reception for persons taken up in the Night, on each side of the Watch House were very inconvenient and unsafe that those confined therein were in danger of being suffocated'.[120] This was no exaggerated fear – on the evening of 15 July 1742, the constables and watchmen of St. Martin in the Fields (while drunk, according to Horace Walpole) had crammed twenty-five or twenty-six women into the parish round-house, leaving them overnight without water and with the doors and windows of the house locked shut. By the morning, four of the women were dead; another two died soon after. The officers of the law fled as an enraged crowd attacked and all but demolished the round-house.[121] The committee's proposed improvements included removing the privies from the cages, raising the floors on joists and altering the roofs from the present concave shape to straight.[122]

In law, the women were required to be held overnight before being brought before a justice of the peace the following morning. In practice, however, prostitutes who were taken up by the watch were frequently expelled from the watch house after a few hours' confinement, without seeing any magistrate. In 1785, for example, two of the watchmen employed by St. Martin in the Fields entered a formal complaint against the substitute constables Shirly and Cooper 'for Suffering persons brought by them to the watchhouse and charged as Disorderly to go immediately at large again without first carrying them before a Magistrate'.[123] As an entry in the St. James' beadles' report book for 21 June 1774 makes plain, this was 'apparently' regular practice: 'The Constable & Lantern Bearer went to the Castle in Swallow Street after twelve o'clock and brought out of the house twelve disorderly girls and in the morning at four let them all go without going before the Justice which is often'.[124]

120. WCA E26448 Minutes of the proceedings of the committee of the watch of the vestry of St. Margaret and St. John the Evangelist, 7 Sep. 1791–3 May 1808, meeting 26 Sep. 1792.

121. WCA F2028 Vestry and watch committee minutes, 3 May 1736–6 Aug. 1754, vestry meeting 17 Jul. 1742.

122. WCA E2648 Minutes of the proceedings of the committee of the watch of the vestry of St. Margaret and St. John the Evangelist, 7 Sep. 1791–3 May 1808, meeting 26 Sep. 1792.

123. WCA F2280 St. Martin in the Fields, Draft vestry and watch committee Minutes, 16 Apr. 1778–4 Nov. 1785, meeting 10 Feb. 1785.

124. WCA D2094, St. James, Piccadilly, Beadles' reports on activities during night patrol with the constables and at the watch houses, 24 Jun. 1773–3 Nov. 1778, entry 21 Jun. 1774.

An earlier constable of the same parish discharged someone in similar circumstances having first extracted promises from them 'not to keep late hours again'.[125] Indeed, such were the discretionary powers with which many constables invested themselves in regard to the decision as to which prisoners were to be released and which were not, that they came to be known popularly as 'Midnight Magistrates'.[126]

Nevertheless, many – almost certainly most – prostitutes did appear before a magistrate as a result of having been arrested. Within the City, this necessitated the transfer of the prisoner from either the Wood Street or the Poultry compter to one of two courts. Depending on the part of the City in which the arrest had taken place, the woman was taken either to the Mansion House to be judged by the Lord Mayor, or to the Guildhall Justice Room, where the Aldermen took turns in presiding.[127]

The number of women brought into the Guildhall Justice Room each week and accused of prostitution varied, but was never very great.[128] Table 5.1 shows the number of days for which records of sitting survive in each year between 1775 and 1796, as well as the number of streetwalking offences recorded. From these a weekly average has been calculated. It was a rare week that saw more than half a dozen such charges recorded.

In 1817, the Select Committee on the Police put it to James Wade, a former constable of St. Anne, Soho, that watchmen made more arrests on Saturday evenings than on any other day of the week. He agreed. As he did – though less readily – with their further suggestion that the reasons for this were not simply that 'its being pay-day for the lower orders, and consequently there being more drunken and riotous persons found in the streets, but that there being also another four-and-twenty hours to lie in the watchhouse, [before seeing a magistrate on the Monday] the watchman is induced to take up persons, in order that they may pay more for their liberation?'.[129] That Saturday night in the City saw more arrests of streetwalkers than any other night is confirmed by the

125. WCA D2092, St. James, Piccadilly, Beadles' reports, 12 Mar. 1739–11 Nov. 1742, entry 4 Aug. 1742.

126. Anon., *Low Life*, 3rd edn. (1764) p.101.

127. The general rule – not always observed – was for persons arrested east of King Street to be taken before the Lord Mayor at the Mansion House, while those taken to the west appeared at the Guildhall: *P.P.* (1822), Vol.IV, Police Committee, p.4.

128. As in the St. James charge books, the term 'accused of prostitution' used here, covers a variety of accusations, from 'disorderly' to 'picking up men'.

129. *P.P.* (1817), Vol.VII, Police Committee, 2nd report, p.397.

TABLE 5.1   *Total prostitution charges at the Guildhall Justice Room, 1775–96*

Year	Recorded sittings (days)	Total charges	Weekly average
1775	34	22	4.5
1776	15	5	2.3
1777	107	86	5.6
1778	27	63	16.3
1779	69	93	9.4
1780	65	78	8.4
1781	173	42	1.7
1782	99	43	3.0
1783	97	49	3.5
1784	148	59	2.8
1785	42	20	3.3
1786	81	77	6.7
1787	53	19	2.5
1788	59	40	4.7
1789	80	34	3.0
1790	51	49	6.7
1791	126	42	2.3
1792	65	46	5.0
1793	41	84	14.3
1794	56	29	3.6
1795	34	19	3.9
1796	39	24	4.3

Source: CLRO 204B Guildhall Justice Room Minute Books of Proceedings, 1752–96

numbers appearing before the Alderman at the Guildhall Justice Room on the Monday morning.

Between 1783 and 1796, while the Alderman sat each day bar Sunday, the Monday sitting accounted for over a quarter of the week's prostitution-related charges. How much of this was due to the venality of the watch, how much to Saturday being the payday for streetwalkers' potential customers (and hence for the women also), and how much a simple reflection of the fact that the Monday sitting dealt with Saturday and Sunday arrests together, cannot be discovered with any certainty. That corruption did not play a large part in it is suggested by an analysis of the figures generated during the heyday of William Payne. Whatever else he may have been, Payne was almost certainly not open to bribery.[130] Between

130. His reporting of another constable for just that offence has already been noted.

1762 and 1782, when Payne was responsible for around three-quarters of all arrests of prostitutes in the City, the Monday sitting saw a third of all such cases – the fact that this was a greater proportion than prevailed after Payne's death reflects the absence of a Saturday morning sitting to deal with the Friday evening arrests. This was not introduced until 1783.

All the figures quoted above include prostitutes facing a wide variety of charges – although each depended ultimately on the woman having been identified as a streetwalker actively soliciting for custom at the time of her arrest. That such charges were so variously worded is symptomatic both of the relatively informal nature of the Guildhall Justice Room's proceedings and of the ambiguous state of the law as it related to prostitution. As with the complaints against watchmen discussed above, a few examples must suffice.

> Ann Perry 'Picking up a Person in the Street & Insulting & Abusing the Constable she appearing not to be a Common offender Discharged'.[131]

> Charlotte Price 'strolling in Fleet Str. & picking up sevl. Men – this was the first time she had been here, she was therefore reprimanded & DS' [i.e. Discharged].[132]

> Mary Knight 'for sitting at a door in Cornhill' committed to Bridewell for seven days.[133]

> Mary Spaughton 'for being in company with a Gentleman' Discharged.[134]

> Sarah Lambert [& nine others] 'apprehended picking up men in the streets of this City – and being Loose Idle and disorderly Women and common night walkers'. All discharged 'having in the Opinion of the Alderman suffered by Imprisonment & promising to keep out of the Streets'.[135]

> Sophia Wilson & Ann Rogers charged by John Ballard 'for asking him to treat him [sic] with a Glass of Wine'. Wilson discharged and Rogers 'recommended to the Hospital being afflicted with the veneral distemper'.[136]

> Mary Green [and nine others] charged as 'disorderly Women' – six sentenced to six days in Bridewell before being passed to their parishes of settlement, four 'excused from some favourable circumstances'.[137]

---

131. GJR/M1, sitting 3 Jun. 1752.   132. GJR/M3, sitting 3 May. 1762.
133. GJR/M10, sitting 28 Sep. 1780.   134. GJR/M17, sitting 5 Aug. 1782.
135. GJR/M10, sitting 4 Sep. 1780.   136. GJR/M18, sitting 20 Sep. 1782.
137. GJR/M45, sitting 2 Sep. 1790.

Jane Byron, Margaret George and Elizabeth Wingood charged with disorderly conduct 'are Com. Prost. [i.e. common prostitutes] & constantly about the neighbourhood' – committed to Bridewell for seven days.[138]

Mary Ann Collins, Susana Gess and Ann Harris, 'disorderly conduct in the Streets last Night at a late Hour' – Gess discharged, Harris committed to Bridewell for correction before being discharged, Collins remanded before being brought up again the following day to be discharged into the care of her mother 'who promises to keep her out of the Streets . . . [the Alderman] . . . ordering her Things to equip for service'.[139]

Apart from giving some indication of the variety of ways in which the charge could be worded, these examples also demonstrate that the magistrate did not always – or even usually – limit his role to a simple decision as to the guilt or innocence of the woman before him. Patrick Colquhoun told the 1816 Select Committee on the Police that when prostitutes appeared before him,

I generally admonish them, inquire where their parents live, commit for the seven days, endeavour to send for their parents or relations, if they have any in town, or offer them a pass to go into the country from whence they originally came, if their settlement is not in the Metropolis.[140]

That the City magistrates followed much the same practice is illustrated by Figure 5.1, which shows the full range of outcomes arising from the 1,076 cases heard at the Guildhall Justice Room – and of which record survives – between 1775 and 1796.

The decisions of the sitting Alderman were not made in a random manner. Nor, for the most part were they solely based on whether or not the woman was adjudged to have committed the offence of which she stood accused. Her guilt – that is, that she had in truth been soliciting for custom as a prostitute was by and large taken for granted once the arresting officer had sworn an oath to that effect. Many who were so 'proved', however, were discharged – indeed, as Figure 5.1 shows, that was the most likely consequence of the hearing.

Those who were so discharged were in general – though by no means exclusively – those who had never come before the court before and whom the constable was not able to swear as 'an old

138. GJR/M53, sitting 1 Sep. 1794.   139. GJR/M55, sitting 14 Mar. 1796.
140. *P.P.* (1816), Vol.V, Police Committee, p.50.

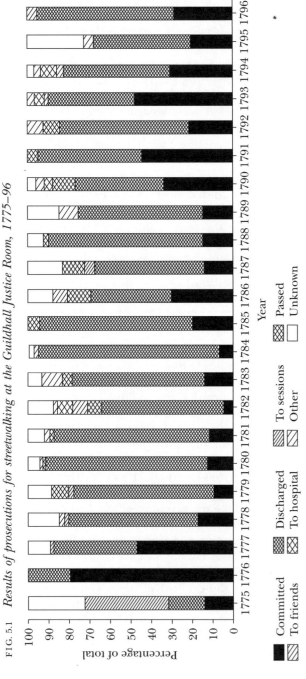

FIG. 5.1   *Results of prosecutions for streetwalking at the Guildhall Justice Room, 1775–96*

Source: CLRO 204B Guildhall Justice Room Minute Books of Proceedings, 1752–96

offender'. Aldermen Crosby and Plomer, for example, in January 1778, discharged Ann Evans (charged by Payne with 'wandering abroad and picking up men') as she 'app'd a poor ignorant Welch Girl, just come from the Country'.[141] Scores of other women were similarly discharged from the Guildhall Justice Room, with the words 'not known' entered beside their names in the minute books.[142] Even those accused who were 'known' to the court or its officers were frequently discharged, albeit after having received a reprimand and promising 'amendment'. Indeed, this was thought by some to be such a common occurrence as to undermine the authority of the watch. In a report to the City committee on prostitution in 1818, the beadle and deputy beadle of the southern precinct of Farringdon Without ward complained that the practice of freeing even 'Prostitutes of the most flagrant Character . . . hardens them in their Iniquity, so much, that some of them, when again taken, become almost unmanageable and their gross abuse and opposition much worse than before'.[143] Smaller numbers of women were also spared imprisonment, instead being handed into the care of 'friends' or relatives, passed to the parishes of settlement, or sent to the hospital after being discovered to be 'diseased'.[144]

Between 1752 and 1796 at the Guildhall, some 274 charges (25.5 per cent) resulted in the immediate conviction and committal of the woman to Bridewell – as against 622 (57.8 per cent) which resulted in unconditional dismissals. (This dismissal rate does not include those passed, sent to hospital or handed to friends – it does include those discharged after a reprimand.) The women who were committed generally fell into one of two groups, and sometimes both. Some had compounded their original offence in some way. Hannah Hall and Elizabeth Harris, for example, might have expected no more than a reprimand on being accused of 'hustling' a young man (especially as their accuser failed to make an appearance in court to press the charge) but the fact that 'they behaved very bad in the Watcho.' brought them ten days' confinement in the Bridewell.[145] Overly intrusive soliciting was equally likely to be

141. GJR/M6, sitting 21 Jan. 1778.
142. The rendering of judgement in accordance with the woman's reputation was, unsurprisingly, a commonplace.
143. CLRO Mss.113.1 Returns of the wards to the committee re. prostitutes of their systems of watchmen and patroles, 1818, Return of St. Bride's and St. Martin's, Ludgate, parishes, 17 Sep. 1818.
144. Total numbers, 1752–96 are: passed to parish of settlement, 39; delivered into care of 'friends' or relations, 14; and sent to the hospital, 13.
145. GJR/M53, sitting 27 Aug. 1794.

punished. Mary Harris was committed to Bridewell for an unspecified length of time, despite being 'very penitent', after being convicted of 'endeavouring to seduce him [her accuser] to her Lodgings – and clasping him in her Arms'.[146] This was the other side of the policy that dismissed the case against Elizabeth Rigby and Margaret Strutton in April 1779 on the grounds that despite 'asking him to treat them – they did no more'.[147]

It did not help Hall and Harris's cases that they were identified as 'common prostitutes', and it is to this group – particularly those named as 'notorious' or 'old' offenders – that the majority of those committed belong. The practice, equally common at other tribunals, was spelt out for the 1817 Select Committee on the Police by the watch house keeper of St. Giles and St. George, who stated that, among others, those arrested 'for disorderly conduct in the street as common prostitutes . . . are taken before the magistrate, and he disposes of them as he thinks proper; if they are old offenders, and we wish to press it, the magistrate commits them'.[148]

A very small number of women charged with prostitution offences (of the Guildhall sample just fourteen, a little over one per cent) were 'committed till a Court' – that is, held in custody to appear at the City of London sessions of the peace. At these, and other, higher courts the outcome of a case was far less likely to be in favour of a defendant on a charge of streetwalking. In sharp contrast to the committal rate of around one quarter at the Guildhall Justice Room, of those held in the Southwark compter between 1814 and 1829 and tried at the Surrey Quarter Sessions as streetwalkers, all against whom a prosecution was pressed were convicted. Only those few women (eight out of sixty-seven) whose prosecution was dropped were discharged.[149] Committal to the sessions on a streetwalking charge virtually guaranteed conviction, although it is worth noting that even known prostitutes were unlikely to be convicted when facing other charges. Sarah Jones, for example, appeared before the Surrey sessions twelve times between 1815 and 1821 on charges of varying seriousness. Three separate charges of

---

146. GJR/M30, sitting 8 Feb. 1785.   147. GJR/M8, sitting 19 Apr. 1779.
148. *P.P.* (1817), Vol.VII, Police Committee, 1st report, p.164.
149. CLRO SC1/8 Commitments for trial at the sessions, Jul. 1814–Oct. 1842. Although the majority of the charges included in this number are given in SC1/8 as 'Idle and Disorderly', the related CLRO Southwark Box 13.1, Calendars of prisoners for trial at the quarter sessions and prisoners upon orders, Oct. 1814–Oct. 1842 – listing the identical cases – shows the full charge in these cases to read 'being a loose, idle & disorderly person, and a Common Street Walker, walking the streets to pick up Men'.

theft – of £20 in 1815, a handkerchief in 1819, and a watch worth £4 in 1821 – each resulted in her discharge after the jury had found 'no true bill'. Two charges of assault were similarly dealt with, while one of riotous and disorderly was not pressed. Of six charges of disorderly, idle and disorderly, and being a common streetwalker, however, four saw the case taken to its conclusion and her committal to the house of correction of one month on each occasion.[150] One month was the usual sentence handed down to prostitutes by the Surrey sessions. Indeed, of the fifty-nine sentences recorded between 1814 and 1829, fifty-six were for one month, two for seven days (one of these including the rider that the woman was to be passed to her home parish on completion of her term), and one for fourteen days. As with the process of decision making, the comparison with the Guildhall Justice Room reveals the greater flexibility of the lower court. Of the 274 cases resulting in committal to Bridewell, just 166 record the length of the sentence imposed (none being from before 1775). These are shown in Table 5.2 below. Combining the sentences for six days and seven days, and doing the same with those for fourteen and sixteen days, it can be seen that sentences of roughly one week and two weeks together account for 85.55 per cent of the whole.[151]

TABLE 5.2 *Lengths of sentences handed down at the Guildhall Justice Room, 1775–96*

Sentence	Number	Percentage of whole
6 days	7	4.2
7 days	69	41.6
10 days	11	6.6
14 days	65	39.1
16 days	1	0.6
28 days	2	1.2
1 month	11	6.6
Total	166	99.9

Source: CLRO 204B Guildhall Justice Room Minute Books of Proceedings, 1752–96

150. CLRO SC1/8 Commitments for trial at the sessions, Jul. 1814–Oct. 1842, sessions dated 4 Oct. 1815 and 1 Jan. 1816(single offence), 3 Jun. 1816, 4 Oct. 1816, 4 Oct. 1817, 3 Jun. 1818, 4 Oct. 1818, 3 Jul. 1819, 1 Jan. 1820, 3 Jun. 1820, 4 Oct. 1820, 1 Jan. 1821, 4 Oct. 1821.
151. Prisoners receiving sentences of more than seven days were put to work – generally picking oakum, although the Bridewell replaced this with working at

Such relatively brief sentences were subjected to criticism on two grounds. The deterrent value of one or two weeks' imprisonment was doubted by the magistrate William Fielding. Fielding questioned whether 'the length of the imprisonment being trifling . . . would contribute to any alteration of their [i.e. the prostitutes'] inclination',[152] although he weakened his case somewhat by stating his opinion that people were in general the worse for being incarcerated and that 'with respect to the prostitutes, there are such innumerable instances of such extreme misery, that I could almost cut my hand off before I could commit such a poor wretch to additional misery'.[153] The Reverend Henry Budd, the chaplain of Bridewell Hospital from 1800, on the other hand, considered sentences of one or two weeks – or even a month – too short to allow him to guide the women to a morally acceptable way of life.[154] Recidivism was rife, Budd claimed, citing one woman who had been committed thirty-nine times during his tenure of the chaplaincy.[155] When pressed on the point by the members of the Select Committee on Mendicity and Vagrancy in the Metropolis, however, he decided that the conditions prevailing in Bridewell had a tendency to improve rather than to harm the morals of its prostitute inmates. This he attributed to the use of solitary confinement and separating the younger from the older women, meaning that 'if the rules are adhered to, they have but few opportunities of communicating with each other'.[156]

None of the women held in the Southwark compter who appeared either at the Guildhall Justice Room or the Surrey quarter sessions was sentenced to be publicly whipped. Evidence from the records of the petty sessions held in the Westminster parish of St. Clement Danes in the 1750s indicates, nevertheless, that in the middle of the century this remained a common punishment for prostitutes. Of seventy recorded cases between 1752 and 1756, involving women charged as common streetwalkers, common prostitutes, loose, idle and disorderly, and similar descriptions, thirty-one

---

spinning machines toward the end of 1817: *P.P.* (1818), Vol.VIII, Committee of the prisons, 1st report, p.135.

152. *P.P.* (1817), Vol.VII, Police Committee, 2nd report, p.405.

153. Ibid., p.405.

154. *P.P.* (1814–15), Vol.III, Minutes of the evidence taken before the Select Committee to Enquire into the State of Mendicity and Vagrancy in the Metropolis and its Neighbourhood, pp.64–5.

155. *P.P.* (1814–15), Vol.III, Select Committee to Enquire into Mendicity and Vagrancy, p.62.

156. Ibid., pp.65 and 68.

resulted in the woman being sentenced to a public whipping before being discharged or passed to her parish of settlement.[157] John Beattie has noted the decline in use of this form of punishment for other offences during the second half of the eighteenth century, particularly where the offender was female.[158] Its complete absence from the Guildhall Justice Room's armoury suggests that prostitutes benefited from this change sooner than most.

A small number (nineteen, or 6.9 per cent of the 274 given custodial sentences by the Guildhall Justice Room) were, however, sentenced to receive 'the correction of the House' – that is, to be privately whipped by the keeper of the Bridewell or, under supervision, his deputy. Richard Weaver, keeper from 1806, told the 1818 Prisons Committee that this was done on the woman's back with a cat o' nine tails. The exact number of lashes and the severity with which they were administered were decided by Weaver on the basis of the prisoner's behaviour and physical condition but in any case never exceeded thirty strokes. Such punishment was in decline for both sexes by the time whipping of female prisoners was abolished in 1818 – Weaver himself estimating that no more than fifteen or sixteen prisoners of either sex (out of roughly 2,000) had been whipped in 1817.[159]

Conclusion

The policing of streetwalking prostitutes in eighteenth- and early-nineteenth-century London was extremely complex. Although statute law was by no means clear, the Watch Acts and local regulations were unambiguous in their requirement that plying for trade by prostitutes was not to be tolerated on the streets of the metropolis. Nevertheless, the relationship between streetwalkers and the various officers of the policing agencies, especially the watchmen, was characterised throughout this period by compromise and the attempted accommodation of each party's needs within a relatively stable yet exceptionally flexible framework. While the fundamental ability of the watch to enforce its dominance was usually – though, importantly, not always – recognised by both sides, prostitutes and law officers were able through their individual and collective actions greatly to influence events.

157. WCA B1066–B1070 St. Clement Danes petty sessions plus vestry, 1740–67.
158. J.M. Beattie, *Crime and the Courts in England 1660–1800* (1986), pp.612–14.
159. *P.P.* (1818), Vol.VIII, Committee of the Prisons, 1st report, p.163.

This flexibility continued to some extent even after an arrest had been made. Once in the watch house, however, power was tilted decisively in favour of the police – in this case, as represented by the constable of the night. While the law remained vague – or overlooked – enough to allow the constable to exercise considerable discretion in deciding whether or not a charge would be pressed, the ability of the woman to influence the outcome was greatly lessened. With her appearance before a justice of the peace, that ability almost entirely disappeared. Here, the capacity to decide on the course of events rested almost entirely with the magistrate. Equally significant, however, is the fact that so little formal limitation was placed on the decisions at which the magistrate could arrive. The individual circumstances of each case counted for much and there were many different routes by which a prostitute could leave such a tribunal. It is only with an appearance at the sessions (to which few women prostitutes were removed) that the evidence points to a more inflexible approach on the part of the judiciary. With this was lost the possibility of numerous different outcomes to any case.

Flexibility, compromise, and absence of system were almost defining characteristics of the policing of street prostitution in this period. The process of policing itself constituted a relationship between police and policed, the nature of which was determined by the needs and activities of both sides. This was equally true of the attempts by the authorities to suppress or, at least, to control, the houses of resort, the bawdy and disorderly houses around which much of the trade revolved.

CHAPTER SIX

Policing Disorderly Houses

Disorderly and bawdy houses were represented, like streetwalking, as threats to the cohesion and well-being of society. They had become, declared Henry Fielding in 1749, 'in a Manner the Seminaries of Education', were the cause of endless mischief, and tended directly to 'the overthrow of Men's Bodies, to the wasting of their Livelihoods, and to the indangering of their Souls'.[1] Petitioning City residents in the early nineteenth century saw in the continued existence of brothels the subversion of every moral and religious principle and the general corruption of society. Less grandiloquently, they were also concerned at the habits of viciousness such houses might foster in their servants and apprentices – habits they felt sure could only be funded through fraud and robbery.[2]

As already noted, the great majority of such houses did not conform to the popular view of the traditional brothel as a building wholly given over to prostitution, tightly controlled by a bawd or brothel keeper, with resident prostitutes whom male clients visited. Some such houses did exist, particularly at the more expensive end of the trade, but most prostitutes, rather than have clients brought to them, solicited for custom in the streets, parks and drinking places of London before retiring with their 'culls' to private rooms in public houses or hotels or to one of the many cheap lodging houses with which the capital abounded.

Commentators used a variety of terms fairly indiscriminately when referring to such houses. Patrick Colquhoun, for instance, classed those who owned 'houses of ill fame, brothels, lodging houses for prostitutes' in a single category in his 1796 *Treatise on the Police of the*

1. H. Fielding, *A Charge Delivered to the Grand Jury* (1749), p.49.
2. CLRO Petition Rolls nos.7 & 9.

Metropolis.[3] Others wrote, most broadly, of houses for the reception of prostitutes or of disorderly houses. For the purposes of supervision and suppression, the chief distinction lay between those which were liable, for one reason or another, to come under the jurisdiction of the licensing authorities and those which were not.

Use of the licensing laws

The members of the 1816 and 1817 Select Committees on the Police showed much concern at the spread of cheaper licensed houses which, the committee alleged, catered mainly if not wholly for thieves and prostitutes. In fact, many (though not all) police and judicial witnesses to the committees denied that such establishments – known as 'Flash Houses' – persisted in any great numbers in the capital. Sir Nathaniel Conant, the chief magistrate at Bow Street police office, protested that he would immediately take steps to suppress any house harbouring criminals and prostitutes should it be proven to him that such existed within his district – though under repeated questioning he stopped short of claiming that all the public houses in the neighbourhood of Bow Street were uniformly respectable.[4] Conant's clerk John Stafford, less concerned perhaps with the niceties of the argument, contented himself with a firm denial that any flash houses operated around the Covent Garden area.[5] The Middlesex magistrate J.T.B. Beaumont, on the other hand, believed that his own Tower Hamlets police division was home to many such houses, as did other officers when speaking of their districts.[6]

Beaumont told the committee that repeated complaints had been made against the most notorious of the houses in his division with the intention of having them deprived of their licences to retail alcoholic drinks. Any house selling such drinks required a licence if it was to remain within the law. The licensees of those establishments – whether alehouses, public houses or gin shops – that had significant numbers of prostitutes amongst their customers were thus vulnerable to a threatened loss of livelihood at the capital's regular licensing sessions.

Within London, responsibility for issuing and revoking licences was divided among a number of different authorities, largely

3. P. Colquhoun, *A Treatise on the Police of the Metropolis* (1796).
4. *P.P.* (1816), Vol.V, Police Committee, p.19.   5. Ibid., p.38.
6. Ibid., pp.71, 147.

depending upon the type of licence required. Primary responsibility rested with the local justices of the peace who, since the late seventeenth century, had established the custom of granting licences only at special sessions (the so-called brewster sessions) – a practice encouraged by Parliament from 1729.[7] Before 1792, it was possible to circumvent this procedure at least partially by the simple purchase of a wine licence from the Stamp Office – a practice widely condemned as allowing disorderly houses and brothels to remain open in defiance of the magistrates.[8] After 1792, however, the loophole was closed, establishments desiring a wine licence having first to obtain a certificate of licence from the local justices.[9] Similarly, the Gin Act of 1743, confirmed and strengthened in 1751, forbade any but tavern, victualling house, inn, coffee house or alehouse keepers to hold a licence to sell spirituous liquors – that is to say that in practice a beer licence had first to be obtained from the magistrates before a spirit licence would be granted by the Excise.[10]

The process of applying for the issue or renewal of a victualler's licence brought other agencies and individuals into play.[11] At licensing time, the usual course was for the constable of each ward or parish to present to the magistrates in session a list of those houses requiring a renewal of their licences. Each constable was then placed on oath and questioned as to the conduct of the houses in his district, if the neighbours had made any complaints, and the results of his investigations into them. Whether the constable spoke well of a house or not, the question was thrown open and any other person present was able to state their objections to the relicensing of the establishment.

This was in theory (and occasionally in practice) the moment for any aggrieved neighbour to come forward, though the majority of such objections were raised by the representatives of the parish or ward authorities. Most bodies responsible for the watch of a district possessed regulations requiring the officers of the watch habitually to check the conduct of the neighbourhood's licensed houses, with

7. P. Clark, *The English Alehouse: a Social History 1200–1830* (1983), pp.52, 179.
8. M.D. George, *London Life in the Eighteenth Century* (1925), pp.296, 392; J. Fielding, *Extracts from such of the Penal Laws, as particularly relate to the Peace and Good Order of this Metropolis, with Observations for the Better Execution of some and on the Defects of others* (1768), p.66.
9. Ibid., p.296; *P.P.* (1816), Vol.V, Police Committee, p.24.
10. *P.P.* (1817), Vol.VII, Police Committee, 1st report, p.29.
11. The following description of the process of renewing a licence owes much to the accounts given by witnesses to the 1817 Select Committee on the Police of the Metropolis, *P.P.* (1817), Vol.VII, Police Committee, 1st report, pp.37, 48, 131–48.

any complaints being recorded so that appropriate action could be taken to attempt to stop the offending house's licence at the next sessions. If no objection was made at the sessions, then the licence would be renewed. If an objection was lodged, however, and some evidence of impropriety or 'disorderly' behaviour shown, the licence of the house in question would be temporarily suspended while the magistrates investigated the matter before gathering again on a later date to give their decision. Providing that the magistrates were satisfied that the complaints were unfounded, or that the house had sufficiently reformed, then a new licence would be issued (although the magistrates might subsequently order a closer surveillance of a house about which they remained suspicious). Failure to satisfy the magistrates would result in the removal of the licensee's right to trade. (New houses applying for a licence for the first time could not, of course, be investigated in this way; rather the aspiring licensee was required to produce a certificate as to his or her good character signed by three local worthies.)[12]

Although the keepers of some houses undoubtedly did lose their licences in the manner described above, in practice there were many ways in which the process could be undermined or altogether circumvented. Chief among these was the marked reluctance of many magistrates to act at all against suspected houses. J.T. Barber, a magistrate in Tower Hamlets, partly explained his own inactivity by stating that he was of course unwilling to do something so serious as remove a man's licence where he could not have the benefit of a fair trial. He also cast doubt on the integrity of his fellow magistrates by saying that, in any case, for him to have resisted, at a recent licensing session, the relicensing of two particular houses which he knew to harbour prostitutes would have been 'a waste of breath'[13] Beaumont, the Middlesex magistrate, claimed that complaints were frequently not even investigated but were rejected out of hand.[14] Whether the magistrates' refusal to force the closure of a house arose from principle (it was not uncommon for them to voice the opinion that 'there must be prostitutes, and are they not better in the back rooms of houses than in the public streets . . . these poor creatures must be somewhere')[15] or because they were as corrupt and as easily bought as was often alleged, the fact that the final decision rested with them meant that unless the bench could be

12. *P.P.* (1816), Vol.V, Police Committee, p.19.
13. *P.P.* (1817), Vol.VII, Police Committee, 1st report, p.38.
14. *P.P.* (1816), Vol.V, Police Committee, p.71.
15. *P.P.* (1817), Vol.VII, Police Committee, 1st report, p.140.

brought to agree with the substance of the complaints, parish and ward authorities were almost powerless to force the removal of a licence.

Undoubtedly, the most effective way to persuade a justice that he had little choice but to deny a licence application was to present him with irrefutable evidence of disorderliness and wrongdoing associated with a house over a prolonged period. It was for this reason among others that the various policing authorities in the capital had laid down regulations requiring their officers to watch over the behaviour of all licensed houses within their jurisdiction. Ensuring that such regulations were adhered to, however, was not an easy task. While the parish of St. Anne, Soho, enjoyed some success by rewarding its watchmen with 2s 6d each time they reported a house as disorderly, a report on the conduct of the City's marshalmen in 1816 found that they completely neglected their duty to inspect licensed houses and enforce 'good order and regularity' upon them.[16] Indeed, the Bow Street police were habitually accused of tolerating the existence of licensed houses harbouring prostitutes and thieves on the grounds that they were a fruitful source of criminal information.[17]

Where sufficient evidence was gathered to persuade the magistrates temporarily to suspend a licence and to investigate the house themselves (such investigation usually taking the form of a much advertised judicial visit to the offending establishment), complainants claimed they were often frustrated by the fraudulent replacement of the original licensee by another which rendered their objections, which had to be made against a named individual rather than against the house itself, null and void.[18] The larger brewers, with their networks of tied houses, were held to be particularly guilty of this practice. However, the historian of the English alehouse suggests that such complaints were mistaken and that in fact the brewers were anxious not to see their tenants' licences threatened and thus 'were keen to send packing licensees whose conduct jeopardised the licensing of their houses'.[19]

---

16. WCA A2053, 2 Apr., 2 Jul., 5 Nov., 3 Dec. 1812; CLRO Misc.Mss 283.4 Committee papers 1814–25: committee appointed 16 Dec. 1813 to consider petition of householders, Orders and regulations for conduct of the marshalmen of the City of London; CLRO Misc.Mss 245.5 Special committee in relation to the police and nightly watch, Printed minutes of the Common Council, 17 Oct. 1816, containing the Lord Mayor's observations on police and nightly watch, p.140.
17. *P.P.* (1816), Vol.V, Police Committee, p.19. 18. Ibid., p.19.
19. See, e.g., Ibid., p.71; Clark, *The English Alehouse*, p.264.

Occasionally, a hard-pressed parish would find itself facing almost all these problems simultaneously. In 1813, various complaints were made by residents of the parish of St. Paul, Shadwell, to the magistrates at the Shadwell Police Office and to the trustees for regulating the parish's nightly watch about the conduct of a number of public houses in the parish. It was claimed that these houses had for a long time past been 'the constant resort of the most abandoned and profligate women' and the cause of a great increase in the number of houses of ill fame in the neighbourhood.[20]

At a loss as to the most effectual measures to pursue in their efforts to force the closure of such houses, the watch trustees themselves patrolled the parish's streets, checking on the demeanour of the houses and summoning the licensees before them to be warned of the consequences of allowing their establishments to be frequented by prostitutes and their clients. Faced with the refusal of the licensees to reform their houses, and sure by now that they had sufficient evidence of wrongdoing, the parochial committee resolved to present to the bench of magistrates at the next licensing session a memorial calling for the removal of the publicans' licences. The threatened licensees, however, responded by covering the walls of the parish with copies of 'a profane and libellous placard, reflecting on the character and conduct of Mr Fletcher' (a churchwarden and the most zealous opponent of the houses' continuation).[21] The parish officers, together with the publicans, attended the ensuing licensing day. Their memorial was greeted, the officers claimed, with 'taunting . . . sneering . . . [and] . . . a variety of sarcastic observations' on the part of some of the magistrates present.[22] On the intervention of others among the bench, however, the licences of three of the 'most notorious' houses were taken away (having previously been suspended at an earlier session). The parish officers claimed to have subsequently come under immense pressure from the brewers Meux & Co., the owners of one of the houses, to raise no objection to their placing a new tenant in a nearby house they had recently purchased to take the place of the one now closed. Resisting such pressure, the officers were horrified when the magistrates licensed the man in the new house, the King's Arms, and 'within a month all the evil practices of the Duke of York [the closed house] were revived'.[23] Other landlords in the area were thus encouraged, claimed the officers, to attract a similar clientele.

20. *P.P.* (1817), Vol.VII, Police Committee, 1st report, p.130.
21. Ibid., pp.131–2.   22. Ibid., p.132.   23. Ibid., p.135.

The parish refused to accept defeat. The presentation of another memorial at the 1814 licensing day again brought the suspension of a number of houses' licences (including that of the King's Arms) so that the magistrates could investigate the complaints. The bench duly visited the parish where, it was alleged, they refused to enter any of the houses, were abusive to the assembled parish officers, and declared their determination to restore the suspended licences – all in the riotous presence of 'all the persons passing the street [and] very many of the prostitutes and others concerned in the bad houses'.[24] The magistrates were as good as their word. All the houses which had been suspended were relicensed at the subsequent appeal session – which was, by the parish officers' accounts, even rowdier than the first. An immediate attempt by the parish to file a criminal suit at the King's Bench against some of the magistrates (whose behaviour the parish ascribed to 'the secret influence of the brewers and distillers')[25] was advised against by the Attorney General who informed them that although the magistrates had certainly, in his view, acted unwisely, there was no proof that they had done so from 'any corrupt or improper motive'.[26]

In such circumstances, and in the much more numerous cases where the establishment under suspicion – whether a coffee-house, cheap hotel or lodging house – sold no drink and hence escaped the jurisdiction of the licensing laws, a parish or ward's only legal remedy was to gather sufficient evidence to justify proceeding against the proprietors by indictment for keeping bawdy or disorderly houses.

Legislation governing bawdy and disorderly houses

The laws governing such houses were relatively precise. Keeping a brothel or bawdy house was a nuisance under the common law. In 1749, Henry Fielding delivered a charge to the Westminster Grand Jury.[27] Basing his remarks on Burn's *Justice of the Peace*, Fielding carefully laid out the legal position for the jurymen. After confirming that the offence was indeed punishable by the common law, he pointed out that 'notwithstanding the Favour which the Law in many Cases extends to married Women, yet in this Case the Wife is

24. Ibid., p.139.   25. Ibid., p.144.   26. Ibid., p.145.
27. Fielding, *Charge Delivered to the Grand Jury*, pp.46–9.

equally indictable, and may be found guilty with her Husband'. Citing precedent, he went on to state that 'nor is it necessary that the Person be Master or Mistress of the whole House; for if he or she have only a single Room, and will therewith accommodate Lewd people to perpetrate Acts of Uncleanness, they may be indicted for keeping a Bawdy-House'. According to Burn's manual this emphasis on the role of married women arose both from the belief that brothel keeping was 'such an offence as may generally be presumed to be managed by the intrigue of her sex' and from the more formal legal notion that it was 'an offence as to the government of the house in which the wife has a principal share'.[28] Fielding concluded his remarks by reminding the assembled jurymen of their obligation to present to the court any whom they knew to be committing such a crime.

The necessity for such a reminder was underlined by the introduction of the Disorderly Houses Act in 1752.[29] This act, applying only to London and its environs, aimed to encourage the prosecution of disorderly and bawdy houses by providing for the payment of a reward of £20 upon conviction of the keeper. The money was to be found by the local overseers of the poor and divided equally between the two informants required by the law for the bringing of a charge. Constables who failed to press such charges were to be fined £20, which sum would again go to the informants.

The Disorderly Houses Act implied that interested private individuals were principally responsible for reporting the existence of a disorderly house to the local authorities (whom they could then have bound over to prosecute) and, indeed, were competent to initiate and conduct a prosecution themselves. In practice, however, the majority of the policing agencies in the capital possessed their own regulations governing the overlooking, reporting and indicting of such houses. Those concerning the checking of unlicensed houses likely to harbour prostitutes were by and large the same as, or similar to, the regulations requiring the watch to report on the conduct of licensed houses as at this level little distinction was made between the two. The justices of the peace acting in the parish of St. James, Westminster, placed notices in the press stating their willingness to receive verbal or written information 'as well against Licensed Victuallers, as any other inhabitants, who

28. Burn, *The Justice of the Peace and Parish Officer*, 2nd edition, Vol.1, p.132.
29. An Act for the Better Preventing Thefts and Robberies, and for Regulating Places of Public Entertainment, and Punishing Persons Keeping Disorderly Houses (25 Geo.II, c.36).

shall . . . keep any house of ill fame' in addition to a range of other public order offences.[30] Outside the City, whether a house was reported by a parish or ward's own constables or watchmen, by the officers employed by the police offices set up in the last quarter of the eighteenth century (though this may have been unlikely – a Queen's Square office patrolman told the 1816 Select Committee on the Police that he did not consider it part of his duties to do so),[31] or by indignant ratepayers, once a disorderly or bawdy house had been brought to the attention of the parish authorities they were bound to move against it by indictment.

Within the City of London boundaries, the process was slightly different. The City was divided into twenty-six wards which were responsible for the preservation of the peace, supervision of trading, sanitation and local upkeep. Ward meetings were called wardmotes. Chief responsibility for finding out and acting against brothels was devolved onto the twenty-six wardmote inquest juries, which operated as standing sub-committees. They could take action in a number of ways. Occasionally, officers of the City or ward watch forces would report the existence of a disorderly or bawdy house directly to the inquest, as happened in the case of Thomas Keen in 1752, who was reported to the Bishopsgate ward inquest by two of the ward's constables for keeping a house of ill fame in St. Botolph's parish.[32] The jury could also discover such houses in the course of their annual perambulations about the ward. Most commonly, the neighbours of a house would inform the inquest jury of its existence, sometimes accompanying their complaint with a formal petition for action to be taken. In 1786, for example, twenty neighbours of Mary Jackson, John Payne, Ann Warn and Betty King signed a petition to the Coleman Street ward inquest complaining that all four kept houses in Little Swan Alley and Langthorne Court wherein lodged 'bad and disorderly women' whose conduct was such that 'no Gentleman can pass the said Houses even in open Daylight without every method being used to decoy them in or insult them'.[33]

Upon receiving a report, the inquest jury would generally direct the constables of the ward to investigate the house, to ensure that the complaint had foundation and to find the necessary witnesses

---

30. *The Times*, 8 Nov. 1788.   31. *P.P.* (1816), Vol.V, Police Committee, p.148.
    32. CLRO 242–246 A–E, Ward presentments, 1668–date, presentment of Bishops-gate ward, 1752.
    33. Ibid., Presentment of Coleman Street ward, 1786.

to acts of bawdry or disorder. These witnesses could either be members of the watch force, such as the City marshal, two constables and four watchmen who stood witness against three houses in the St Dunstan's precinct of Farringdon Without in 1817,[34] or the residents who made the initial complaint, as in the case of the widow Elizabeth Grout of Philip Lane in the ward of Cripplegate Within, whose neighbours Mrs Wright, John Elliot and Thomas Grove (the last two a jeweller and a glass grinder) offered themselves in 1770 as witnesses to her having kept a disorderly house for upwards of two months.[35]

Once the inquest jury was convinced of the justice of an allegation (and had gone some way toward gathering the necessary evidence) it would include the name of the keeper and the location of the house in its annual Plough Monday list of presentments to the City's Court of Aldermen. This was combined with a request that the person be proceeded against and, often, the names of witnesses and two or more individuals (generally members of the inquest) who agreed to be bound over to prosecute. The Court would in its turn refer the matter back to the Alderman representing the ward in question for confirmation. Should he raise no objection, and be satisfied that the house had been operating for at least the previous six months, he would then order the City solicitor to prepare a prosecution, to be paid for by the City. On completing the collection of evidence, the solicitor would go on to lay an indictment before the Grand Jury at the next sessions (generally for two counts, the first for keeping a bawdy house; the second – in recognition of the difficulty of gaining a conviction under the first – for the less severe offence of keeping a disorderly house). Should the Grand Jury be convinced there was a case to answer they would declare 'a true bill'. At this point a warrant would be issued for the arrest of the parties named in the indictment, who would be brought to trial at the subsequent sessions. By the third quarter of the eighteenth century, exhibiting convicted bawdy house keepers in the pillory was falling into disuse (though it was not entirely unknown) and those found, or pleading, guilty were liable to a relatively small fine, usually accompanied by a term of imprisonment.[36]

Those outlining this procedure for the benefit of the 1817 Select Committee on the Police of the Metropolis were adamant that it was filled with difficulties for the prosecuting authorities and

---

34. Ibid., Presentment of St. Dunstan, Farringdon Without ward, 1817.
35. Ibid., Presentment of Cripplegate Within ward, 1770.
36. J.M. Beattie, *Crime and the Courts in England 1660–1800* (1986), pp.614–6.

frequently allowed the guilty parties to escape retribution altogether. Nevertheless, it is not hard to find examples of the law being used successfully – particularly where prosecutions occurred as part of a concerted campaign against houses catering to prostitutes in a localised area.

A petition against prostitution signed by upwards of 2,000 City householders in 1813 provoked the Common Council of the City into establishing a committee (which remained in existence until 1825) whose task it was to investigate the extent of the problem and suggest solutions. Having satisfied itself that the presence of large numbers of houses of ill fame in the City could no longer be tolerated, and having taken legal advice as to the sufficiency of the laws governing the same, the committee began by urging the Common Councils of the twenty-six wards to set up their own committees with the aim of assisting the inquest juries to discover and remove such houses from their immediate jurisdictions.[37] Many wards complied by simply designating their inquest jury as the committee,[38] but others took the matter more seriously and founded new committees. That of Bishopsgate ward was especially active. It consisted of the ward deputies and Common Councilmen together with fourteen other respectable inhabitants of the ward. Its tasks were defined as discovering the number of houses of ill fame in the ward and forwarding that information to the ward inquest so that legal measures could be taken to remove them; inquiring 'as to the persons of the Character alluded to in the said petition frequenting the public streets of this Ward'; and ensuring that the constables, patrols and watchmen of the ward were fulfilling their duties in respect of keeping the streets clear of prostitutes.[39] In their first report to the Bishopsgate wardmote, in December 1815, the committee disclosed that they had gained evidence of several houses of ill fame within the ward and had laid the same before the inquest jury, asking the jury to present the owners or occupiers to the Court of Aldermen for prosecution. As a result nine bills of indictment were preferred, of which seven were found to be true bills. Three individuals were brought to trial, convicted and

37. GL Common Council reports 1816–21 no.1, *Report of the Committee appointed to consider the Petition of Sundry Inhabitant Householders of the Principal Streets of this City, relative to Common Prostitutes infesting the same* (1816).

38. See, for example, GMR Ms.60 Cheap ward wardmote court and inquest minutes, 1701–1829, meeting 21 Dec. 1814; GMR Ms.3039 Farringdon Within ward wardmote court minutes, 1806–63, meeting 21 Dec. 1814.

39. GMR Ms. 1428/1 Bishopsgate wardmote court minute book, 1737–1839, meeting 23 Dec. 1814.

imprisoned. Three others pleaded guilty and were discharged on their own recognisances, having quit the ward; while two were tried under a single indictment and acquitted due to insufficient evidence.

In all, the committee reported with enthusiasm, nine houses of ill fame had been suppressed, leading to a great diminution in the number of prostitutes frequenting the public streets of the ward.[40] Thereafter, the committee's energies seem to have been directed at preventing the appearance of any other bawdy houses in the ward – an aim in which they claimed to have been successful in their second report to the wardmote, made in December 1818, although they had to admit that they had failed in their further efforts to close the house whose keepers had been found not guilty three years before.[41]

Taken together, the City launched prosecutions against thirty-five houses between 1814 and 1817. Of these, twelve or thirteen were tried and either pleaded guilty or were convicted – most for the lesser offence of keeping a disorderly house. Those admitting guilt and abating the nuisance were subject to a small fine before being discharged upon recognisances of future good behaviour.[42]

By the early nineteenth century, this kind of co-ordinated campaign was seen as the best method of enforcing the laws against houses of ill fame. The parish of St. Sepulchre in the ward of Farringdon Without, active in the campaign of 1814–16, founded a special vestry committee in 1825 to move against the brothels and disorderly houses which had lately re-established themselves in the parish. The ward beadle compiled a list of houses of ill fame and within little over a year the committee claimed to have done away with all sixteen houses on the list.[43] Nor were such committees limited to the City. The residents of St. Martin le Grand, a liberty within the City of Westminster (later being brought within the City of London as part of Aldersgate ward under the Post Office Act), elected eight 'commissioners for the pavement' from amongst their number, with the job of proceeding against acknowledged disorderly houses within the liberty. Four houses were indicted of which the keepers of three quit the parish, one only being convicted and sentenced to three months' imprisonment and a spell in the

40. Ibid., meeting 21 Dec. 1815.   41. Ibid., meeting 23 Dec. 1818.
42. *P.P.* (1817), Vol.VII, Police Committee, 2nd report, p.454.
43. GMR Ms. 3189, Parish of St. Sepulchre, Farringdon Without, vestry committee appointed to enquire into the most efficient means of removing brothels, disorderly houses, which exist in this parish: Minutes, 28 Jun. 1825–20 Oct. 1826.

pillory; the latter was set aside on the woman successfully pleading her belly (that is, proving she was pregnant).[44]

Individual prosecutions, not undertaken as part of a general campaign, could still be effective. The St. Sepulchre committee learned with interest of an individual named Williams who had successfully prosecuted several houses of ill fame in his own parish, gaining sufficient evidence to get convictions for keeping bawdy houses by 'giving a Person a few shillings to go to a house suspected, in the company of a Girl of the Town, & paying for the use of a room – & satisfying himself for what purpose the house was used'.[45]

Such a success rate was, however, unusual – particularly for the serious charge of keeping a bawdy house. Of the twenty-one persons so charged in Southwark between 1817 and 1821 (in itself a very low figure given the area's reputation as a centre of prostitution) just four were found guilty, receiving sentences of between fourteen days' and three months' imprisonment. Three were tried and acquitted (including the only two also facing the lesser charge of keeping a disorderly house). These results cast doubt on the claim of William Newman, the City solicitor, that he would expect to win convictions on such a charge in five cases out of six.[46] In one instance the prosecution was dropped as the case came to court, two others were discharged by proclamation, while eleven of the twenty-one defendants chose to forfeit their bail by failing to appear to answer the charges.[47]

Quitting the parish and, if only temporarily, closing down a brothel was one way of avoiding the full force of the law. Those responsible for enforcing the legal procedures were vociferous in their complaints both at the law's inadequacy and at the skill with which this was exploited by the capital's brothel keepers. These complaints illustrate yet another aspect of the shifting problems of law enforcement.

Many of the problems associated with the suppression of bawdy houses were of long standing. The framers of the Disorderly Houses Act of 1752 had referred to 'the many subtle and crafty contrivances . . . by which means many notorious offenders have escaped punishment', and the act itself had been introduced with the specific intention of closing some of the more glaring avenues of escape

44. *P.P.* (1816), Vol.V, Police Committee, pp.252–4.
45. GMR Ms. 3189, meeting 18 Sep. 1826.
46. *P.P.* (1817), Vol.VII, Police Committee, 2nd report, p.453.
47. CLRO SC1/8 Commitments for trial at the sessions, Jul. 1814–Oct. 1842.

offered under the common law offence of bawdry. Despite the act's apparent success, however, there is much evidence that the authorities continued to be frustrated in their attempts to diminish, if not entirely eradicate, London's stock of houses of ill fame.

One of a number of petitions presented to the Lord Mayor and Aldermen of the City in the early nineteenth century listed what the petitioners believed to be the central problems with the law as it then stood.[48] They complained of the difficulty of obtaining sufficient evidence to win a conviction; of the ease with which convicted bawdy house keepers were able to transfer possession of the house to 'others of the same description whereby the nuisance is not abated'; and of the difficulty in producing legal evidence as to the real owner of such houses – this despite a clause in the 1752 Act deeming the legal keeper of the house to be anyone who appeared to act as such. Most vigorously, they complained of the great expense involved in laying a prosecution before the courts. Instances of all these problems – and others – can be found in the surviving ward and parish records.

Difficulties in implementing legislation

The regulations which were laid down to ensure the maintenance of at least a minimum of supervision over both licensed and unlicensed premises were easier to enact than to enforce. There is little reason to suppose that the richly ambiguous relationship between watchmen and streetwalkers ceased to operate at the bawdy house door; especially when the rigorous execution of the rules might lead to the officer being burdened with the expense of a prosecution – an outlay which he could not be absolutely certain the parish would defray.[49] Neighbours were often equally reluctant to come forward and initiate a complaint, principally, thought the constable of St. Giles and St. George, 'for fear of the trouble and loss of time'.[50]

Once a house was identified as being suspected of harbouring prostitutes, gathering sufficient evidence to commence a prosecution

48. CLRO Petition Roll No.8, Petition of the inhabitants of the ward of Bishopsgate relating to disorderly houses and the need for legislation. For similar petitions see CLRO Petition Rolls 6, 7, 9 and 24.

49. WCA F2028 Vestry and watch committee minutes, 3 May 1736–6 Aug. 1754, vestry meeting 18 Apr. 1738; *P.P.* (1818), Vol.VIII, Police Committee, 3rd report, pp.136–7.

50. *P.P.* (1817), Vol.VII, Police Committee, 2nd report, p.360.

posed further difficulties for the authorities. The conviction of an individual for keeping a bawdy house required eyewitness testimony that repeated acts of bawdry had taken place within the establishment during the period referred to in the indictment.[51] It has already been seen that one determined prosecutor procured such testimony by paying another to visit suspected houses in the company of prostitutes and 'satisfying himself for what purpose the house was used'. This was no guarantee of success, however, and it is not difficult to see how such a paid informant might fall into that category of witnesses considered by the magistrate William Fielding to be 'of such a description, as to hazard the verdict' in trials of alleged brothel keepers.[52]

Less exacting standards of proof were required to press a charge of keeping a disorderly house, but even here the difficulties were considerable and there was little agreement as to what exactly constituted the offence – especially as the parish authorities were usually looking for evidence of bawdry as well as disorderly behaviour and at this early stage made little distinction between the two. Harmer, the solicitor employed as legal advisor to the St. Sepulchre vestry committee in 1825, told the committee members that in his opinion the fact that a cry of 'Murder!' had been heard from a house in Turnagain Lane was, when coupled with other circumstances, sufficient to prove it a disorderly house.[53]

What those other circumstances might be is indicated by the testimony of James Webb, a patrol officer of Walbrook ward, who was questioned by the ward inquest in 1828 about a supposed house of ill fame in Ball Alley. Webb said that 'he knew it to be a house of that description by seeing Common Street Walkers go in on several occasions'. He cited particular instances of women whom he knew to be prostitutes entering and leaving the house before concluding that 'from the time he first observed the House it has been frequented in the same manner by loose Women nightly with the exception of two or three nights and that Persons are constantly going in and out until One O Clock in the Morning'. He was supported by the constable Thomas Dennet who three months previously had followed a man and a woman who 'he knew . . . by sight as a Woman of the Town' from nearby Charlotte Row to the house in question, witnessing them enter the house by a private door in

51. *P.P.* (1817), Vol.VII, Police Committee, 2nd report, p.457; *P.P.* (1822), Vol.IV, Police Committee, p.87.
52. *P.P.* (1816), Vol.V, Police Committee, p.128.
53. GMR Ms. 3189, meeting 11 Jul. 1825.

Ball Alley at which point the man had asked 'Is this the place?' to which the woman had replied in the affirmative.[54] Certainly, testimony of this sort could bring success. St. Martin le Grand had proceeded against the houses within its borders on the basis of eyewitness accounts of 'continually girls standing at the door enticing young people in, and at all times fighting and quarrelling, giving charge, and sometimes men taken out'.[55] Yet similar prosecutions often failed, too. Mary Barker was tried before the Recorder of the City of London for keeping a disorderly house in Cradle Court in St. Mary Axe in November 1808, evidence being given to show that 'men and women had been seen going in and out, apparently as if for meretricious purposes'. The jury had retired for an hour before sending its foreman back into court to ask whether such evidence was enough to prove the house disorderly. The recorder had replied that it was not and reminded the jury that they were to decide the case on the facts before them (rather than, presumably, what they knew of the house's local reputation). Fifteen minutes later the jury brought in a verdict of not guilty.[56]

Despite his advice to the jury, the recorder plainly considered Mary Barker to have been extremely fortunate to have escaped conviction, warning her in his post-verdict remarks 'to seek a reputable livelihood and not place herself again in such a situation'. Others were equally sure that they knew a brothel when they saw one, though unable to prove it so in law. William Newman, the City solicitor, spoke in 1817 of houses which 'though there is no particular sign upon them, yet, from the door being kept upon the jar, the particular manner in which they are fitted up, the manner in which they are painted, the blinds and curtains, it is very well known what sort of houses they are'.[57] Such establishments, he complained, though they drew into the surrounding area great numbers of streetwalkers, were almost impossible to come at via the law as in recent years they had tended to be kept 'in a very quiet state', rendering useless the formal indictment which spoke of 'disorderly men and women frequenting them . . . drinking, tippling, whoring, quarrelling and fighting'. William Vale of Farringdon Without ward agreed that the keepers of many houses of ill fame (which he considered

54. GMR Ms. 463/1 Walbrook ward inquest minute book, 1731–1834, meeting 5 Jan. 1828.

55. *P.P.* (1816), Vol.V, Police Committee, p.252.

56. GL SL71/061 Collection of newspaper cuttings relating to the City of London 1771–1830, 28 Nov. 1808.

57. *P.P.* (1817), Vol.VII, Police Committee, 2nd report, p.456.

to be as numerous as ever) had taken to managing their establishments in a more orderly manner, though he placed a more optimistic interpretation upon this development, feeling it to be due
– in his ward at least – to the fact that the authorities held 'a great
terror over them'.[58]
Terrified or not, the keeper of a bawdy or disorderly house was
not always readily identifiable, presenting the authorities with the
problem of not knowing which individual to prosecute. In 1815 the
City jointly indicted a Mr and Mrs Levi together with two of their
servants as keepers of a bawdy and disorderly house at 2 Cavendish
Court. The grand jury dismissed the charges against the servants,
finding a true bill against the Levis alone. On coming to trial the
couple contested neither the bawdy nor the disorderly house
charges. Rather, through their counsel, they challenged the City to
prove conclusively that they were the legal owners of the house.
Despite having demonstrated that the Levis' actual place of residence was not only adjacent but connected by a clearly visible and
much-used passage to the suspected house; that the same servants
were employed in both houses (and had never heard of the name
given by the Levis as that of the real owner of No.2); that Mr Levi
had threatened the foreman of the Bishopsgate inquest jury with a
law suit after the latter had entered the house; and that Levi had
entered into negotiations to sell the lease; the City's case against
the couple was dismissed – although they were (illogically in view of
the verdict) warned by the court to remove the nuisance.[59]
    Patrick Colquhoun told the 1816 Select Committee on the
Police that in his experience it was necessary to prove that the
occupier of a suspected house paid the tax on the house before
a charge could be successfully pressed home.[60] Whether this was
so in all cases, there can be little doubt but that the clause in the
1752 act stating that anyone who appeared to act the part of keeper
should be considered the keeper for the purpose of indictment
had only a limited impact and could on occasion even be used to
frustrate a prosecution. The parish of St. George, Southwark, took
advantage in 1816 of the fact that the law allowed a wife to be
convicted of keeping a bawdy or disorderly house, even if it were
shown that the husband had been present when the offence was
committed, by naming the former on an indictment, having first
questioned alienated former residents of the house and been

58. *P.P.* (1816), Vol.V, Police Committee, p.265.
59. *P.P.* (1817), Vol.VII, Police Committee, 2nd report, p.449.
60. *P.P.* (1816), Vol.V, Police Committee, p.49.

assured by them that the man took no part in the running of the place. The indictment was subsequently quashed by the court, with the comment that it should have been laid against the man, on the defendant's counsel showing that on one occasion the husband had urged the female inmates of the house to get out about their business.[61]

The Levis chose to contest the case against them. But many others preferred to attempt to defer any charges coming to court or evade the trial altogether. The fact that an arrest warrant was not issued until a grand jury had deliberated and found a true bill (possibly months after the commencement of an investigation into a house) gave ample time for the accused to quit the parish before proceedings could formally begin.[62] Those who were arrested and were able to afford bail frequently failed to appear for trial. Those who did appear had the power to transfer the hearing to the subsequent sessions.[63] Given that a house had to have been open for six months before it was possible for a ward inquest to present it to the Common Council, it was thus common, as Edward Forster complained to the 1817 Select Committee on the Police, for a bawdy or disorderly house to be in operation for a year or more before being brought to trial – even making the large assumption that the authorities acted against it at the earliest possible moment.[64]

The results of twenty-two cases prosecuted by the City in 1816 give some backing to the complaints of the authorities. In that year, just two defendants were tried and convicted of keeping disorderly houses, receiving sentences of two and six months in the City compter. Two had managed to delay their trial for the best part of a year before being acquitted; while two more, Thomas Stevens and his wife Janet, although under recognisances to appear, had still not been tried by the time the solicitor gave his report to the City committee on prostitution in December 1816. Six persons had pleaded guilty, five of whom were fined the nominal sum of one shilling each and discharged, the other entering into a bond for £200 not to repeat the offence. Nine had absconded (one, it was thought, as far as France) and had not been found; the remaining keeper had died before her case had come to court.[65]

61. *P.P.* (1817), Vol.VII, Police Committee, 2nd report, p.465.
62. Ibid., p.448.   63. Ibid., p.448.   64. Ibid., p.448.
65. CLRO Misc.Mss.S 283.4 Committee papers 1814–25 (Committee appointed 16 Dec. 1813 to consider petition of householders), Statement of the solicitor of the prosecutions of houses of ill fame during the present year, read before the committee 18 Dec. 1816.

In one way, of course, most of the above cases represented successes for the prosecuting authorities as – with the possible exception of the four defendants who had either been acquitted or had not yet come to trial – all those indicted, whether they had subsequently been convicted, had pleaded guilty and been discharged, or had fled, had been forced to close their houses. The committee members were unlikely to have been convinced, however, that matters rested there. In 1816, Farringdon Without ward presented Ann Hill of 5 Shoe Lane before the Common Council. The former occupant of the house had only recently been proceeded against by the City solicitor and the ward inquest jury was convinced that Hill had taken over not just the tenancy but also the trade of the house as 'her apparent Business of a Milliner therein is a mere cloak and . . . the said house is still a resort to and receptacle for lewd females and common prostitutes'.[66] The seeming ease with which the transfer of tenancies or even ownership of known bawdy and disorderly houses could be accomplished was a recurrent complaint of magistrates and local authorities.[67] Yet even where such a transfer – or, as the frustrated prosecutors preferred to believe, an apparent transfer – did not take place, houses frequently reopened under their original (convicted) keepers.

One reason why keepers felt able to take the risk of returning was the reluctance of parishes to suffer the financial consequences of further legal action. St. Martin le Grand had spent almost £300 in prosecuting the keepers of houses of ill fame within its jurisdiction only to see them all restored to their places 'although there was some process of law hanging over the heads that they were liable to be punished'.[68] The parishioners of the diminutive liberty balked at the likely expense of reopening the cases.[69] Indeed, the cost of undertaking a prosecution was held to be sufficient on its own, quite apart from the complications of the law and of evidential requirements, to discourage many parishes and wards from laying a first indictment, let alone a second, against any bawdy house within their boundaries.[70]

The £300 spent by St. Martin le Grand in initiating proceedings against ten houses (although only four came to trial and conviction)

66. CLRO 242–246 A–E, Ward presentments, 1668–date, Presentment of St. Dunstan, Farringdon Without ward, 1815.
67. *P.P.* (1816), Vol.V, Police Committee, pp.38, 266; *P.P.* (1817), Vol.VII, Police Committee, 2nd report, p.455.
68. *P.P.* (1816), Vol.V, Police Committee, p.252.   69. Ibid., p.253.
70. Ibid., p.49; *P.P.* (1817), Vol.VII, Police Committee, 1st report, p.162; *P.P.* (1817), Vol.VII, Police Committee, 2nd report, pp.369, 462.

was by no means an unusually large amount. The most expensive case brought by the City against a brothel keeper between 1814 and 1817, involving a much-protracted trial with many witnesses, cost £72, against an outlay of £15 for the cheapest. The average cost was reckoned at £35.[71] William Fielding agreed that a prosecution made by a parish could probably not be done for less than around £30, although he considered a privately undertaken proceeding, demanding the employment of an attorney and a counsel as well as the collection of witnesses, could be brought home for between £14 and £16.[72]

Creative accounting and manufactured delays by lawyers, police and watch officers, vestry clerks and others with a pecuniary interest in a case were frequently credited with further increasing the cost of prosecuting.[73] Within the City boundaries, the wards and parishes generally expected the Corporation to shoulder the financial burden of any proceedings, although they were occasionally disappointed and were obliged to fund the cost of a prosecution themselves.[74] This could prove particularly onerous for the less affluent wards, whose indebtedness and relatively large numbers of poor inhabitants often precluded any action being taken.[75]

The question of which body was legally responsible for meeting the expense of proceeding against brothels in the City came to a head in the early nineteenth century with a sustained rise in the number of presentments being made. The Court of Aldermen informed the wards in 1818 that the City Exchequer was not capable of sustaining all the prosecutions of houses of ill fame being thrown upon it by the various inquest juries and that the Court therefore expected the precincts or parishes within each ward to act at their own cost. St. Andrew, Holborn, replied that as a consequence it would no longer present such houses, neither having the necessary funds nor, to its knowledge, any legal power to raise them.[76]

The widely-held perception that the law was inadequate, time-consuming and – above all else – costly led to steady pressure for its reform. Concentrating licensed bawdy houses in specific areas of the capital was a recurrent suggestion, and although such proposals never won serious consideration by the legislature, the efforts of

71. *P.P.* (1817), Vol.VII, Police Committee, 2nd report, p.454.
72. *P.P.* (1816), Vol.V, Police Committee, p.128.
73. Ibid., p.148; *P.P.* (1817), Vol.VII, Police Committee, 2nd report, pp.465–9.
74. GMR Ms. 1229/1 Broad Street wardmote court minute book, 1780–1808, meeting 30 Aug. 1792.
75. CLRO 242–246 A–E, Ward presentments, 1668–date, presentment of Queen-hithe ward, 1830.
76. Ibid., Presentment of St. Andrew, Holborn, Farringdon Without ward, 1818.

individual justices of the peace and some local policing authorities to limit the public visibility of prostitution sometimes achieved a comparable effect. When sitting on the licensing bench for the Tower Hamlets division, for example, Caston Rohde preferred to confine 'those kind of houses' to the St. Catherine district 'where no person need go unless they went on purpose'.[77] The impact of such a policy on many of those who lived in an affected area can be gauged by the impassioned plea addressed to the inquest jury by residents of Coleman Street ward in 1786 who blamed what they saw as an alarming increase of prostitutes on the number of cheap houses for rent in the ward and, more especially, on the practice of allowing streetwalkers to solicit in and around the Royal Exchange.[78]

Most calls for the reform of the laws dealing with houses of ill fame urged not toleration, however, but suppression, principally through the extension of summary jurisdiction to the offence of brothel keeping. But despite the optimism often displayed by the advocates of such changes that proposals for toughening the law on brothels would soon gain legislative approval, the legal procedures for acting against bawdy and disorderly houses remained unchanged after the introduction of the Disorderly Houses Act in 1752.[79] As a result, local authorities were obliged to employ a wide range of alternative methods when attempting to control or suppress the disorderly houses within their perimeters – methods which they hoped would prove both more effective and less financially ruinous than the cumbersome process of indictment before the sessions.

Policing in practice

Ward inquest juries frequently complained that they might include a particular house of ill fame in their presentments to the Court of Aldermen for a number of years running and still see no action taken against it. In such circumstances, the inquest, in an attempt somehow to bring the house within the compass of the law, would often couple a charge of running a disorderly or bawdy house with some other, usually lesser, offence. In 1773, Aldgate ward presented Robert Nugent of Billiter Lane and Sarah Bunny of Sugar Loaf

77. *P.P.* (1817), Vol.VII, Police Committee, 1st report, p.49.
78. CLRO 242–246 A–E, Ward presentments, 1668–date, presentment of Coleman Street ward, 1786.
79. CLRO Misc.Mss. 283.4 Committee papers 1814–25: (Committee appointed 16 Dec. 1813 to consider petition of householders).

Court for keeping houses of ill fame as well as for selling wine by short measure.[80] In 1801, Aldgate presented Hannah Isaacs of Bookers Gardens for keeping a disorderly house and for allowing her 'Necessary' to overflow onto the adjoining public footpath.[81] Other offences frequently combined with the principal included selling strong liquor without a licence, not being free of the City, having a smoky chimney, and walls or pavements in need of repair.[82]

More common, perhaps, was the simple procedure of issuing a warning to those suspected of – or known to be – keeping disorderly houses. Broad Street ward inquest ordered Abraham Warner to appear before it to answer the charges of his neighbours that his house in London Wall was a receptacle for lewd and dissolute women. Warner refused and was promptly served with a summons.[83] After similar complaints against The Fleece, in Wells Court, Cheap ward cautioned the house's keeper, a Mrs Mancor, to shut her doors by 11 p.m. and not to allow women of the town to assemble there.[84] The patrolmen of Langbourne ward noted in the watch house minute book that they had been roundly abused by the landlady of The Anchor in Bell Court after they had remonstrated with her for allowing prostitutes to enter her house at past midnight.[85] The vestry committee appointed by St. Sepulchre to suppress brothels and disorderly houses within the parish visited each suspected house in turn, giving each three days to close down after which time proceedings would begin against them.[86]

These warnings were all made to the keepers of houses under suspicion. Occasionally, the authorities went over the head of the keeper, giving notice to the owner of the house not to renew the lease to the individual concerned;[87] or issued a general directive, such as that given by the Lord Mayor when part of the parish of St. Martin Le Grand came under the City's jurisdiction, ordering all public houses in the parish to be shut up by 11 p.m.[88]

---

80. CLRO 242–246 A–E, Ward presentments, 1668–date, presentment of Aldgate ward, 1773.

81. Ibid., presentment of Aldgate ward, 1801.   82. Ibid., passim 1700–1829.

83. Ibid., presentment of Broad Street ward, 1700.

84. GMR Ms. 3462 Cheap ward Common Council minute book, 1789–1821, meeting 1 May 1812.

85. GMR Ms. 461, Langbourn ward Fenchurch Street watch house minute book, 1817, entry Thursday 28 Aug.

86. GMR Ms. 3189, meeting 18 Sep. 1826.

87. See e.g., GMR Ms. 51/2 Billingsgate wardmote court minute book, 1821–82, meeting 9 Feb. 1830; and Walbrook ward inquest minute book, 1731–1834, meeting 5 Nov. 1828.

88. *P.P.* (1816), Vol.V, Police Committee, p.254.

Such warnings were often supplemented, or replaced, by regular observation of a house by watchmen and patrols.[89] In 1815, Bishopsgate ward stationed constables from 10 a.m. until one or two the following morning outside the doors of the eleven known disorderly houses in the ward. Members of the ward committee formed to suppress brothels visited each house in turn, in part to ensure that the constables remained at their posts and in part to speak to the keepers of the houses who 'by threatening and persuading, began to see that we were in earnest'.[90] Surveillance had the dual purpose of ensuring that a warning was being heeded and of gathering evidence for any subsequent prosecution – as we have seen, reliable testimony that known prostitutes had been seen entering and leaving a house was considered, by the ward authorities at least, sufficient proof that an offence was being committed.[91] Should the offence continue, the watchmen were empowered to enter the house and turn the inmates out.[92]

Apparently no less effective was the practice known as 'burning out' the keeper of a brothel.[93] Less dramatic than the term implies, this involved the posting of a watchman with a lighted lantern at the door of a suspected house with the aim of shaming potential customers. In 1819 Cordwainer ward placed watchmen, night and day, outside two houses in Little St. Thomas Apostles, with candles, lanterns and a painted sign reading 'Beware of Bad Houses', the cost being met out of the watch rates.[94] *The Times* ridiculed such procedures, suggesting that parish officers who authorised such activities were simply 'determined that no one shall sacrifice to Love in the dark'.[95] In 1789, the paper published an article entitled, with ponderous wit, 'Chastity of Church Wardens: A Fact'. The article retold an incident in which a Mr Wheeler – a respected glazier – was called to repair a window in a bawdy house in Shire Lane: 'And he was not a little surprised,' (the paper declared) 'when he came to the entry

89. Surveillance could be ordered by justices of the peace, particularly as part of the licensing procedure, by wards or by parish watch committees, or be an accepted element of local watch regulations.

90. *P.P.* (1817), Vol.VII, Police Committee, 2nd report, p.448.

91. GMR Ms. 463/1 Walbrook ward inquest minute book, 1731–1834, entry 5 Nov. 1828.

92. J. Shaw, *Parish Law: Or, a guide to Justices of the Peace, Ministers, Churchwardens, Overseers of the Poor, Constables, Surveyors of the Highways, Vestry-Clerks, and all Others Concern'd in Parish Business* (1750), p.361.

93. *P.P.* (1816), Vol.V, Police Committee, p.128.

94. GMR Ms. 8634 Cordwainer wardmote court minute book, 1812–1907, entry for 29 Jan. 1819.

95. *The Times*, 14 Aug. 1788.

of the house, to find two of the nightly guardians of the peace, at half past twelve at noon day, with their poles and lighted lanterns, to conduct him in; and, after he had returned, to light him out . . . with "This way, Sir" – "Across here, Sir" – "How were you pleased, Sir?" and such like salutations, the populace laughing at him as he went along.' Unsurprisingly, Wheeler promptly assaulted one of the watchmen – an offence of which he was subsequently acquitted.[96]

Despite the derision of the press, parish authorities continued to believe in the effectiveness of the practice. As, it appears, did many bawdy house keepers – such as Sarah Moss, who signed an undertaking to Walbrook ward to discontinue the proceedings in her house on condition the watchman with his lantern be withdrawn;[97] or Thomas Dawson, whose letter to the St. Sepulchre vestry committee begging that the watchmen with bells and lanterns be removed from the entrance to his lodging house was ignored and who subsequently quit the parish.[98]

Other measures could be, and were, employed by the parishes and wards in their efforts to suppress disorderly houses although, unfortunately, less can be discovered of either their detail or their prevalence. In 1790, for example, the parish of St. Andrew Undershaft went so far as to purchase the lease of a house of ill repute in Greyhound Alley in order that the tenants might be ejected;[99] while in 1821, the inquest of Portsoken ward made application to the Commissioners of Sewers and Pavements to be allowed to brick up the entrance to Still Alley off Houndsditch on the grounds that it was 'a receptacle and resort of Thieves, Prostitutes and other profligate characters'[100] and other wards advised residents to have locked iron gates erected across the entrances to their streets on the same grounds.[101]

96. *The Times*, 28 Nov. 1789.
97. GMR Ms. 463/1 Walbrook ward inquest minute book, 1731–1834, entry for 5 Nov. 1828.
98. GMR Ms. 3189, entry for 6 Oct. 1826; see also GMR Ms. 1229/1 Broad Street wardmote court minute book, 1780–1808, entry for 6 Mar. 1781.
99. GMR Ms. 4151 Parish of St. Andrew Undershaft, Deeds relating to parish property in the church 114–116 etc., Bundle 1 (1693–1837).
100. 'To the Honourable the Commissioners of Sewers and Pavements of the City of London, The Memorial of the Foreman and Inquest of the Ward of Portsoken in the said City of London', dated 6 Dec. 1821: loose sheets placed in GMR Ms. 2649/2 Portsoken wardmote inquest minute book, 1799–1840.
101. See, e.g., GMR Ms. 466 Memorial of the Alderman, Deputy, Common Council and other Inhabitants of the Ward of Walbrook to the Honorable the Commissioners of Sewers etc., (undated but early nineteenth century); and GMR Ms. 3037/1 Farringdon Within wardmote inquest minute book, 1779–1810, entry for 22 Jan. 1808.

Conclusion

This chapter has been devoted to an examination of the legal procedures open to the authorities in their attempts to control or suppress the capital's houses of ill fame. It has also described the methods employed by the keepers of those houses to evade the prescribed consequences of those procedures. In effect, there existed an active dialogue between the parish authorities and the bawdy house keepers – as there was between the prostitutes and the watchmen. This dialogue had two principal effects. The first was to allow many bawdy and disorderly houses to continue operating successfully in London throughout the eighteenth and early nineteenth centuries. The second was to encourage the recognition on the part of London's policing agencies that their capacity effectively to intervene in and disrupt the lives of bawdy house keepers was dependant less on the specific powers available to them under the law (whether common or, after 1752, statute law) than on their ability to initiate and develop diverse strategies of control and the willingness or otherwise of individuals at different levels to enforce – and accept – them.

CHAPTER SEVEN

Attitudes towards Prostitution

A 'whorish woman' is one who 'hunts for the precious life'; – She is one, whose infamous conduct marks the diabolical depravity of her heart.[1]

Tho' the profession of a prostitute is the most despicable and hateful that the imagination can form; yet the individuals are frequently worthy objects of compassion.[2]

The debates on prostitution in the eighteenth century present an intricate network of conflicting arguments and analyses. Apparently contradictory beliefs as to the importance of sexual desire among the motives that led a woman to become a prostitute, the extent and consequences of the trade, and the best means to curtail it, for example, could all be voiced by a single commentator – frequently within a single text. Some ideas surfaced, became momentarily fashionable, and then all but disappeared from the sources. Others maintained a more permanent presence, although reshaped and redeployed under different circumstances and in the service of different arguments.

Of the myriad images of prostitution and prostitutes thus produced, this chapter is concerned with just two of the more widely held and influential collections of ideas – it would be wrong to ascribe to them any greater coherence than that. The first portrayed the prostitute as an agent of destruction. She had chosen her calling and through her actions she fouled society, spreading

1. W. Hale, *Reply to the Pamphlets Lately Published in Defence of the London Female Penitentiary: With Further Remarks Upon the Dangerous Tendency of that Institution* (1809), p.47.

2. Anon., *The Histories of Some of the Penitents in the Magdalen House, as Supposed to be Related by Themselves* (1760), Vol.1, p.v.

physical ruin and moral disintegration. She was one of those 'Impudent Harlots [who] by their Antick Dresses, Painted Faces, and Whorish Insinuations, allure and tempt our Sons and Servants to Debauchery'.[3] Resolutely vicious and beyond redemption, she was the woman as predator.

The second reversed this image. While the horror with which the trade was viewed remained (indeed, in some of its aspects, grew), the individual prostitute, far from being the wilful catalyst of her own, and society's, downfall, was depicted as prostitution's first victim. Both her entry into vice and her remaining within it were represented as involuntary – the result of specifically feminine weakness and male sexual voracity: 'Tho' forced to act the harlot's wretched part, Virtue ne'er quite forsook my wounded heart'.[4] She retained her virtue if not her innocence – the sin remained, but the sinner was forgiven. Both sets of ideas share a belief in the speedy decline into poverty and death of prostituted women, but for those who saw such women as the awful victims of circumstance, that decline was pitiful and undeserved and, more importantly perhaps, could be prevented by the intervention of moral and rational philanthropy.

The prostitute as agent of destruction

It is difficult to overstate the degree of horror with which many writers regarded prostitution's apparent ability to undermine and destroy first the individuals, female and male, most directly involved in the trade, then their families, and ultimately the entire social edifice. 'We may without exaggeration assert,' wrote the author of *An Account of the Institution of the Lock Asylum* in 1792, 'that a common Prostitute is, in a Community, an Evil, not dissimilar to a Person infected with the Plague; who, miserable himself, is daily communicating the Contagion to those, that will propagate still wider the fatal Malady.'[5] The bawdy houses of Tower Hamlets were 'Nurseries of the most horrid Vices, and sinks of the most filthy Debaucheries . . . publick Nusances and common destructive pests to Thousands of Families'.[6] In such 'Hellish Families . . . Hirelings consume their Wages . . . thereby Families are begger'd and Parishes

3. Anon., *Antimoixeia: Or, the Honest and Joynt Design of the Tower Hamblets for the General Suppression of Bawdy Houses, as Encouraged by Publick Magistrates* (1691), s.s.fol.
4. *The Times*, 6 Nov. 1786.
5. Anon., *An Account of the Institution of the Lock Asylum for the Reception of Penitent Female Patients when Discharged Cured from the Lock Hospital* (1792), p.3.
6. Anon., *Antimoixeia*.

much impoverished'.[7] If left unchecked, the trade would visit ruin upon the city, the nation and the state.

Such fears of the dangers presented by a vice that was perceived as growing ever more widespread throughout the eighteenth century were articulated in a number of different ways. One of the most direct, and one which equipped the writer with a peculiarly lurid language of metaphor, was through the prostitute's capacity to transmit disease – particularly venereal.

The comprehensive diffusion of venereal disease throughout society made the army useless and the gentry weak and sickly.[8] Worst of all, wrote Bernard Mandeville in 1724, the innocent suffered alongside the guilty, for: 'Men give it to their wives, women to their husbands or perhaps their children, they to their nurses and the nurses again to other children, so that no age, sex, or condition can be entirely safe from infection'.[9] Despite this listing of the many different ways in which the contagion could be disseminated – and the underlying suggestion of an undetectable, almost miasmic danger from which none could be successfully protected – the originator and primary transmitter of the disease was held to be the prostitute. Her guilt lay not simply in the extent of her promiscuity, but in the very nature of her trade. Such women, Mandeville believed, more commonly infected men than vice versa. For each prostitute, there were many male clients and hence she was able to infect the larger number.[10] Moreover, whereas a man's desire for sex was likely to subside upon his catching the disease, a similarly infected prostitute would attempt to increase the number of clients she had connection with in order to raise the money to pay the surgeon's fees. 'The spreading of this Distemper', therefore, 'must be owing to the neglect of cure in the woman.'[11]

In a century much concerned with the false spectre of falling population levels, the likelihood that sufferers from venereal disease would be rendered infertile or, at best, beget sickly and short-lived offspring was of the greatest importance. 'The great use of Women in a community, is to supply it with members that may be serviceable, and keep up a succession', according to the anonymous author of *Some Considerations upon Streetwalkers*.[12] Yet prostitutes were

---

7. Ibid.   8. Mandeville, *A Modest Defence of Public Stews* (1724), pp.2–3.
9. Mandeville, *Modest Defence*, p.3. And again Anon., *Antimoixeia*: 'Many a Housekeeper is Infected with a Venomous Plague, which he communicates to his Honest and Innocent Wife'.
10. Mandeville, *Modest Defence*, pp.20–1.   11. Ibid., p.22.
12. Anon., *Some Considerations upon Streetwalkers*, p.6.

believed to be almost wholly barren; in part as a result of venereal disease, and in part because too frequent sexual connection with different men was considered to so 'agitate' the female reproductive organs as to make conception impossible.[13] One of the more optimistic estimates suggested that all the prostitutes in London might bring forth 100 children each year, and those born disordered, in place of the 2,000 healthy children they might otherwise have mothered. (These figures were predicated on a total prostitute population for London of some 20,000 women – Saunders Welch, writing almost thirty years earlier, had given the more modest figure of 3,000 women within the Bills of Mortality living wholly by prostitution – of whom 2,500 were barren. He described this situation as 'a national and moral evil'.)[14] A decline in the number of people, quite apart from its military implications in the face of the much more populous France, would at length involve the arts, manufacture and commerce in a common distress.[15]

The author of *Some Considerations upon Streetwalkers* further condemned prostitutes for failing to fulfil the secondary function of women in society, that of labouring either for their own maintenance or for that of their husbands or parents. Consumed with vanity and pride and determined to do little and yet gain much, prostitutes had chosen their occupation through indolence. He argued that while their mode of life and susceptibility to disease prevented their mothering children, the tendency toward idleness which had led them to become prostitutes incapacitated them for honest industry. They remained a pernicious charge upon the wealth and resources of their country, while their lives and services were irrevocably lost to it.

Quite apart from the loss of productive and reproductive resources represented by the prostitutes themselves, their activities were also depicted as diminishing the industrious capacities of the other classes in society. Henry Fielding voiced his concern at the debilitating effect of prostitution on the mental and physical health of the ruling class:

> in an age when brothels are become in a manner the seminaries of education, and that especially of those youths whose birth makes

13. M. Ludovicus [pseud.], *A Particular but Melancholy Account of the Great Hardships, Difficulties and Miseries, that those Unhappy and Much-to-be-Pitied Creatures, the Common Women of the Town, are Plunged into at this Juncture* (1752), p.5.

14. *The Times*, 8 Dec. 1786; S. Welch, *A Proposal to Render Effectual a Plan, to Remove the Nuisance of Common Prostitution from the Streets of the Metropolis* (1758), p.13 fn.

15. J. Hanway, *Letter V to Robert Dingley* (1758), p.14.

their right institution of the utmost consequence to the future well being of the public: for whatever may be the education of these youths, however vitiated and enervated their minds and bodies may be with vices and diseases, they are born to be the governors of our posterity.[16]

Like the great empires of the past, a nation whose ruling elite was physically, intellectually and morally degenerate would rapidly collapse into impotence.

From the point of view of the majority of the commentators – many of whom were drawn from among the prosperous manufacturing and commercial classes – prostitution's role in the demoralisation of the middling and plebian orders was even more insidious. The reformer Jonas Hanway argued that once the poor, through indulgence in vice, lost their sense of shame they became idle and abusers of charity, corruption and bad example turning new-felt wants into needs.[17] Justices of the peace and the City authorities were similarly concerned at the mixing of London's apprentices and prostitutes in low taverns and bawdy houses, those 'constant Fountains that furnish the courts of Justice with offenders and the place of execution with victims'.[18] Numerous petitions addressed to the Lord Mayor of London deplored the 'malignant influence of abandoned women [by which] the youth of both sexes are seduced and corrupted, shopmen, apprentices and servants are enticed to defraud or rob their masters [and] those juvenile delinquents with which our jails are thronged, are tutored . . .'; the whole leading to 'the subversion of every religious and moral principle and the general corruption of the Community'.[19]

It was above all else the very public nature of much prostitution that was objected to. 'When a Person unacquainted with the Town, passes at Night thro' any of our principal Streets, he is apt to wonder, whence that vast Body of Courtezans . . . can take its Rise. Where the Devil do all these B——hes, come from?'.[20] *The Times* complained

---

16. H. Fielding, *A Charge Delivered to the Grand Jury* (1749), pp.49–50.
17. Hanway, *Letter V to Robert Dingley*, p.9.
18. J. Fielding, *An Account of the Origin and Effect of the Police* (1758), p.41.
19. CLRO Petition Roll no.7, Petition of the Inhabitants of Farringdon Within Relating to Legislation concerning Prostitutes (no date given on petition, but early nineteenth century).
20. Father Poussin, *Pretty Doings in a Protestant Nation: Being a View of the Present State of Fornication, Whorecraft, and Adultery, in Great Britain, and the Territories and Dependencies thereunto belonging* (1734), p.1. The work was republished anonymously some years later as *Satan's Harvest Home: Or the Present State of Whorecraft, Adultery, Fornication, Procuring, Pimping, Sodomy, and the Game at Flatts* (1749). The *Game at*

in 1787 that 'the indecencies practised by the crowds of prostitutes before Somerset-House, every night, not only put modesty to the blush, but absolutely render it dangerous to pass'.[21] The 1816 Select Committee on the State of the Police of the Metropolis considered it common knowledge that in no other capital in the world was there the same 'outrageous behaviour' on the part of prostitutes soliciting in the streets as there was in London.

Such negative comparisons with foreign cities were often drawn throughout the eighteenth and early nineteenth centuries, and not just by English writers anxious to demonstrate the need for action against prostitution. In *A Tour to London: or, New Observations on England and its Inhabitants*, translated from the French in 1772, P.J. Grosley observed that 'Women of the Town . . . are more numerous than at Paris, and have more liberty and effrontery than at Rome itself'.[22] The seeming rarity with which prostitutes were found on the major thoroughfares of other nations' capitals was not, some writers suggested, because their women were more modest, but was the result of deliberate policy in those countries. In Paris, Venice, Amsterdam and other cities, streetwalkers were by law confined to certain areas of the town so that although 'the Dutch may give liberties in their Speel Huisen, or music houses, as so many rendezvous of harlots, we exceed them in appearance of common women in the open streets'.[23] Mandeville had suggested the setting up of a similar – though more rigidly controlled – system in London in his *Modest Defence of Public Stews*, in which he had argued that properly regulated prostitution would virtually eradicate all other (for Mandeville, more pernicious) forms of extra- or pre-marital sex, thereby drastically lessening the incidence of venereal disease.[24] Mandeville described London's streetwalkers ('poor strolling Damsels') as 'those Drains and Sluices . . . to let out Lewdness . . . those Horn-works and breast-works of Modesty . . . Those ramparts and Ditches within which the Virtue of our Wives and Daughters lay so

---

Flatts 'was the practice of Lesbian love': F. Henriques, *The Immoral Tradition: Prostitution and Society, Vol.3, Europe and the New World* (1966). p.148.

21. *The Times*, 2 Jun. 1787.

22. P.J. Grosley (trans. Thomas Nugent), *A Tour to London: Or, New Observations on England, and its Inhabitants* (1772), Vol.1, p.55.

23. J. Hanway, *Letters Written Occasionally on the Customs of Foreign Nations in Regard to Harlots, the Lawless Commerce of the Sexes, the Repentance of Prostitutes, the Great Humanity and Beneficial Effects of Magdalen Charity in London, and the Absurd Notions of the Methodists* (1761), 'Letter III: The Inefficacy of Laws to Prevent Unlawful Commerce', p.17.

24. Mandeville, *Modest Defence*, pp.2 and 20.

conveniently entrenched'.[25] In 1758, Jonas Hanway, more tentatively, wondered aloud whether the evil effects of prostitution might be made less immediately harmful to the state and to private individuals if brothels were confined to a certain spot and there tolerated by the authorities. He reasoned, in part, that one of the benefits of such a system might lie in its removal of temptation from the eyes of young men who were, under the present state of affairs, in constant danger of being led astray from the paths of virtue.[26] If prostitution could not be made less vicious, then it could at least be rendered less visible.

The conviction that the men who went with prostitutes were essentially innocents abroad was an important part of the arguments put forward by those who advocated legalised districts for prostitution, although it enjoyed considerable currency on all sides. *Some Considerations upon Streetwalkers* began with a verse in which a 'Man of Frailty' was urged to fly from the 'dang'rous Beauty of the Wanton' if he wanted to escape utter ruin;[27] while the anonymous author of an open letter to the Bishop of London in 1808 quoted from the Book of Proverbs: 'For a whore is a deep ditch . . . she lieth in wait as for a prey and increaseth the transgressors among men.'[28] Those residents of Cornhill ward who petitioned the City authorities against female prostitutes in 1819 complained that their sons and apprentices, their shopmen and servants, were unavoidably exposed to aggressive soliciting whenever they entered the street: 'Thus assailed by temptation they are seduced into vice, their morals are corrupted and vicious habits are established.'[29] Men bringing prosecutions for theft against prostitutes at the Old Bailey were anxious to ensure that the court understood that they had been deceived into communication with the women. Thus William Fife informed the Old Bailey in 1716 that he had been walking across Tower Hill on the evening of January 3rd 'and there met Katherine Ely, who told him it was very cold, and desir'd him to

25. Ibid., p.ii. The author of *Harris's List of Covent-garden Ladies*, unsurprisingly, agreed, commenting that 'were there no common women, young fellows would be more earnest and assiduous in their attacks of [sic] the virtuous': J. or B. Harris [attrib.], *Harris's List of Covent-garden Ladies: Or, New Atlantis for the year 1764* (1764), p.viii.

26. Hanway, *Letter V to Robert Dingley*, p.19.

27. Anon., *Some Considerations upon Streetwalkers*, title-page.

28. Proverbs ch.23, verses 27, 28: quoted on the title-page of Anon., *Letter to the Right Rev. the Lord Bishop of London* (1808).

29. CLRO Petition roll no.9, Petition of the Inhabitants of the Ward of Cornhill Against Female Prostitutes and the Existing Laws Against Them, 11 Feb. 1819.

make her drink; which he, not being acquainted with such sort of Persons, complied with'. Ely and her co-defendants Elizabeth White and Anne Bartley, accused of assaulting Fife and stealing his silver buckles, called in their defence 'a most impudent Prostitute, whose extraordinary Progress in all sorts of Wickedness had gain'd her the name of 'Trolly Lolly', to swear, that Fife chuck'd her under the Chin, as she was standing at her Door, and ask'd if she had any Fire'. They had then gone to bed together and 'he gave her the Buckles for Satisfaction'. Trolly Lolly's testimony appears to have done more harm than good – Ely, White and Bartley were found guilty of felony and ordered to be burnt in the hand, Lolly was imprisoned by the court 'for her extraordinary Impudence'.[30] Few prosecutors admitted to having solicited the women themselves and spoke of having been lured, tricked and tempted into criminal connection. The image thus presented emphasised the essential honesty and artlessness of the male, whose body and soul were endangered by the guile and corrupt sophistication of the prostitute woman.

Not all women were portrayed in this manner, and it was not only men who stood at risk of moral and physical pollution from too close contact with women of the town. Many of those who objected to the presence and behaviour of prostitutes in the public arena stressed the corrupting effect of such a presence on the modest, chaste and innocent woman. It had become 'utterly impossible for a modest woman to pass the streets after dusk, without being insulted in the grossest terms and frequently obliged to suffer the hearing of horrid expressions too shocking to relate'. The respectable householders of Lambeth demanded from the Surrey magistrates more forthright action against prostitutes in order to 'prevent their wives and daughters from having their eyes and ears offended with indecencies'.[31] This desire to segregate the virtuous woman from the abandoned extended into indoor public spaces. The frequent presence of procuresses and prostitutes in the lobbies and auditoria of theatres was felt to be particularly objectionable. The boxes at Drury Lane were, *The Times* declared, 'licensed stews for the abandoned and profligate to meet and pair off from'.[32] It is interesting, however, that few proposals were made to prohibit their attendance entirely. In an echo of the arguments of those who advocated the confinement of prostitution to out-of-the-way areas

30. OSBP, 13–14 Jan. 1715/16.   31. *The Times*, 29 Feb. 1788.
32. Ibid., 8. Oct. 1785.

of the capital, it was felt sufficient for the managements of the playhouses to restrict prostitutes to certain relatively secluded parts of the building.[33]

The fear of the consequences of the intermingling of the respectable with the unrespectable was especially acute within the public domain. On the streets, in the parks, the theatres and public gardens of the city, prostitution was a visible, material presence. Vice was no longer some secret miasmic threat but an overt and personified adversary. As Lynda Nead has commented when discussing nineteenth-century streetwalking, it was also within this public space that the distinction between vice and virtue was most liable to be eroded, to break down.[34]

The absence of physical boundaries between the pure and the corrupt could lead to the disintegration of the moral divide between the two. *The Times* expressed in extreme form the fear of such a collapse of identities in its attack on an exhibition of paintings held at Somerset House in the spring of 1786 in which portraits of what the paper described as 'notorious prostitutes, triumphing as it were in vice' were placed alongside those of modest women 'of rank and virtue'.[35] The French, the paper claimed, would never have allowed such an exhibition in their academy. It nevertheless used the opportunity to strengthen the supposedly intrinsic difference between purity and depravity by drawing attention to the ease with which an observant audience might distinguish 'the vicious courtezan from the modest maiden or chaste wife'. Once again, the emphasis is placed upon the prostitute's outward appearance as a reflection of her essential depravity. This sat somewhat uneasily alongside an earlier complaint from the paper that should a policy of barring prostitutes from public places be adopted by the authorities it would prove impossible to operate as fashionable women were too much in the habit of copying the make-up and clothing adopted by the women of the town, falsely advertising their own lack of virtue and making it impossible to distinguish between women of the town and modest women.[36]

33. *The Times*, 8 Oct. 1785.

34. L. Nead, *Myths of Sexuality: Representations of Women in Victorian Britain* (1988), p.114.

35. *The Times*, 10 May 1786.

36. Ibid., 8 Oct. 1785. William Hutton, visiting London in the 1810s, embarrassed himself on at least one occasion by his inability to differentiate between 'girls of the town' and 'ladies of beauty, elegance, and modesty': W. Hutton, *A Journey to London: Comprising a Description of the Most Interesting Objects of Curiosity to a Visitor of the Metropolis* (1818), p.43.

The language used by commentators expressed the tensions generated by this and similar confusion of categories, as it was employed to erect an uncrossable barrier between prostitute and wife or daughter. A report in the press in 1786 that a prostitute had been rescued from a mob in St. James's Square by an officer described the woman as 'a beautiful impure' and 'a frail fair one' and condemned her attackers for abusing one of those whom men were born to defend.[37] Criticism of the attitude taken in the report derided the view that men were born to defend common prostitutes, referring to them as 'wretches who have forfeited the character of women', 'banes of society, enemies of mankind and the curses of every age' and described them as the very reverse of the type of a good woman. A description of a violent confrontation in the Strand between 'a young lady' and 'a young harlot' who had, according to the report, mistaken the former for a fellow streetwalker had the episode end when 'the virgin was conveyed home in a fit, and the prostitute dragged to the watchhouse in a frenzy'.[38] Each word in the first half of the sentence can be matched against its opposite in the second: virgin – prostitute; conveyed – dragged; home – watch house; fit – frenzy. The sentence could hardly be more efficiently constructed in order to reinforce the distinction between vice and virtue which the prostitute had by her actions threatened.

As the terms 'streetwalker' and 'woman of the town' suggest, prostitution was understood as an essentially urban phenomenon.[39] Indeed, it was seen as being almost uniquely localised to the capital. If the image of the countryside had not yet developed into that of a pre-lapsarian garden of Eden that it was to achieve in the later nineteenth century, then it was at least seen as a place where temptations to vice were rare. London, by contrast, with its great population, many of them crammed into teeming rookeries, its places of entertainment from theatres to gin shops, and its massive inequalities of wealth, was the centre of vice, moral pollution and criminality. The principal effect of the urban environment, according to the German-born Londoner Pastor Freidrich Wenderborn in 1791, was to increase the individual's natural propensity for vicious behaviour.

37. *The Times*, 10 Aug. 1786.
38. *The Times*, 7 Jun. 1787.
39. 'Women of the Town' was not the most pejorative title attached to prostitutes, although it moved one writer in 1799 to lament that 'the very title seems to level them with the pavement on which they wander – they are a property equally regarded as common, equally base, equally to be trampled on': Anon., *Thoughts On the Means of Alleviating the Miseries Attendant Upon Common Prostitution* (1799), p.2.

(Not everybody saw this as something to be condemned, however – 'How silly your resolution of absconding a wicked town for a more virtuous country . . . For God's sake, George, leave their hypocritical company, and come to town and sin like a gentleman.')[40] Both the possibility of acquiring riches which London offered, and the more bitter experience of anonymity and destruction which the city was believed to hold out to the immigrant from the country, led women into prostitution. 'In that state of society in which we live', wrote Wenderborn, 'everything almost may be done with money, and all that is desirable may be bought with it; health, tranquility of mind, and immortality excepted.'[41] Jonas Hanway declared that nothing 'tends to pervert the female heart so much as the habit of spending much time and money in amusement, and the decoration of their persons, following the example of the superiors in fortune'.[42] He claimed that such frivolity and emulation accounted for at least half the prostitutes on London's streets. John Fielding preferred to emphasise the ease with which, in such a populous city, vast numbers of people might sink, unknown, into idleness, destitution and crime.[43]

It was prostitution's apparently intimate link with crime and public disorder that came most to exercise the minds of those in authority by the beginning of the nineteenth century. Many of the poorer, more wretched areas of the city in which prostitutes were said to congregate already possessed venerable reputations as centres of criminality. The Spitalfields–Whitechapel district to the east of the City, Chick Lane to the north, and the St. Giles Rookery in the heart of the West End, for example, were all regarded – and much-feared – as sites of lawlessness and prostitution. The already insufficiently rigorous segregation of these areas from those frequented by the fashionable and the virtuous (Drury Lane itself, for instance, running alongside Covent Garden and down into the Strand, formed part of the St. Giles Rookery) was further undermined by the necessary movement of prostitutes between respectable and unrespectable districts. Indeed, the figure of the prostitute was the link between the two, the conduit through which the squalor of the gin shop

40. F.A. Wenderborn, *A View of England Towards the Close of the Eighteenth Century* (1791), Vol.1, p.290; Anon. *The Humours of Fleet-Street, Covent-Garden and the Strand: Being the Lives and Adventures of the Most Noted Ladies of Pleasure, By An Old Sportsman* (c.1745), p.4.
41. Wenderborn, *A View of England*, p.290.
42. J. Hanway, *The Defects of Police the Cause of Immorality, and the Continual Robberies Committed: Particularly in and about the Metropolis* (1775), p.xxiii.
43. Fielding, *Account of the Origin*, pp.42–3.

might soil the elegance of the promenade. More prosaically, perhaps, she was also seen as both the cause and the focus of much of
the capital's crime. John Fielding's evidence given before the House
of Commons Committee on burglaries and robberies in London
and Westminster in 1772 blamed the current disorders on 'the
immense number of common prostitutes who . . . infest the streets
of . . . Westminster and parts adjacent'.[44] Certainly, by the last quarter of the eighteenth century complaints against soliciting by streetwalkers along the major thoroughfares were as likely to emphasise
the dangers thus presented to the wallets and purses of passers-by
as to their souls. Fielding had stressed to the select committee the
connection between prostitutes and 'soldiers and other bullies'. It
had come to be seen as inevitable that prostitutes and thieves would
combine 'in the destruction of the public peace'. In *Serious Thoughts
on the Miseries of Seduction and Prostitution*, published in 1783, Charles
Horne deplored the two groups' 'mutual and joint ravages on the
honest and industrious part of society'; 'the more firm their friend-
ship and alliance', he wrote, 'the more we suffer'.[45] As criminals
themselves, as the allies of criminals, and as the cause of criminality
in others, prostitutes were seen as an evil whose eradication would
bring peace, stability and public order.

Counting prostitutes

Central to the idea that prostitution represented a serious threat to
the well-being of the nation was the belief that its practitioners
existed in huge numbers. For the greater part of the century, writers
made no attempt to quantify the number of prostitutes working
the streets of the capital. Instead, they wrote of the 'incredible
numbers', the 'vast body of courtezans as plenty as mackrel after
thunder', the 'hosts of half-naked prostitutes'. The town was 'over-
stocked with harlots' and each year added to their number. Streetwalkers were so numerous, thought Hanway, that come evening
one should think every woman met with was a prostitute, 'were they
not distinguished for the most part, by that sort of conduct which is

44. Quoted in *P.P.* (1812), Vol.II, Police Committee, Appendix 8.
45. C. Horne, *Serious Thoughts on the Miseries of Seduction and Prostitution, with a Full
Account of the Evils that Produce them: Plainly Showing Prostitution to be Contrary to the Laws
of Nature, And a Method Pointed Out, whereby These Two Dreadful Evils May be Totally
Exterminated, Fairly Deduced from the Laws of God and Nature* (1783), p.59.

totally devoid of *honor, decency* or *shame*.[46] Much of the language used reflected the almost ubiquitous imagery of contagion and disease with an additional stress on what was perceived as the irrational, irredeemably beast-like behaviour of the women. 'Herds' of prostitutes filled the town; the Strand and Drury Lane 'swarmed' with them; most commonly, prostitutes were said to 'infest' the streets.

By the turn of the century, however, it had become common to affix a definite figure to accounts of the trade's enormity. Hanway had spoken only in general terms when considering the numbers of prostitutes in 1758, but the Magdalen Hospital for the Reception of Penitent Prostitutes – of which Hanway was a co-founder – was very soon issuing regular reports on the number of women entering and leaving the Hospital, breaking the figures down by age, origin and experience.[47] Estimates of the number of prostitutes operating in the capital varied widely with 20,000, 30,000 or 40,000 all being cited with equal confidence. Archenholz, writing in the late 1790s, reckoned there to be 50,000 prostitutes in London, of whom 13,000 resided in the parish of Marylebone alone.[48] The figure of 50,000 'females of all descriptions who support themselves chiefly or wholly by prostitution', had first appeared in Patrick Colquhoun's *Treatise on the Police of the Metropolis* in 1796 – the year the Society for Bettering the Condition of the Poor was founded with the stated intention of providing 'improvement' with a scientific basis – and had rapidly become the most widely quoted sum. Those who cited Colquhoun's figure in later years suggested that as London had grown both more populous and more vicious in the intervening period, so 50,000 had if anything to be considered an underestimate of the number of women walking the streets. Even the advocates of the lower totals were agreed that the number of prostitutes was rising. The various parliamentary Committees into the Police of the Metropolis set up in the early years of the nineteenth century were insistent both that prostitution was increasingly extensive and that the behaviour of the capital's streetwalkers had grown more offensive over the preceding fifty years. An examination of the testimony of witnesses to the committees reveals a somewhat more complex situation, however, some agreeing that the vice had become worse, others that it had remained much the same, and still others suggesting it had in fact diminished.

46. Hanway, *Letter V to Robert Dingley* (1758), p.23.
47. See, for example, W. Dodd, *An Account of the Rise, Progress and Present State of the Magdalen Charity* (1761).
48. W. Von Archenholz, *A Picture of England* (1797), p.302.

Despite the rhetorical advantages of being able to cite statistical 'fact' in this way, the earlier language of metaphor was too powerful to be entirely given up and writers and the authorities continued to refer to the metropolis being 'infested' with crowds of prostitutes; sometimes combining the two languages to produce 'hosts of mercenaries forty thousand strong' – an emotive vocabulary joining with the language of scientific 'truth' in order to reinforce the fear of the invasive threat that prostitution presented.

Critical to this way of thinking, then, was the belief that prostitution was the product of a growing urban environment, that it was becoming an increasingly large and powerful system, and that through the physical and moral contamination of the mass of the population it posed a substantial menace to the maintenance of order, propriety and wealth. That much it shared with those who saw the prostitute herself as the chief victim of the trade. It held a very different view, however, of the prostitute herself, believing her to have entered prostitution willingly, to remain within the trade by choice, and in consequence to be so spiritually degraded as not to want, nor deserve, nor be able, to quit her occupation and return to the paths of virtue and industry.

One possible reason for the inability of commentators to agree on the exact numbers of prostitutes lies in the absence of any single agreed definition of who or what was a prostitute. Colquhoun, for example, included within his total of 50,000, an estimate of all women living with men without having undergone a recognised marriage ceremony. The far more modest figure of around 7,000 prostitutes for the entire capital put out by the newly established Metropolitan Police in the 1830s, relied on uncertain extrapolations from the number of streetwalkers arrested each year.[49]

The prostitute as victim

One particular definition of prostitution, however, did emerge and become amplified during the eighteenth and early nineteenth centuries. That definition played an important part in the structuring and development of the second of the two dominant ways of thinking about prostitutes in this period – that is, the representation of the prostitute as the victim, rather than the malign agent, of

49. J. Edgar, DD, *Female Virtue – Its Enemies and Friends: A Discourse on the Statistics, Evils and Cure of Prostitution* (1841), pp.6–8.

prostitution, who had despite the vile degradation visited upon her, retained a vestigial purity of heart.

The advocates of social reformation in the late seventeenth and early eighteenth centuries did not discuss prostitution in isolation. Significantly, the word 'prostitution' was not then in common usage; nor indeed did any other term exist which referred exclusively to the selling of sex. 'Whoring', and its permutations, were the most common appellations and were used to describe almost all extra-marital heterosexual activity. To denounce a woman as a whore was to accuse her of sexual immorality and carried no necessary implication of payment.[50] To speak or write of 'common whores' narrowed the field somewhat; even so it referred as much to promiscuity as to commerce and a woman who appeared to others as insufficiently discriminating in her choice of partners was liable to be so named whether or not any money had changed hands. 'Common whoring' referred equally, if not more, to the actions of the man – the client – as to those of the woman. Mandeville, although one of the first writers to draw a distinction between paid and unpaid fornication, nevertheless defined whoring as the action of the male in 'lying in with a certain Set of Women'. The term lacks the institutional and organisational connotations of 'prostitution', marking at most a series of events rather than a trade or an identity.[51]

Of the scores of pamphlets published and distributed by the Societies for the Reformation of Manners after 1680, none addresses itself exclusively to the question of 'common whores'. A large number, however, deal with the subject of 'Lewdness'. A vague and necessarily flexible term, it embraced all sexual acts, and states, which were, as John Disney put it in 1722, 'Inconsistent with the Character and Safety of a Christian'.[52] These usually included adultery, fornication, uncleanness (that is, masturbation), lasciviousness, sodomy, obscene talk, lewd books or pictures, procuring, concubinage, incest, rape and polygamy. The diversity of such a list is apparent and it is not the intention here to suggest that the pamphlets' authors were unable to distinguish between, for example, adultery and lewd talk. More particularly, the Societies were

50. For a discussion of this popular slander, see J.A. Sharpe, *Defamation and Sexual Slander in Early Modern England: The Church Courts at York* (Borthwick Institute of Historical Research, Borthwick papers No.58).

51. Mandeville, *Modest Defence*, p.8. Mandeville's use of the phrase 'a certain Set of Women', however, indicates the extent to which he differed from other writers of this period.

52. J. Disney, *Fleshly Lusts Inconsistent with the Character and Safety of a Christian* (1722).

obviously aware of streetwalking – indeed expended vast amounts of time and effort in attempting to stamp out the practice – and a number of their publications reflected that awareness.[53] Nevertheless, it would be true to say that the Societies conceived of both the streetwalker and the woman discovered in a pre- or extra-marital sexual relationship as fundamentally alike. The two women were united both in their flouting of the moral injunction against fornication and in their shared possession of a promiscuous sexuality; 'public' and 'private' whoring were to be condemned impartially as component parts of the larger category of lewdness.

Where a distinction was made, it was one of degree only and one that tended to censure public whoring as the greater evil. Disney was of the opinion that 'the Lewdness of Common Whores' was the more offensive 'for surely, Impudence, and open profession in Vice, increase the guilt'.[54] He was, however, reluctant to make too much of this. The pamphlet in which it appears was written in 1729, six years after the reissuing of Mandeville's *Fable of the Bees*, in which the Dutchman had first rehearsed the arguments afterwards elaborated in *A Modest Defence of Public Stews*.[55] In the introduction to *A View of Ancient Laws Against Immorality and Prophaneness* Disney fiercely attacked Mandeville's thesis. With regard to the latter's contention that prostitution safeguarded the virtue of 'Women of Honour', Disney roundly declared that such women 'are guided by Principles, either of Conscience or Reputation, which will not suffer them to be lewd, tho' no Common Whore were permitted'.[56] Given that it is unlikely that Disney believed that *only* 'Common Whores' experienced illicit sexual connection, it appears that he was here not distinguishing between prostitutes and all other women but rather refusing to differentiate between prostitutes and any woman sexually active outside marriage.

Mandeville's *Modest Defence* was published in 1724. Later students of the work have followed Disney in concentrating on Mandeville's declared purpose of demonstrating prostitution's worth in preserving the virtuous chastity of the generality of women.[57] Of equal

---

53. For example, Anon., *An Account of the Societies for the Reformation of Manners in England and Ireland: With a Persuasive to Persons of All Ranks to be Zealous and Diligent in Promoting the Execution of the Laws Against Prophaneness and Debauchery* (1701).
54. J. Disney, *View of Ancient Laws* (1729), p.4.
55. B. Mandeville, *The Fable of the Bees* (1714); the second, extended, edition appeared in 1723.
56. Disney, *View of Ancient Laws*, preface.
57. For example, see S. Schama, *The Embarrassment of Riches: An Interpretation of Dutch Culture in the Golden Age* (1987), pp.467–80.

significance, however, is Mandeville's attempt to make explicit the object of his polemic. Over several pages, Mandeville explained what he meant by the terms 'public whoring' and 'private whoring'. The defining characteristic of the former, that which set it apart from 'private whoring', was that the 'certain Set of Women' involved 'for such a Sum of Money, more or less, profess themselves always in a Readiness to be enjoy'd'.[58] This emphasis on the centrality of a cash payment was new. Whereas previous writers had distinguished only between those women who experienced sexual contact outside the marriage bed and those who did not, Mandeville further divided the first of these two categories; prostitutes were not simply especially active fornicators. The reformers of the Societies recognised few motives for fornication other than sexual lust. Mandeville, while acknowledging the importance of 'the Violence of Female Desire' in the propagation of private whoring, saw those women who engaged in public whoring as driven primarily by an economic need.[59]

By the time Disney published his attack on Mandeville, the latter's views on the reasons why women entered prostitution, if not his analysis of the social advantages of the trade, were already gaining in popularity. Mandeville was no longer alone in recognising a difference, for women, between desire and prostitution. As early as the 1690s, Thomas Bray, a leading member of the Societies for the Reformation of Manners, had indicated some awareness of that difference by drafting a plan for a penitentiary solely for prostitutes, where they were to be shown the error of their ways (though, significantly, it was never published).[60] A similar scheme had been hinted at by Robert Nelson in 1715.[61]

Nevertheless, it was not until 1735 that a work was published dealing with the question of prostitution in isolation from that of lewdness. The author of *Some Considerations upon Streetwalkers* continued to refer to London's prostitutes as 'lewd abandon'd Women' and to reproach them for their idleness and scandalous behaviour but, importantly, he dissented from the beliefs expressed by almost all previous commentators by blaming the women's entry into prostitution not on their extreme sexual appetites but rather on their

58. Mandeville, *Modest Defence*, pp.8–11.
59. Ibid., p.9, '. . . nothing but mere Necessity obliges them to continue in that Course . . . That they themselves in Reality utterly abhor.'
60. T. Bray, 'General Plan of a Penitential Hospital for the Imploying and Reforming Lewd Women', referred to in H.P. Thompson, *Thomas Bray* (1954), p.24.
61. R. Nelson, *An Address to Persons of Quality and Estate* (1715), p.12.

economic needs.[62] The meaning of much of his argument is ambiguous; the author suggested that women become prostitutes after failing to marry and thus '. . . not provided for by their Kindred, prompted by Nature, and urged by Wants, are forced to become the Instruments of satisfying those desires which are given for a better Use'.[63] Whilst the sinfulness of the initial step into prostitution was not denied, continuation in the trade was not seen as wilfully immoral; 'Necessity succeeds Sin, and Want puts an End to Shame.'[64] For the first time, the misery of life as a prostitute was evoked and 'charitable Compassion' pleaded for such women 'as may find themselves reduc'd to this Condition, which they must know and feel to be the Extremity of Unhappiness'.[65] Not only were prostitutes no longer seen as simply the most blatant example of female sexual waywardness but the outright condemnation that such extreme waywardness attracted was be replaced by expressions of pity and the call to reform.

Partly because of the decline and eventual demise of the Societies for the Reformation of Manners, little was published on the subjects of either prostitution or lewdness in the 1730s and 1740s. With the appearance of a new array of writings in the 1750s it appears that a fundamental change had taken place in the way in which prostitution was perceived. The ambiguities and hesitant urge to compassion of writings such as *Some Considerations upon Streetwalkers* have gone; as the title of a piece published in 1752 by the pseudonymous M. Ludovicus makes plain. *A Particular but Melancholy Account of the Great Hardships, Difficulties and Miseries, that those Unhappy and Much-to-be-pitied Creatures, the Common Women of the Town, are Plung'd into at this Juncture* attacked 'the late severe Edict issued forth against these unfortunate Fair Ones' (this was an allusion either to the Disorderly Houses Act of 1752, or to the practice of London's Lord Mayors of pledging to clear the City of streetwalkers on taking office).[66] For 'Ludovicus', the issue was not one of sexuality but of poverty. The wealthy could deplore the women's lack of virtue but were unqualified to pronounce on such matters:

> it is easy talking of being virtuous with a Coach and Six, but it is difficult, nay I may say impossible, being really so, without either Friends, Money, Character, or Subsistence . . . Pray then what must they do to get Bread? . . . They will use what God, and his Handmaid

62. Anon., *Some Considerations upon Streetwalkers.*
63. Anon., *Some Considerations upon Streetwalkers*, p.7.   64. Ibid., p.8.
65. Ibid., p.5.   66. Ludovicus, *Particular but Melancholy Account*, p.3.

Nature, have bestowed upon [them], in order to get Subsistence, seeing the poor Women Cannot starve, and I think it very unreasonable in any to imagine they should, whilst they have got any Commodity to dispose of that can bring them in a Penny.[67]

In *A Modest Defence of Public Stews* Mandeville had criticised the methods used by the Societies in suppressing streetwalking. Public whippings and imprisonment would only further decrease the ability of a prostitute to obtain gainful employment; he pointed out the implausibility of a scheme of reform that involved reducing a woman to greater poverty in order to make her chaste when it was lack of money that had led her into living otherwise.[68] His proposed alternative however – placing such women in state-run brothels – was received with scepticism. Twenty-eight years later, 'Ludovicus' made a somewhat garbled appeal for the construction of a 'Reception House' for prostitutes who wished to quit the trade.[69] This proposal was confused and – as the author's chosen name implies – presented in a semi-humorous style. In 1751, however, more serious suggestions had been made along similar lines in the form of pseudonymous letters to *The Gentleman's Magazine* and Samuel Johnson's *The Rambler*. These deplored the miserable appearance of the large numbers of prostitutes operating in London's streets and alleys. 'Amicus' wondered at the fate of the mothers of the children filling Thomas Coram's Foundling Hospital.[70] 'Sunderlandis' proposed 'reclaiming' the women via 'a foundation upon the plan of the convents in foreign countries'.[71] The editor of *The Gentleman's Magazine* also reminded his readers that the author of *The Vices of the Cities of London and Westminster* had proposed that:

> it would be an act of great benevolence, if among the many noble charities established in this metropolis, some foundation were made for the support of penitent prostitutes, who might be employ'd to publick advantage, in a manufacture of *Dresden* work, and after a probation of some years recover their character.[72]

In 1758 there appeared a remarkable assemblage of pamphlets (some of whose authors were supposed to have drawn their inspiration from the letters of seven years before), all advocating the creation of a refuge, an asylum, with the aim of rescuing from the

---

67. Ibid., pp.9–10.   68. Mandeville, *Modest Defence*, p.xi.
69. Ludovicus, *Particular but Melancholy Account*, p.10.
70. *The Rambler*, no.107, 26 Mar. 1751.
71. *The Gentleman's Magazine*, Apr. 1751, pp.163–5.
72. Ibid., Mar. 1751, pp.128–9.

misery of prostitution as many women as was humanly possible.[73] The authors – Robert Dingley, Jonas Hanway, John Fielding and Saunders Welch – were well known and respected figures. Hanway and Dingley, the principal movers of the project, were prominent businessmen, active in the Russian fur trade and, in the case of Hanway, a director of the Bank of England. Fielding was perhaps the leading magistrate of his day and Saunders Welch the High Constable of Holborn. They were deeply religious men, favouring Evangelicalism, and much concerned with a wide variety of social and moral issues; in many ways, they were heirs to the activist, reforming tradition of the Societies for the Reformation of Manners.

They differed fundamentally from the Societies, however, over the extent to which they believed that a life of prostitution obliterated the moral sensibilities of women. Whereas the men of the Societies had conceived of 'streetwalking strumpets' as wholly corrupt figures who had voluntarily cast off all sense of shame and female honour, the founders of what was to be the Magdalen Hospital for the Reception of Penitent Prostitutes stressed each woman's retention of an inner spark of virtue. Hanway wrote that:

> It is a great mistake to imagine that those whom we are now recommending, are lost beyond redemption. There is a *native* ingenuousness in the female mind; and *virtue* will charm as well as *vice*. All who have been hurried into these excesses, are not deaf to the calls of conscience. Strength of passion, and strength of reason, often meet in the same person, and there have been instances of the worst sinners becoming the greatest saints.[74]

The prostitute was the victim, not of her own unbridled sexuality but of material want and male heedlessness. Seduced reluctantly into vice and loss of reputation, unable to find employment as a result, she was incapable of returning to respectability through her own efforts – 'the seeds of virtue would assert themselves', pleaded Dingley 'but alas, the possibility is removed'.[75] The prostitute was fashioned into the antithesis not of the chaste and modest woman – with whom she shared a powerful sense of shame – but of the adulterous and incontinent female. The poverty-stricken, pitiable,

73. Hanway, *Letter V. to Robert Dingley*; idem, *A Plan for Establishing a Charity-House, for the Reception of Repenting Prostitutes, to be called the Magdalen Charity* (1758), and idem, *Thoughts on the Plan for a Magdalen House* (1758); R. Dingley, *Proposals for Establishing a Public Place of Reception for Penitent Prostitutes* (1758); J. Fielding, *A Plan for a Preservatory and Reformatory for the Benefit of Deserted girls and Penitent Prostitutes* (1758); and Welch, *Proposal to Render Effectual a Plan*.
74. Hanway, *Letter V. to Robert Dingley*, p.22.   75. Dingley, *Proposals*, p.4.

above all *powerless* and hence *forgivable* character of the prostitute was counterposed to the salacious, threatening, wilful sexuality of the 'promiscuous' woman.

Within a year of the initial appeal, funds had been raised, premises acquired, an asylum opened. Candidates for entry had to be prostitutes or 'in danger' of becoming so and be able to convince the committee of their sincere desire to reform. Inmates were to receive moral and religious instruction and, perhaps more practically, were to be taught a suitable trade with the aim of either returning them to their 'friends' or placing them in appropriate positions, which generally speaking meant domestic service. Both courses of action would, it was assumed, remove any financial need for their return to prostitution.

The Magdalen Hospital became a successful charity; one which it was fashionable to support. By the opening years of the nineteenth century it had become the model for other institutions, both in the capital and in provincial towns and cities.[76]

By the middle of the second half of the eighteenth century, the image of the prostitute as victim had become so entrenched in the thinking of the majority of those who wrote on the subject, that a standard narrative of the life of a typical woman of the town had been developed. Although details differed, in its broad outlines this narrative varied little between writers. It required the woman to have been born into the threadbare respectability of the down-at-heel rural middling and lower-middling sort. Her father was most frequently characterised as a half-pay army officer or a clergyman with a poor living. Indebtedness had hurried him to his grave. Her virginity seduced from her by 'the arts and insinuations of those whose rank, fortune, or education, furnish them with the means to corrupt or delude', she was disowned by her surviving family and so accompanied the agent of her downfall to London. Here, after she had enjoyed a single season of uneasy pleasure, her seducer contrived to lodge the girl in a disguised brothel, abandoning her forever. She became indebted to the bawd for her food and lodging. She was thus forced to agree to prostitute herself. The first client introduced to her by the bawd was almost invariably described as an aged Jew (this anti-semitic element grew in importance over the period – first appearing in the 1780s, it developed to the point where serious social investigators of the 1830s baldly declared it 'a

76. Other 'Magdalens' or 'Female Penitentiaries' subsequently opened in Bristol, Bath, Edinburgh, Liverpool and London.

well-known fact' that 80 per cent of London's bawdy houses were run by Jews). The woman's undoubted beauty led the bawd to overwork her. Within a short time, she became disease-ridden and, having turned to drink to alleviate her shame and disgust at her way of life, an alcoholic. She was ejected from the bawdy house. She was thus forced to become a streetwalker. Her physical and moral destruction were almost complete, although it was essential to the outcome of the narrative that a vestige of each remained, and her subsequent decline was rapid. Its close was, however, uncertain. Would she end her days by dying on the scaffold or in some broken-down cellar, or would her 'awakening conscience' lead her to an asylum where her health, her soul and her character could all be regained through industry, modesty and repentance?[77]

By the early nineteenth century, one such asylum was the London Female Penitentiary. This was founded in 1807 and took the Magdalen, then entering its fiftieth year, as its model. Unlike the founders of the Magdalen however, the proponents of the new Penitentiary met with vociferous opposition. The loudest voice was that of William Hale, a prosperous Spitalfields silk manufacturer, who accused the Penitentiary's backers of promoting vice, encouraging sloth and allowing the wicked to go unpunished.[78] Hale argued that by accepting only prostitutes, rather than those 'in danger' of going on the streets, the Female Penitentiary encouraged – even forced – women to augment their sins until they had reached a sufficient depth of depravity to be considered eligible to enter its doors.[79] Once inside, they had, apparently, no prospect of punishment but were instead to be offered consolation and reward.[80] With heavy sarcasm, Hale suggested the extension of the principle to pornographers.[81] His attack provoked allies and critics of the Penitentiary into print. The justifications advanced by each side reveal both affinities with, and departures from, the earlier debates.

Hale's argument rested primarily on an unwavering belief in the wickedness of prostitutes. For Hale, 'females who, having once deviated from the paths of virtue, and are desirous of being restored to religious instructions, are not to be found in the nocturnal walks of

77. See, as just one example of this type of narrative, Anon., *Thoughts on the Means*, passim.
78. W. Hale, *Address to the Public on the Dangerous Tendency of the London Female Penitentiary: With Hints Relative to the Best Means of Lessening the Sum of Prostitution* (1809); and idem, *Reply to the Pamphlets Lately Published in Defence of the London Female Penitentiary: With Further Remarks Upon the Dangerous Tendency of That Institution* (1809).
79. Hale, *Address to the Public*, pp.22–3.   80. Ibid., pp.16, 28.   81. Ibid., p.28.

abandoned prostitution'.[82] The workhouse, he declared, was the proper place of resort for prostitutes wishing to leave the trade.[83] In one of the first replies to Hale, 'Juvenus' – after denouncing 'the baneful effects of luxury' – attempted to refute this idea.[84] He did so by emphasising the relatively elevated social origins of the 'typical' prostitute. This was not a new conception. Both Dingley and Fielding planned to set aside part of their asylums for those of more genteel education. What was new, however, was the degree to which almost a majority of the capital's prostitutes could now plausibly be portrayed in this light. The idea that the majority of London's prostitutes had been raised amidst the threadbare gentility of the down-at-heel middle classes had been gaining in popularity since the middle of the century. By the 1780s, commentators felt able to state with confidence that nine out of ten streetwalkers were the daughters of half-pay officers and poor clergymen.[85] Now 'Juvenus' could affirm his belief that a repenting prostitute was unlikely even to know how to gain admission to a workhouse. In the improbable event of her knowing the correct procedures and being admitted to this 'general receptacle of the miserable, the vicious, and the destitute, to whom could she unbosom her feelings, or the painful sense of her past errors?'[86]

To Hale's accusation that the Penitentiary's policy of only admitting prostitutes – rather than those at risk of becoming so – would serve to encourage women to enter prostitution knowing that the asylum was only open to those who had 'departed from every trace of modesty', 'Juvenus' asked if the opponents of the Penitentiary would have it open its doors to all pregnant women and out of place servants.[87] He further doubted whether knowledge of the Penitentiary's existence and policies would very much influence any woman's decision to embark or not on a career of prostitution.[88] Hale's charge that the Penitentiary would act as a pleasant retreat for prostitutes and leave them unpunished was met with the statement that it was both preferable and more effective to tempt such women toward virtue than coerce them from vice.[89] Although the legal power should continue its application of 'the rod of correction' – indeed might, by so doing, encourage more women to take up what 'Juvenus' admitted to be the numerous vacant places

---

82. Hale, *Address to the Public,* p.12.   83. Ibid., pp.7–9.
84. Juvenus [pseud.], *Cursory Remarks On a Recent Publication, Addressed to the Public, Upon the Dangerous Tendency of the London Female Penitentiary* (1809).
85. *The Times,* 10 Nov. 1785.   86. Juvenus, *Cursory Remarks,* pp.11–12.
87. Ibid., p.29.   88. Ibid., p.30.   89. Ibid., p.37.

within the asylum – it was no business of the Penitentiary either to enforce or remove penal statutes.[90] Besides which, he argued, a woman forced out of prostitution through fear of punishment had still to procure a means of livelihood and was liable to do so by criminal and fraudulent means.[91] One who voluntarily quit the streets through an awakening conscience, on the other hand, would re-enter the world with her principles so fortified and her sense of guilt so thoroughly excited by the teachings of the asylum that descent into her former habits of indolence and vice would be neither necessary nor comprehensible.

By the early nineteenth century, an image of the prostitute as the miserable, pitiable casualty of circumstance had achieved widespread currency. The earlier almost universal description of such women as 'vile harlots' and 'vicious streetwalking whores' lying in wait for unwary males had given way to a picture of abused womanhood, subject to the combined depredations of brothel keepers, clients and police. The change was perhaps most vividly expressed in the increasingly common labelling of prostitutes – both within and outside the circles of self-conscious philanthropic endeavour – as 'misfortunate' or 'unfortunate' women. The contexts within which this term appeared reveal that it was used not in reference to some particular mischance in the individual's life but rather as a means of identifying her as a prostitute. The poor law records of St. Martin Vintry in 1818, for example, described Elizabeth Lively – passed to the parish from a house of ill fame in Stoke Newington – as having been 'unfortunate' for the last two months. Of greater significance, perhaps, is the fact that from the middle years of the eighteenth century, a growing number of prostitutes accused of theft and other offences at the Old Bailey described themselves in the same way. On being asked how they earned their bread, they replied that they were 'misfortunate' or 'unfortunate' women.[92] Miserable ill fate had become almost the defining characteristic of the prostitute.

These changes, however, appeared gradually over many years and too-rigid and over-systematic structures can easily be imposed on what were in reality far looser and more pluralistic collections of ideas and images. If one of the defining characteristics of the

---

90. Ibid., p.42.   91. Ibid., pp.37–8.
92. See, for example *OBSP* 15 Sep. 1790, pp.867–8. According to Hale, 'there is not one instance in a hundred of a woman who becomes a prostitute in consequence of seduction, although it is their constant plea of defence': Hale, *Reply to the Pamphlets*, p.47.

prostitute came to be seen as suffering, then that of those who thought and wrote about prostitution might be eclecticism. The narrative of the 'fallen woman', ruined and then abandoned by a heartless seducer, for example, had centuries-old antecedents – especially in the Catholic countries of continental Europe. It was also in these countries, as the Evangelical Protestant founders of the Magdalen were uncomfortably aware, that the setting up of reformatories, wherein remorseful prostitutes might redeem themselves, had long been practised.

Conclusion

The two prevalent representations of prostitutes presented here were only rarely in direct conflict with each other. Many of the images employed were common to both and apparently contradictory ideas were expressed by many individuals and institutions – sometimes within a single text. This is strikingly evident, for example, in a poem published in 1805, entitled 'Lines for the grave of a prostitute, written by herself in her last illness', in which the poet laments the death of 'the willing victim of a quick decay . . . early seduc'd by men's perfidious snares'. She had fallen 'half-forc'd' on her seducer's bed, and from then until her early death ('the sure and sole asylum of my woes'), 'full seven long years of infamy I pin'd, and fondled, loath'd and prey'd upon mankind'.[93]

That the idea of the prostitute as victim did not simply replace the predatory image is evident from such a poem. The enduring importance of the condemnatory and punitive attitude towards prostitutes is further – and perhaps more powerfully – indicated by the late-eighteenth and early-nineteenth-century revival of 'reformation of manners' type campaigns.[94] Nevertheless, to see this as demonstrating the 'failure' of those who advocated the more self-consciously compassionate approach towards prostitutes is to misapprehend the nature of their 'success'. Not only did the penitential ideal lead to the creation of asylums across the country by the mid-nineteenth century, but the *language* of pity became the most acceptable means

93. *Annual Register*, Vol.47 (1805), pp.968–9.

94. J. Innes, 'Politics and morals: The Reformation of Manners movement in later eighteenth-century England', in E. Hellmuth (ed.), *The Transformation of Political Culture: England and Germany in the Late Eighteenth Century* (Oxford, 1990). For the early nineteenth century, see M.J.D. Roberts, 'The Society for the Suppression of Vice and its early critics', *Historical Journal*, 26 (1983).

of expression – even for those who supported more ruthless reformatory methods. None of these ideas developed in discursive isolation. It would be a mistake, however (despite the imagery's appropriation by prostitutes), to see them as directly reflecting, or having great influence upon, the changing experiences of prostitutes on the streets of London. Indeed, for the law-enforcing agencies (who helped shape those experiences), prostitution remained largely a problem of public order rather than spiritual damnation, and this, more than anything else, governed their actions in relation to the trade. Rather, such ideas developed out of – and, in turn, reshaped – the personal, religious and political concerns of those who saw in prostitution a threat to the well-being both of the individual and of society.

CHAPTER EIGHT

Conclusion

This book has examined three different aspects of female prostitution in eighteenth- and early-nineteenth-century London. The first of these has been the necessarily heavily empirical task of recovering and describing the nature and extent of the trade itself and the experiences of the women who entered into it. The second has been the laws governing the trade – whether on the streets or in the bawdy houses – and, at greater length, the relationship between those charged with implementing the laws and the streetwalkers and brothel keepers of the capital. Finally, the changing and, in many cases, enduring images of prostitution and prostitutes over this period have been analysed.

The nature and extent of the trade

An examination of the trade and its practitioners reveals few fundamental changes between the 1730s and 1830s. Throughout the period, the recruits to prostitution were largely drawn from the most impoverished sections of society. As such, they were unlikely to gain the opportunity to acquire the skills necessary for them to escape from poverty. Those that did enter a trade outside prostitution were for the most part concentrated within the lowest-paid and most insecure sections of the economy such as the clothing industry or domestic service. For many – perhaps the majority – of London's streetwalkers, prostitution was no more than one of a number of means of generating income. Time spent within the trade frequently alternated with, or was undertaken at the same time as, periods of 'respectable' employment, the reception of parish relief or private charity, and overtly criminal activity such as pickpocketing and theft from clients. In this putting together of an economy of makeshift they were far from unique: the construction of a viable income – whether in cash or in kind – from a variety of sources was a common practice among the urban poor of this period.

Despite the insistence of some commentators that London's street-walkers were 'a sacrifice to the metropolis offered by the thirty-nine counties',[1] prostitutes were neither more nor less likely to have been born outside the capital than any other of its inhabitants. Nor was child prostitution as widespread as many in authority believed. The majority of women arrested for various offences connected with prostitution, and whose ages were recorded, were in their late teens or early twenties. Against the repeated assertions of some members of the parliamentary Select Committees on the Police that brothels staffed entirely by infants were common, most police and judicial witnesses denied any knowledge of such establishments.

Central to the belief that child prostitution was rife was the idea that the trade was controlled by tyrannical bawds who dominated every aspect of their charges' lives. Yet the picture that has emerged is not one of a tightly organised traffic in helpless young women. Only a minority of prostitutes worked in brothels. Most of the women were independent of either pimp or bawd. They solicited for custom – frequently in pairs or small groups – on the streets and in the parks and public houses of the city before retiring with their clients to darkened corners of those same streets, to their own lodgings, or to rooms rented hourly in nearby bagnios, lodging houses and hotels.

While many areas of the city possessed above average concentrations both of such 'houses of resort' and, in consequence, of street-walking prostitutes, neither were confined – whether legally or in practice – to specific districts. There is some evidence to suggest that such 'red-light zones' may have been developing by the end of the period, in part through the activities of the various agencies of law-enforcement and in part because of the increasing attractions of some areas. Within the City, for example, 'houses of ill fame' became increasingly concentrated in a small number of wards, while the creation of the docks in the east and the expansion of entertainment centres in the West End and south of the Thames drew many prostitutes to those areas in search of custom. In general, however, the geographical expansion of prostitution mirrored that of the metropolis as a whole.

1. W. Hutton, *A Journey to London* (2nd edn. 1818), p.47.

Prostitutes were not, therefore, geographically separated from the mass of the city's population. Nor were they separated socially. They walked the same streets, drank in the same public houses and gin-shops, frequented the same parks, and in many cases lived in the same houses as Londoners of most, if not all, social classes. In many districts, prostitutes formed an important element in the local economy. It does not, of course, follow automatically from this that the presence of streetwalkers in a neighbourhood was acceptable to the area's other residents and there is no lack of evidence (from petitions to such momentous events as the bawdy house riots of 1749) pointing to a considerable degree of hostility to prostitutes. The 1749 riots arose, however, not from any aversion on the part of the seamen to the prostitutes' deviation from re-spectable sexual mores but rather because of alleged thefts by the inhabitants of one of the houses.[2] Our knowledge and understand-ing of the sexual morality, even the behaviour, of the greater part of the population in this period remain extremely limited. It would be a mistake to perceive it as no more than a confused reflection of middle- and upper-class convictions, acquired by some imperceptible osmotic process. Acceptance and toleration were almost certainly the more common attitudes.

Laws on prostitution and their enforcement

The second aspect covered by this book has involved an examina-tion of the laws concerning prostitution and their implementation – both against streetwalkers and the keepers of disorderly and bawdy houses. Three elements have proved central to this examination. Firstly, not until the very end of the period under discussion, in 1822, did the term 'prostitute' appear in the text of a public act. Prior to this, the women actively involved in the trade were legally subsumed under the general rubric of 'idle and disorderly persons' as employed in the various Vagrancy Acts current during the eight-eenth century, or were brought within the cognisance of the law via local Watch Acts and ward and parish regulations. There was little agreement among the authorities over whether, as John Fielding believed, prostitutes were 'scarce, if at all, within the description of

---

2. These riots saw crowds of enraged sailors and others attack several bawdy houses along the Strand on the nights of 1–2 July 1749.

any Statute now in being',[3] or, as the 1818 Police Committee report preferred, 'a greater degree of vigilance on the part of the watchmen . . . would operate as a more effectual check to it [i.e., prostitution], than any alteration of the existing laws'.[4]

The Police Committee's report points to the second important element – that is, that the law-enforcing agencies were not homogeneous blocks, united in purpose and ability. Rather they were divided both horizontally and vertically. Co-operation between parishes in questions of policing was minimal, that between the City of London and Westminster, or the City and Bridewell, almost non-existent. Within districts, justices of the peace, watch committees, constables and watchmen all had differing priorities. It was largely within the interstices of this 'system' that London's streetwalkers and brothel keepers were able to operate.

The final element in the question of the law and policing was perhaps the most significant of the three. It is that the implementation of the law at all levels, from watchmen to magistrates, was characterised by compromise, informality, and the making of decisions on a case-by-case basis. This was not unique to the policing of prostitution, being fundamental to the law's dealings with all types of petty offending.[5] It may, however, have been even more prevalent in the case of prostitution. As streetwalking was a 'victimless crime', the decision to initiate legal proceedings of any sort lay not with any aggrieved victim but largely with the officers of the parish, ward or City watch. As has been seen, each of these possessed myriad reasons for the exercise of discretion and flexibility in their dealings with London's prostitutes. That remained true – although to a diminishing extent – as one proceeded up through the judicial process, each step carrying with it the possibility of any one of a large number of outcomes.

It is as well at this point, however, to caution against the attribution of too roseate a glow to this portrayal of the legal process. Certainly, the nature of prostitutes' work brought the women into daily contact with the law and its agents. They were unlikely, therefore, to stand very much in awe of its mysteries. (By contrast, it is

---

3. *P.P.* (1812), Vol.II. Police Committee, II, Appendix 8, quoting the testimony of Sir John Fielding to the 1770 Select Committee to Enquire into the Several Burglaries and Robberies that of late have been committed in and about the Cities of London and Westminster.

4. *P.P.* (1818), Vol.VIII, Police Committee, 3rd report, p.30.

5. See R.B. Shoemaker, *Prosecution and Punishment: Petty Crime and the Law in London and Rural Middlesex, c.1660–1725* (Cambridge, 1991), especially pp.311–19.

probable that many of the prostitutes' social superiors saw the law as being designed for their own protection and were therefore liable to be the more alarmed if they found themselves on the wrong side of it.) To acknowledge these complexities, and to suggest that prostitutes were far from powerless in their dealings with the policing system, is not, however, to subscribe to the view that the law was a neutral tool, as easily wielded by a prostitute as by any other.

Streetwalkers, along with others of the poor to whom the streets and squares of the city were a place of work, were subject to occasional acts of violence – and routine harassment – by officers of the watch. Prostitutes' frequent evasions of the law may have been successful, but they were necessary precisely because the law's weight so often pressed upon them. Similarly, although by far the most likely outcome of any legal proceeding against a woman for streetwalking was her discharge, for those few sentenced to – albeit brief – terms of imprisonment, notions of flexibility, discretion and 'dispersed centres of power' would have appeared strange indeed. Against the examples of women like Katherine Green and Mary Forbes who, as already noted, informed the Roundhouse-keeper of St. James that 'they would do as they please . . . in spite of the watchman',[6] must be set such as Isabella Wright, who was committed to the Bridewell on 23 April 1800 as 'an idle and disorderly person and a common prostitute'. Two weeks later, she was discovered dead, having hanged herself from the bars on the window of her cell.[7]

The fate of Isabella Wright would have provided useful ammunition to those involved in the debates on prostitution which flourished at various times throughout the eighteenth and early nineteenth centuries, and which have been the third aspect of the trade to be discussed.

Debates on prostitution

These debates were at best intermittent, with individual views being canvassed which often had little or no direct connection with each other. Indeed, to characterise some of the commentaries as debates at all is, perhaps, questionable. Nevertheless, it is possible to see

6. WCA D2105 Charge Book of the Parish of St. James, Piccadilly, entry 25 Apr. 1774.
7. CLRO 441B Coroners' Inquests, Prisons: Bridewell Hospital (House of Correction), 1800–38, Bundle 1, Inquisition Taken the 12th Day of May 1800 on Isabella Wright.

'sides' being taken, lines of descent of a particular argument appearing, the dominance or the temporary defeat of one or another set of ideas being established.

In the 1730s, the assumption that had largely governed the practice of the Societies for the Reformation of Manners (that is, that prostitutes were distinguishable from the mass of potentially lewd women only by the greater magnitude of their immorality) began to be questioned. The idea that prostitutes were driven by sexual desire was largely, though never entirely, supplanted by the belief that such women were on the streets through economic necessity – the appetite for food rather than fornication. That they had 'fallen' through their own weakness remained axiomatic, as did the conviction that their continuing as prostitutes was deeply sinful and a crime against God. But the belief now held by many commentators, that the women were frequently unwilling victims of circumstance, led to the rethinking of the means by which to end their dependence on vice. If women were prostitutes, and hence sinful, only reluctantly (indeed, if in their hearts they retained a vestige of purity), then forgiveness was the most appropriate emotional response. If prostitutes remained in the trade in order to feed, clothe and shelter themselves, then they must be enabled to subsist by more acceptable methods. An aptitude for industry, as well as an acceptance of guilt, would bring them closer to God, respectability, and useful labour.

For the founders and promoters of the Magdalen Hospital in the 1750s and the London Female Penitentiary in the 1800s, it was essential that the women be presented as possessed of as little control over, and hence responsibility for, their situations as possible. Such institutions were designed both to confer training in the domestic skills and to effect a spiritual and practical rite of passage. On leaving, achieved by returning to her family or being placed in service, the penitent would be defined by the recovery of her character – both in the sense of having attained a moral resurrection and, more tangibly, through the possession of a written reference acceptable to any future employer.

The institutions themselves, though, had little direct effect on the lives of London's prostitutes. The numbers of prostitutes entering them were relatively small and the Magdalen besides concentrated its efforts on those who were 'at risk' of entering the trade. Their importance for the historian lies more in their being seen as concrete manifestations of the new way of thinking about prostitution and its practitioners.

Prostitutes were increasingly seen as a distinct social group, willing but unable to reform themselves, not the deliberate propagators of vice, but its first victims. Many prostitutes made use of this image, employing its terminology and narratives of seduction and despair in the courts and elsewhere. Although such narratives were not new – indeed they had been common in continental Europe for many centuries – it was the fact that they were now a *significant* element in the discourse about prostitution in England that allowed prostitutes to use them, occasionally to good effect.

For women who were not prostitutes, the effects of these changes are almost impossible to assess. The author of one article on the subject has concluded that the ideological detachment of prostitutes from other women was largely beneficial to both groups; the former because to be no longer condemned outright must have represented some sort of improvement, the latter because it resulted in a loosening of the moral requirements surrounding most women's sexuality since they were no longer 'branded with the automatic suspicion of whoredom'.[8] Attractive as such an argument is in many ways, it is mistaken. By effectively denying to prostitutes the attributes of agency – that is, by declaring them helpless victims of circumstance – and by this means rendering them harmless and thus forgivable, it was implied that other women who offended against sexual morality *by choice* were consequently *unforgivable*. The limits of acceptable sexual practice for the majority of women were thus reinforced, not weakened, by the apparent bestowal of pity and forgiveness on prostitutes.

8. R. Trumbach, 'Modern prostitution and gender in *Fanny Hill*', in G.S. Rousseau and R. Porter (eds.), *Sexual Underworlds of the Enlightenment* (Manchester, 1987), p.82.

Bibliography

The bibliography is arranged as follows:

Primary sources
Manuscript sources:
(a) British Library
(b) Corporation of London Record Office
(c) Guildhall Muniments Room
(d) Westminster City Archives
Printed sources:
(a) Official publications
(b) Newspapers and periodicals
(c) Other contemporary published works

Further reading (secondary sources)
Place of publication is London, unless otherwise stated.

Primary sources

MANUSCRIPT SOURCES

(a) British Library
Add.Mss.27825, Place Papers.

(b) Corporation of London Record Office
204B Guildhall Justice Room Minute Books of Proceedings, 1752–96 (55 vols., broken series).
255E SC1/8 (Southwark Compter) Commitments for Trial at the Sessions, Jul. 1814–Oct. 1842.
242A Book of Summaries of Ward Presentments, 1680–1845.
242–246 A–E Ward Presentments, 1668–present date.
441B Coroners' Inquests, Prisons: Bridewell Hospital (House of Correction), 1800–38.

562A Report Books on the State of the Watch and the Wages of the Watchmen: Daily Reports, 1806–12 (6 vols.).

Mss.113.1 Returns of the Wards to the Committee re. Prostitutes of their Systems of Watchmen and Patroles, 1818.

Misc.Mss 245.4 Miscellaneous Papers re. Serjeants at Mace, Marshalmen, Beadles, etc., 1810–23.

Misc.Mss 245.5 Special Committee in Relation to the Police and Nightly Watch: Rough Minutes, Papers and Returns, 1816–17.

Misc.Mss 283.4 Committee Papers, 1814–25 (Committee Appointed 16 Dec. 1813 to Consider Petition of Inhabitant Householders).

Southwark Box 13.1, Oct. 1814–Oct. 1842: 223–4 F Calendars of Prisoners for Trial at the Quarter Sessions and Prisoners upon Orders.

Petition Rolls.

P.A.R. Book 4, p.111: Abstract of Returns of the Nightly Watch, with Minutes of Evidence taken before the Sub-Committee Appointed in Relation to the Nightly Watch, 1827.

(c) Guildhall Muniments Room

Ms.1163a Aldgate Ward Wardmote Inquest: Minutes, 1758–1804.

Ms.51/1–7 Billingsgate Ward Wardmote Court: Minutes, 1809–82.

Ms.1428/1 Bishopsgate Ward Wardmote Court: Minutes, 1737–1839.

Ms.3461/3 Bridge Ward Within Ward Wardmote Inquest: Minutes, 1689–1747.

Ms.1229/1–2 Broad Street Ward Wardmote Court: Minutes, 1780–1831.

Ms.3462 Cheap Ward Common Council: Minutes, 1789–1821.

Ms.60 Cheap Ward Wardmote Court and Inquest: Minutes, 1701–1829.

Ms.4458/2 Coleman Street Ward Wardmote Court and St. Stephen Coleman Street Parish Vestry: Minutes, 1726–49.

Ms.8634 Cordwainer Ward Wardmote Court: Minutes, 1812–1907.

Ms.4069/2–4 Cornhill Ward Wardmote Court and Inquest: Minutes, 1652–1833.

Ms.1563/1 Cripplegate Within Ward Wardmote Inquest: Minutes, 1827–50.

Ms.1276/1 Dowgate Ward Wardmote Court: Minutes, 1806–50.

Ms.3039 Farringdon Within Ward Wardmote Court: Minutes, 1806–63.

Ms.3037/1–2 Farringdon Within Ward Wardmote Inquest: Minutes, 1779–1841.

Ms.6610/3–4 Farringdon Without Ward Inquest: Presentments, 1702 and 1716.

Ms.3018/1–2 Farringdon Without Ward Parish or Precinct of St. Dunstan in the West Wardmote Inquest: Minutes, 1558–1870.

Ms.1322 Farringdon Without Ward Precinct of St. Martin Ludgate Wardmote Inquest: Minutes, 1808–56.

Ms. 3189 Farringdon Without Ward Parish of St. Sepulchre, Vestry Committee Appointed to Enquire into the Most Efficient Means of Removing Brothels, Disorderly Houses, which Exist in this Parish: Minutes, 28 June 1825–20 October 1826.

Ms.461 Langbourn Ward Fenchurch Street Watchhouse: Minute Book, 1817.

Ms.1169/1–2 Lime Street Ward Wardmote Court and Inquest: Minutes, 1664–1866.

Ms.2649/1–2 Portsoken Ward Wardmote Inquest: Minutes, 1684–1840.

Ms.2843/1 Vintry Ward Wardmote Court: Minutes and Verdicts, 1778–1832.

Ms.463/1 Walbrook Ward Wardmote Inquest: Minutes, 1731–1834.

Ms.466 Memorial of the Alderman, Deputy, Common Council and other Inhabitants of the Ward of Walbrook to the Honorable the Commissioners of Sewers etc. for the City of London, undated (early 19th century).

Ms.4151 St. Andrew Undershaft: Deeds relating to parish property in the church, 114–116 etc., Bundle 1, 1693–1837.

(d) Westminster City Archives
WCA Print Collection.

Liberty of the Rolls
K387 (1) Constable's, Beadle's and Patroles' Nightly Reports, 17 Nov. 1812–7 Mar. 1815; (2) Charges in the Watchhouse, 24 Feb. 1815–24 Oct. 1815; (3) Table of Watchmen's Beats and Dates, Nov. 1815–Mar. 1817.

K388 Directors' and Governors' of the Nightly Watch and Beadles' Minutes, 17 Oct. 1810–9 Sep. 1829.

St. Anne, Soho
A2282–A2287 Records of Petty Sessions held in the Vestry Rooms Touching the Affairs of the Parish of St. Anne, 1749–92.

A2052a Minutes of the Committee of Evening Patrol and Names of Subscribers thereto, November 1792–March 1793.

A2054e/3 Warrant against William Marshall for keeping a disorderly house in the parish, 1 Apr. 1800.

A2054e/4 Warrant against Sarah Gusty for keeping a disorderly house in the parish, 6 Jul. 1804.

A2053 Minute book of the Committee for Regulating the Nightly Watch and Beadles, 6 Jun. 1803–1 Apr. 1819.

St. Clement Danes

B1066–B1070 Petty Sessions plus Vestry, 1740–67.

B1292 (1) Governors' of the Nightly Watch and Beadles' Minutes 7 Nov. 1768–11 Jul. 1785; (2) Summaries of the Duties of the Watch under the Acts of 1764 and 1774.

St. James, Piccadilly

D2075 Rules, Orders and Regulations for the Better Management of the Nightly Watch and Beadles in the Parish, including stands, no. of watch boxes, beats. 1796. Printed with Ms.additions.

D2092–D2096 Beadles' Reports on Activities during Night Patrols with the Constable and at the Watch Houses, 1739–42, 1749–52, 1773–8, 1815–19, 1819–23.

D2099 and D2102 Report Books of the Captain of the Watch Patrols, 2 Nov. 1819–17 Jan. 1824.

D2105–D2108 Charge Books of the Parish of St. James, Piccadilly, 1773–9.

D2116–D2123 Charge Books of the Parish of St. James, Piccadilly, 1821–6.

St. Margaret and St. John (combined parish for civil purposes)

E2643, E2645 and E1932 Minutes of the Vestry of St. Margaret and St. John the Evangelist Relating to the Watch, 1736–79 (broken series).

E2648–E2649 Minutes of the Proceedings of the Committee of the Watch of the Vestry of St. Margaret and St. John the Evangelist, 1791–1822.

E3045–E3051 St. Margaret's Beadles' Report Books, 1774–97.

E3052–E3055 Patrole Watchmen's Report Books for the Whole of the United Parish, 1777–82.

E3074 Constables' Charge Book, Jul. 1793–Nov. 1794.

E3754 Minutes of the Committee Appointed to Place the Watchmen of St. Margarets, 1736.

St. Martin in the Fields

F2028 Vestry and Watch Committee Minutes, 3 May 1736–6 Aug. 1754.

F2280 Draft Vestry and Watch Committee Minutes, 16 Apr. 1778–4 Nov. 1785.

F2282 Draft Vestry and Watch Committee Minutes, 14 Nov. 1785–14 Feb. 1793.

St. Mary le Strand
G1044 Watch Trustees' Minutes, 29 Jun. 1774–1 Oct. 1829.

St. Paul, Covent Garden
H889–H890 Watch Trustees' Minutes, 1794–1829.

H891 (1) Minutes of Vestry Meetings to Consider the Watch, 1757–91; (2) Watch Trustees' or Commissioners' Minutes, 1791–4.

PRINTED SOURCES

(a) Official publications

Statutes of the Realm

Commons Journals (1770), Vol.XXXII, Report from the Select Committee to Enquire into the Several Burglaries and Robberies that of Late have been Committed in and about the Cities of London and Westminster, 878.

Commons Journals (1772), Vol.XXXIII, Report from the Select Committee to Enquire into the State of the Nightly Watch within the City and Liberty of Westminster, 759.

P.P. (1810–11), Vol.IV, Two Reports from the Select Committee on the Laws Relating to Penitentiary Houses, 569 and 691.

P.P. (1812), Vol.II, Report from the Select Committee on the Nightly Watch and Police of the Metropolis, 95.

P.P. (1814–15), Vol.III, Minutes of the Evidence taken before the Select Committee to Enquire into the State of Mendicity and Vagrancy in the Metropolis and its Neighbourhood, 23.

P.P. (1813–14), Vol.IV, Report from the Select Committee to Inquire into the State of the Gaol of Newgate and the Poultry, Giltspur-street, Ludgate and Borough Compters, 249.

P.P. (1814–15), Vol.IV, Report from the Select Committee on the King's Bench, Fleet and Marshalsea Prisons, etc., 533.

P.P. (1816), Vol.V, Report from the Select Committee on the State of Police of the Metropolis, 1.

P.P. (1817), Vol.VII, First Report from the Select Committee on the State of Police of the Metropolis, 1.

P.P. (1817), Vol.VII, Second Report from the Select Committee on the State of Police of the Metropolis, 321.

P.P. (1818), Vol.VIII, Third Report from the Select Committee on the State of Police of the Metropolis, 1.

P.P. (1818), Vol.VIII, First Report from the Select Committee on the Prisons within the City of London and Borough of Southwark, 297.

P.P. (1818), Vol.VIII, Second Report from the Select Committee on the Prisons within the City of London and Borough of Southwark, 545.

P.P. (1819), Vol.XI, Report from the Commissioners Appointed to Inquire into the State, Conduct, and Management of the Prison and Gaol of the Court of His Majesty's Palace at Westminster; and of the Court of Marshalsea of His Majesty's honourable Household; and of the Prisoners in the said Respective Prisons Confined, 325.

P.P. (1821), Vol.IV, Report from the Select Committee on the Existing Laws Relating to Vagrants, 121.

P.P. (1822), Vol.IV, Report from the Select Committee on the State of Police of the Metropolis, 91.

P.P. (1823), Vol.IV, Report from the Select Committee Appointed to Consider the Means of Improving and Maintaining the Foreign Trade of the Country: West India Docks, 489.

P.P. (1828), Vol.VI, Report from the Select Committee on the State of Police of the Metropolis, 1.

(b) Newspapers and periodicals

Annual Register
The Gentleman's Magazine.
The London Magazine.
The Proceedings on the King's Commission of the Peace, Oyer and Terminer, and Gaol Delivery for the City of London: And also the Gaol Delivery for the County of Middlesex, held at Justice-Hall in the Old Bailey.
(Known during the eighteenth century as *The Old Bailey Sessions Papers*, abbreviated here as *OBSP.*)
The Rambler, in W.J. Bate and A.B. Strauss (eds.), *The Yale Edition of the Works of Samuel Johnson* (New Haven and London, 1969).
The Times.
SL 71/061 Guildhall Printed Books Department Collection of Newspaper Cuttings relating to the City of London, 1771–1830.

(c) Other contemporary published works
Anon., *Antimoixeia: Or, the Honest and Joynt Design of the Tower Hamblets for the General Suppression of Bawdy Houses, as Encouraged by the Publick Magistrates* (1691).

Anon., *God's Judgement Against Whoring: Being an Essay Towards a General History of it* (1697).

Anon., *An Account of the Societies for the Reformation of Manners in England and Ireland: With a Persuasive to Persons of All Ranks to be Zealous and Diligent in Promoting the Execution of the Laws Against Prophaneness and Debauchery* (1701).

Anon., *Discourse of Suppressing Vice, and Reforming the Vicious . . . By a Minister of the Church of Scotland* (1702).

Anon., *Some Considerations upon Streetwalkers. With a Proposal for Lessening the Present Number of Them, in Two Letters to a Member of Parliament: to Which is Added a Letter from One of Those Unhappy Persons, when in Newgate, and Who was Afterwards Executed for Picking a Gentleman's Pocket, to Mrs.—— in Great P—ney Street* (c.1735).

Anon., *The Humours of Fleet-Street, Covent-Garden and the Strand: Being the Lives and Adventures of the Most Noted Ladies of Pleasure, By An Old Sportsman* (c.1745).

Anon., *Reflections Arising from the Immorality of the Present Age* (1756).

Anon., *The Histories of Some of the Penitents in the Magdalen House, as Supposed to be Related by Themselves* (2 vols., 1760).

Anon., *Low Life: Or One Half of the World Knows Not How the Other Half Lives, Being a Critical Account of What is Transacted . . . in the Twenty-Four Hours Between Saturday Night and Monday-Morning as it is Usually Spent within the Bills of Mortality* (3rd edition, 1764).

Anon., *The Complete Parish Officer* (1772).

Anon., *An Account of the Proceedings of the Governors of the Lock-Hospital, near Hyde-Park-Corner* (1792).

Anon., *An Account of the Institution of the Lock Asylum for the Reception of Penitent Female Patients when Discharged Cured from the Lock Hospital* (1792)

Anon., *The Evils of Adultery and Prostitution: With an Enquiry into the Causes of their Present Alarming Increase, and Some Means Recommended for Checking their Progress* (1792).

Anon., *Thoughts on the Means of Alleviating the Miseries Attendant upon Common Prostitution* (1799).

Anon., *An Address to the Benevolent Public in Behalf of the London Female Penitentiary* (1807).

Anon., *Letter to the Right Rev. the Lord Bishop of London: Containing a Statement of the Immoral and Disgraceful Scenes which are Every Evening Exhibited in the Public Streets by Crowds of Half-Naked and Unfortunate Prostitutes . . . by a Citizen* (1808).

W. Blair, *Prostitutes Reclaimed and Penitents Protected: Being an Answer to Some Objections Against the Female Penitentiary* (1809).

W. Blair, *Strictures on Mr. Hale's Reply to the Pamphlets Lately Published in Defence of the London Penitentiary* (1809).

W. Blair, *The Pastor and Deacon Examined: Or, Candid Remarks on the Rev. John Thomas's Appeal in Vindication of Mr. William Hale's Character, and in Opposition to the Female Penitentiaries, to which are added a Critique on Mr. Hale's Reply and Five Letters in Confutation of his New Objections* (1810).

T. Bray, *The Tryals of Jeremy Tooley, William Arch and John Clauson, Three Private Soldiers, for the Murder of Mr John Dent, Constable, in the Parish of St. Paul's Covent Garden, March 18 1708–9* (1732).

R. Burn, *The Justice of the Peace and Parish Officer,* (2nd edn., 1756; 18th edn. 1797; 28th edn., 1837).

R. Challoner, *Proposals for Opening a Subscription in Favour of an Asylum to Receive Poor Young Maids, Destitute of Places, for Preserving their Virtue and Innocence, 'till Proper Places can be Procured for Them* (c.1770).

P. Colquhoun, *Observations and Facts Relative to Licensed Ale-Houses in the City of London and its Environs* (1794).

P. Colquhoun, *A Treatise on the Police of the Metropolis: Containing a Detail of the Various Crimes and Misdemeanors By which Public and Private Property and Security are, at Present, Injured and Endangered: And Suggesting Remedies for their Prevention* (1796).

Corporation of the City of London, *The Report of the Committee Appointed to Consider the Petition of Sundry Inhabitant Householders of the Principal Streets of this City, Relative to Common Prostitutes Infesting the Same* (1814).

Corporation of the City of London, *The Report of the Committee to Consider the Petition of the Inhabitants of this City Relative to Prostitutes Frequenting the Public Streets . . . Particularly attending the Important Business of Removing all Houses of Ill-Fame* (1814).

Corporation of the City of London, *The Report of the Committee Appointed . . . to Examine the Allegations contained in the Petition of Sundry . . . Householders . . . Relative to Common Prostitutes Frequenting the Public Streets* (1816).

Corporation of the City of London, *The Report [from the Committee Appointed to Examine the Allegations contained in the Petition of Householders Relative to Common Prostitutes Frequenting the Public Streets] Relative to the Numerous Shops for the Sale of Spiritous Liquors within the City* (1817).

M. Dalton, *The Countrey Justice, Containing the Practice of the Justices of the Peace out of their Sessions: Gathered for the Better Help of Such Justices of Peace as Have Not Been Much Conversant in the Studie of the Lawes of this Realm* (1635).

C. de Saussure, *A Foreign View of England in the Reigns of George I and George II* (translated and edited by Mme. van Muyden, 1902).

R. Dingley, *Proposals for Establishing a Public Place of Reception for Penitent Prostitutes* (1758).

J. Disney, *An Address to Grand Juries, Constables and Church-wardens: Representing their Power in the Repression of Vice and Prophaneness and the Obligation that Lies upon them from their Oaths thereto* (1710).

J. Disney, *A Second Essay Upon the Execution of the Laws against Immorality and Prophaneness* (2nd. edn. enlarged, 1710).

J. Disney, *Fleshly Lusts Inconsistent with the Character and Safety of a Christian* (1722).

J. Disney, *A View of Ancient Laws against Immorality and Prophaneness* (1729).

W. Dodd, *An Account of the Rise, Progress and Present State of the Magdalen Charity* (1761).

J. Edgar, DD, *Female Virtue – Its Enemies and Friends: A Discourse on the Statistics, Evils and Cure of Prostitution* (1841).

J. Evans, *General Redemption the Only Proper Basis of General Benevolence: A Letter Addressed to Robert Hawker . . . suggested by his Defence of the London Female Penitentiary* (1809).

H. Fielding, *A Charge Delivered to the Grand Jury, at the Sessions of the Peace held for the City and Liberty of Westminster* (1749).

H. Fielding, *A True State of the Case of Bosavern Penlez, Who Suffered on Account of the Late Riot in the Strand* (1749).

J. Fielding, *An Account of the Origin and Effect of the Police* (1758).

J. Fielding, *A Plan for a Preservatory and Reformatory for the Benefit of Deserted Girls and Penitent Prostitutes* (1758).

J. Fielding, *Extracts from Such of the Penal Laws, as Particularly Relate to the Peace and Good Order of this Metropolis: With Observations for the Better Execution of Some, and on the Defects of Others* (1768).

E. Fowler, *A Vindication of an Undertaking of Certain Gentlemen, In order to the Suppressing of Debauchery and Prophaneness* (1692).

J. Gay, *Trivia: Or, the Art of Walking the Streets of London* (1716), in V.A. Dearing (ed.), *John Gay: Poetry and Prose* (Oxford, 1974), Vol.1.

P.J. Grosley (trans. Thomas Nugent), *A Tour to London: Or, New Observations on England, and its Inhabitants* (2 vols., 1772).

W. Hale, *Address to the Public on the Dangerous Tendency of the London Female Penitentiary: With Hints Relative to the Best Means of Lessening the Sum of Prostitution* (1809).

W. Hale, *Reply to the Pamphlets Lately Published in Defence of the London Female Penitentiary: With Further Remarks Upon the Dangerous Tendency of that Institution* (1809).

J. Hanway, *Letter V to Robert Dingley, Esq: Being a Proposal for the Relief and Employment of Friendless Girls and Repenting Prostitutes* (1758).

J. Hanway, *A Plan for Establishing a Charity-House, for the Reception of Repenting Prostitutes, to be called the Magdalen Charity* (1758).

J. Hanway, *Thoughts on the Plan for a Magdalen House* (1758).

J. Hanway, *Letters Written Occasionally on the Customs of Foreign Nations in Regard to Harlots, the Lawless Commerce of the Sexes, the Repentance of Prostitutes, the Great Humanity and Beneficial Effects of Magdalen Charity in London, and the Absurd Notions of the Methodists* (1761).

J. Hanway, *The Defects of Police the Cause of Immorality, and the Continual Robberies Committed: Particularly in and about the Metropolis* (1775).

J. or B. Harris (attrib.), *Harris's List of Covent-Garden Ladies: Or, New Atlantis for the Year 1764* (1764).

A. Highmore, *Pietas Londinensis: The History, Design, and Present State of the Various Public Charities in and near London* (1810).

G. Hodson, *The Remonstrant: Being a Letter to Mr. William Hale in Reply to His Address to the Publick upon the Injurious Tendency of the London Female Penitentiary* (1809).

C. Horne, *Serious Thoughts on the Miseries of Seduction and Prostitution, with a Full Account of the Evils that Produce them: Plainly Showing Prostitution to be Contrary to the Laws of Nature, And a Method Pointed Out, Whereby These Two Dreadful Evils May be Totally Exterminated, Fairly Deduced from the Laws of God and Nature* (1783).

W. Hutton, *A Journey to London: Comprising a Description of the Most Interesting Objects of Curiosity to a Visitor of the Metropolis* (2nd edn., 1818).

Juvenus (pseud.), *Cursory Remarks on a Recent Publication, Addressed to the Public, upon the Dangerous Tendency of the London Female Penitentiary* (1809).

S. Leigh, *New Picture of London* (1823).

M. Ludovicus (pseud.), *A Particular but Melancholy Account of the Great Hardships, Difficulties and Miseries, that those Unhappy and Much-to-be-Pitied Creatures, the Common Women of the Town, are plunged into at this Juncture* (1752).

M. Madan, *An Account of the Triumphant Death of F.S., a Converted Prostitute, who Died Apr. 1763, Aged Twenty-Six Years* (1763).

M. Madan, *Thelyphthora: Or, a Treatise on Female Ruin, in its Causes, Effects, Consequences, Prevention, and Remedy* (3 vols., 1780–1).

B. Mandeville, *The Fable of the Bees* (1714).

B. Mandeville, *A Modest Defence of Public Stews: Or, An Essay Upon Whoring, As it is Now Practis'd in these Kingdoms* (1724).

A. Morton [pseud. for Daniel Defoe], *Every-Body's Business is No-Body's Business: or Private Abuses, Public Grievances: Exemplified in the Pride, Insolence, and Exorbitant Wages of our Women Servants, Footmen, etc.* (1725).

R. Nelson, *An Address to Persons of Quality and Estate* (1715).

W. Nelson, *The Office and Authority of a Justice of the Peace* (1718).

T. Penant, *Some Account of London: The Fifth Edition, with Considerable Additions* (1813).

J. Popham, *Reports and Cases Collected by the Learned Sir John Popham* (1656).

Father Poussin, *Pretty Doings in a Protestant Nation: Being a View of the Present State of Fornication, Whorecraft, and Adultery, in Great Britain, and the Territories and Dependencies thereunto belonging* (1734).

Robert, Lord Raymond, *Reports of Cases Argued and Adjudged in the Courts of King's Bench and Common Pleas* (4 vols., 4th edn., 1792).

M. Ryan, *Prostitution in London, with a Comparative View of Paris and New York* (1839).

J. Shaw, *Parish Law: Or, a Guide to Justices of the Peace, Ministers, Church-wardens, Overseers of the Poor, Constables, Surveyors of the Highways, Vestry-Clerks, and all Others Concern'd in Parish Business* (1750).

W. Shrubsole, *A Defence of the London Female Penitentiary in Reply to the Charge of 'Dangerous Tendency', Brought against it by Mr. William Hale* (1809).

A. Smith, *An Inquiry into the Nature and Causes of the Wealth of Nations* (1776).

J. Thomas, *An Appeal to the Public: Or, a Vindication of the Character of Mr. William Hale from the Calumnious Aspersions of the Reviewer in the Evangelical Magazine; With a Candid Statement of Objections Against the London Female Penitentiary* (1809).

W. Von Archenholz, *A Picture of England: Containing a Description of the Laws, Customs and Manners of England* (1797).

S. Welch, *A Proposal to Render Effectual a Plan, to Remove the Nuisance of Common Prostitution from the Streets of the Metropolis* (1758).

F.A. Wenderborn, *A View of England towards the Close of the Eighteenth Century* (2 vols., 1791).

J. Woodward, *Sodom's Vices Destructive of Other Cities and States* (1697).

J. Woodward, *An Account of the Progress of the Reformation of Manners, in England and Ireland, and other Parts of the World . . . To which is Added, The Special Obligations of Magistrates to be Diligent in the Execution of the Penal-Laws against Prophaness and Debauchery, for the Effecting a National Reformation* (1701).

J. Woodward, *Young Man's Monitor* (1706).

Further reading

This book derives from my doctoral thesis and as such is very largely based upon primary sources. This bibliography highlights some of the numerous secondary works which I found most valuable. A word of caution: many of the following books and articles could have been placed with ease in all of the categories into which the bibliography has been divided, others with difficulty into any. Some of the categorisations may, therefore, appear somewhat arbitrary and I advise any reader seeking further reading on a particular topic to peruse the entire bibliography rather than rely wholly on my judgement as to the central concern of any one text.

SOCIETY, WORK AND THE URBAN EXPERIENCE

Excellent, general introductions to the social history of the period can be found in P. Langford, *A Polite and Commercial People: England 1727–83* (1989), R. Porter, *English Society in the Eighteenth Century* (1982) and L. Stone, *The Family, Sex and Marriage in England, 1500–1800* (1977).

In the course of researching and writing this book, I became fascinated by the ways in which policemen, prostitutes and pedestrians manoeuvred for control of London's streets. Of the many theoretical studies of the uses of urban space, I found S. Anderson (ed.), *On Streets* (1978) and B.B. Greenbie, *Spaces: Dimensions of the Human Landscape* (New Haven, 1981) the most stimulating. Two studies which explicitly theorise the eighteenth-century public space are P. Borsay, 'The rise of the promenade: the social and cultural use of space in the English provincial town, c.1660–1800', *British Journal for Eighteenth-Century Studies*, 9 (1986) and P.J. Corfield, 'Walking the city streets: the urban odyssey in eighteenth-century England', *Journal of Urban History*, 16, 2 (1990).

While P.J. Corfield, *The Impact of English Towns, 1700–1800* (1982) offers an invaluable overview of English urban life, the best single study of London in this period remains the exceptional M.D. George, *London Life in the Eighteenth Century* (1925). Other useful works include G.E. Mingay, *Georgian London* (1975) and H. Phillips, *Mid-Georgian London: A Topographical and Social Survey of Central and Western London about 1750* (1964). For the difficult relationship between the Londons south and north of the Thames, see D.J. Johnson, *Southwark and the City* (1969). G.M. Still, 'Rogues, strumpets and vagabonds: Defoe on crime in the City', *Eighteenth-Century Life*, 2, 4

(1976) discusses one writer's view of London's 'undeserving poor', while for another's, see the marvellous F.A. Pottle (ed.), *Boswell's London Journal, 1762–3* (New Haven, 1950). P. Clark, *The English Alehouse: A Social History, 1200–1830* (1983) examines the establishments within which many of Boswell's more louche experiences occurred.
No historian of London can afford to be without R. Hyde (ed.), *The A to Z of Georgian London* (1982); P. Laxton and J. Wisdom (eds.), *The A to Z of Regency London* (1985) and B. Weinreb and C. Webb (eds.), *The London Encyclopaedia* (1983).
Many of the above titles, particularly M.D. George, *London Life in the Eighteenth Century* (1925), examine the world of work. Other useful studies include P. Earle, 'The female labour market in London in the late seventeenth and early eighteenth centuries', *Economic History Review*, 2nd ser., 42, 3 (1989); D.A. Kent, 'Ubiquitous but invisible: female domestic servants in mid-eighteenth-century London', *History Workshop Journal*, 28 (1989); I. Pinchbeck, *Women Workers in the Industrial Revolution* (1930) and J.S. Taylor, *Poverty, Migration and Settlement in the Industrial Revolution* (Palo Alto, Calif., 1989).

THE LAW, POLICING AND CRIMINALITY

It sometimes seemed that the hardest part of researching this book lay in trying to make sense of the labyrinthine structures and procedures of the English legal system in this period. That I was able to make any progress at all is largely due to the following studies: S. Amos, *A Comparative Survey of the Laws in Force for the Prohibiting, Regulation, and Licensing of Vice in England and Other Countries* (1877); J.H. Baker, 'Criminal courts and procedure at common law, 1550–1800', in J.S. Cockburn (ed.), *Crime in England, 1550–1800* (1977); J.M. Beattie, *Crime and the Courts in England, 1660–1800* (1986); T.R. Forbes, 'A Study of Old Bailey sentences between 1729 and 1800', *Guildhall Studies in London History*, 5, 1 (1981); J.H. Langbein, 'Criminal trial before the Lawyers', *University of Chicago Law Review*, 45 (1983); J.H. Langbein, 'Shaping the eighteenth-century criminal trial: a view from the Ryder sources', *University of Chicago Law Review*, 50 (1983); R.H. Spearman, *The Common and Statute Law Relating to Highways in England and North Wales* (1881); S. & B. Webb, *English Local Government: the Manor and the Borough, I* (1924); J. Innes, 'Prisons for the poor: English Bridewells, 1555–1800', in F. Snyder and D. Hay (eds.), *Labour, Law and Crime: An Historical*

Perspective (1987); S. & B. Webb, *English Prisons under Local Government* (1922) and the absolutely essential L. Radzinowicz, *A History of English Criminal Law and its Administration from 1750, Vol.II* (1956). For the scarcely less complicated church courts, see J.A. Brundage, 'Prostitution in the medieval canon law', *Signs: Journal of Women in Culture and Society*, 1, 4 (1976); P.E.H. Hair (ed.), *Before the Bawdy Court, 1300–1800* (1972) and M. Ingram, *Church Courts, Sex and Marriage in England, 1570–1640* (Cambridge, 1987).

To comprehend the law is by no means always, or even ever, to understand its implementation. The complex processes of policing the city before the invention of the Metropolitan Police are described and analysed in V.A.C. Gatrell, 'Crime, authority and the policeman-state', in F.M.L. Thompson (ed.), *Cambridge Social History of Britain, 1750–1950: Vol.3, Social Agencies and Institutions* (Cambridge, 1990); G. Howson, *It Takes a Thief: The Life and Times of Jonathan Wild* (1987); R. Paley, 'An imperfect, inadequate and wretched system? Policing London before Peel', *Criminal Justice History*, 10 (1989); E.A. Reynolds, 'St. Marylebone: local police reform in London 1755–1829', *The Historian*, 51, 3 (1989); M.J.D. Roberts, 'Public and private in early nineteenth-century London: the Vagrant Act of 1822 and its enforcement', *Social History*, 13, 3 (1988); D. Rumbelow, *I Spy Blue: The Police and Crime in the City of London from Elizabeth I to Victoria* (1971) and J.J. Tobias, *Crime and Police in England, 1700–1900* (1979).

The following titles discuss far more than just 'crime', but they are grouped together here in part because of the strength of their various dissections of that difficult concept: P. Linebaugh, *The London Hanged: Crime and Civil Society in the Eighteenth Century* (1991); J.L. McMullan, *The Canting Crew: London's Criminal Underworld, 1550–1700* (New Jersey, 1984); J.A. Sharpe, *Crime in Early Modern England, 1550–1750* (1984); R.B. Shoemaker, *Prosecution and Punishment: Petty Crime and the Law in London and Rural Middlesex, c.1660–1725* (Cambridge, 1991). The specific application of that concept to women is subject to a rare examination in J.M. Beattie, 'The criminality of women in eighteenth-century England', *Journal of Social History*, 6 (1975).

A number of texts dealing with Victorian or present-day policing proved to be fruitful sources of ideas, including R.D. Storch, 'The policeman as domestic missionary: urban discipline and popular culture in Northern England, 1850–80', *Journal of Social History*, 4, 9 (1976); R.D. Storch, 'Police control of street prostitution in Victorian London: a study in the contexts of police action', in D. Bayley (ed.), *Police and Society* (1977); O. Gill, 'Urban stereotypes and delinquent incidents', *British Journal of Criminology*, 16, 4 (1976); S. Welsh, 'The manufacture of excitement in police–juvenile encounters', *British Journal of Criminology*, 21, 3 (1981) and C. Werthman and I. Piliavin, 'Gang members and the police', in D.J. Bordua, (ed.), *The Police: Six Sociological Essays* (New York, 1967).

SEXUALITY

Studies of sexuality abound. The best introduction for this period is the excellent T. Hitchcock, *English Sexualities, 1700–1800* (1997). The following studies proved among the most useful in the writing of this book: P.G. Boucé, 'Aspects of sexual tolerance and intolerance in eighteenth-century England', *British Journal for Eighteenth-Century Studies*, 3 (1980); P.G. Boucé, (ed.), *Sexuality in Eighteenth-Century England* (1982); A. Clark, 'Whores and gossips: sexual reputation in London, 1770–1825', in A. Angerman *et al.* (eds.), *Current Issues in Women's History* (1989); R.P. Maccubbin (ed.), *Unauthorised Sexual Behaviour During the Enlightenment* (Cambridge, 1988); P. Meyer-Sacks, ' "Ev'ry woman is at heart a rake" ', *Eighteenth-Century Studies*, 8 (1974); L. Nead, *Myths of Sexuality: Representations of Women in Victorian Britain* (1988); G.S. Rousseau and R. Porter (eds.), *Sexual Underworlds of the Enlightenment* (Manchester, 1987) and J. Weeks, *Sex, Politics and Society: Regulation of Sexuality since 1800* (1981; 2nd edn., 1989).

PHILANTHROPY, SUPPRESSION AND REFORM

The best recent study of philanthropic endeavour in the eighteenth century is D.T. Andrew, *Philanthropy and Police: London Charity in the Eighteenth Century* (New Jersey, 1989). The treatment of venereal disease among the poor is examined by J. Bettley, 'Post Voluptatem Misericordia: The rise and fall of the London Lock Hospitals', *The London Journal*, 10, 2 (1984); M.A. Waugh, 'Attitudes of hospitals in London to venereal disease in the eighteenth and nineteenth centuries', *British Journal of Venereal Disease*, 47, 2 (1971) and T.J. Wyke, 'Hospital facilities for, and diagnosis and treatment of, venereal disease in England, 1800–70', *British Journal of Venereal Disease*, 49, 1 (1973). For the Magdalen Hospital for the Reception of Penitent Prostitutes, see H.F. Compston, *The Magdalen Hospital: The Story of a Great Charity* (1917); S.B. Pearce, *An Ideal in the Working: the Magdalen Hospital, 1758–1958* (1958); S. Nash, 'Prostitution and charity: the

Magdalen Hospital, a case study', *Journal of Social History*, 17 (1984) and S. Lloyd, 'Pleasure's golden bait: poverty and the Magdalen Hospital in eighteenth-century London', *History Workshop Journal*, 41 (1996).

Very general and showing its age, E.J. Bristow, *Vice and Vigilance: Purity Movements in Britain since 1700* (1977) is nevertheless a useful introduction to the various anti-vice movements of the eighteenth century and later. More particular studies include T. Curtis and W. Speck, 'The Societies for the Reformation of Manners: a case study in the theory and practice of moral reform', *Literature and History*, 3 (1976); J. Innes, 'Politics and morals: the Reformation of Manners movement in later eighteenth-century England', in E. Hellmuth (ed.), *The Transformation of Political Culture: England and Germany in the Late Eighteenth Century* (Oxford, 1990); T. Isaacs, 'The Anglican hierarchy and the Reformation of Manners, 1688–1738', *Journal of Ecclesiastical History*, 33 (1982); W.K. Lowther Clarke, *A History of the S.P.C.K.* (1959) and M.J.D. Roberts, 'The Society for the Suppression of Vice and its early critics', *Historical Journal*, 26 (1983).

PROSTITUTION

Many books and articles which proved useful in the writing of this book are studies of prostitution in other countries and other periods. As such, they have been omitted from this bibliography and may be found in the footnotes. The works cited below include only a very few general histories of the trade together with some studies whose periods and places are at least adjacent to eighteenth-century London.

L. Basserman, *The Oldest Profession: A History of Prostitution* (1967) and F. Henriques, *Prostitution and Society: A Survey* (3 vols., 1962–68) are very general histories and a cautious reading of either produces many useful nuggets of information and opinion. V. Bullough, *A Bibliography of Prostitution* (1977) is dated and oddly partial but still useful.

Of more direct relevance to this study are V. Bullough, 'Prostitution and reform in eighteenth-century England', in R.P. Maccubbin (ed.), *Unauthorized Sexual Behaviour during the Enlightenment*, special issue of *Eighteenth-Century Life*, vol.9, no.3 (1985); J.B. Radner, 'The youthful harlot's curse: the prostitute as symbol of the city in eighteenth-century English literature', *Eighteenth-Century Life*, 2 (1976); S.J. Rogal 'The selling of sex: Mandeville's *Modest Defence of Public Stews*', *Studies in Eighteenth-Century Culture*, 5 (1976); W.A. Speck,

'The harlot's progress in eighteenth-century England', *British Journal for Eighteenth-Century Studies*, 3 (1980); R. Trumbach, 'Modern prostitution and gender in *Fanny Hill*: libertine and domesticated fantasy', in G.S. Rousseau and R. Porter (eds.), *Sexual Underworlds of the Enlightenment* (Manchester, 1987). There are very many studies of Victorian prostitution. Among those which I found most useful are F. Finnegan, *Poverty and Prostitution: A Study of Victorian Prostitution in York* (1979); L. Mahood, *The Magdalenes: Prostitution in the Nineteenth Century* (1990) and J. Walkowitz, *Prostitution and Victorian Society: Women, Class and the State* (Cambridge, 1980) – the last, in particular, is essential reading for anybody interested in the subject.

Many studies of prostitution spend time considering the difficult relationship between historian, subject and sources. Two articles which explicitly examine the question are A.R. Henderson, 'Prostitution and the city: a review essay', *Journal of Urban History*, 23, 2 (1997) and L. White, 'Prostitutes, reformers and historians', *Criminal Justice History*, 6 (1985).

Index